Urban Ministry
Reconsidered

R Drew Smith
sept 16, 2019

Urban Ministry Reconsidered

Contexts and Approaches

Edited by

R. Drew Smith,

Stephanie C. Boddie,

and

Ronald E. Peters

WJK WESTMINSTER
JOHN KNOX PRESS
LOUISVILLE • KENTUCKY

© 2018 Westminster John Knox Press

First edition
Published by Westminster John Knox Press
Louisville, Kentucky

18 19 20 21 22 23 24 25 26 27—10 9 8 7 6 5 4 3 2

Scripture quotations from the New Revised Standard Version of the Bible are copyright © 1989 by the Division of Christian Education of the National Council of the Churches of Christ in the U.S.A. and are used by permission.

Scripture taken from *The Message.* Copyright © 1993, 1994, 1995, 1996, 2000, 2001, 2002. Used by permission of NavPress Publishing Group.

Figure 1: Gun Ownership in America is used by permission of Robert P. Jones.

Good-faith efforts have been made to trace the owner or holder of each copyright and to acquire permission where necessary. If any rights have been inadvertently infringed upon, the publisher asks that the omission be excused and agrees to make the necessary corrections in future printings.

Book design by Sharon Adams
Cover design by designpointinc.com

Library of Congress Cataloging-in-Publication Data

Names: Smith, R. Drew, 1956– editor.
Title: Urban ministry reconsidered : contexts and approaches / edited by R. Drew Smith, Stephanie C. Boddie, Ronald E. Peters.
Description: Louisville, KY : Westminster John Knox Press, 2018. | Includes index. |
Identifiers: LCCN 2018007907 (print) | LCCN 2018016650 (ebook) | ISBN 9781611648454 (ebk.) | ISBN 9780664263928 (pbk. : alk. paper)
Subjects: LCSH: City churches. | City clergy. | Cities and towns—Religious aspects—Christianity.
Classification: LCC BV637 (ebook) | LCC BV637 .U73 2018 (print) | DDC 253.09173/2—dc23
LC record available at https://lccn.loc.gov/2018007907

Contents

II. Urban Community Formation

III. Urban Social Policy

Introduction

R. Drew Smith

"Urban ministry" has become well-established terminology within the theological lexicon, although there is a wide range of thinking about its meaning. This is not surprising, given there is no uniform understanding of what is meant by "urban" or "ministry." As outlined below, "urban" has acquired both empirically and socially descriptive usages, referring to forms of collective living where certain numerical thresholds, structural configurations, or cultural patterns obtain. Whether numerically small or large, key characteristics of urban populations have included a spatial concentration; an economic, political, and cultural variegation; and a developmental intensity and dynamism resulting from the interactions between diverse individuals, institutions, and ideas.

A growing proportion of the global population resides in urban spaces, even as the intensity and dynamism characteristic of those spaces has been multiplied by technologies that have facilitated vastly increased communications, information gathering, and social intersectionality. Given the intensifying nature of these urban dynamics, Christian ministries have struggled to account for urbanization's growing force, complexities, and reach—and to formulate theologically and sociologically appropriate responses. Rapidly evolving urban circumstances have fueled Christian efforts, for example, to reassess and reenvision ministry forms and functions; reaffirm and reinvigorate spiritual grounding in response to social forces; and reconsider and reformulate moral, ethical, and theological foundations of community life.

Nevertheless, in doing so, ministry approaches have varied in the extent to which urban social-contextual factors have been accounted for explicitly and systematically within their ministry analysis and practice—for

1

instance, accounting for the complex ways personal lifestyles, livelihoods, worldviews, and behaviors may be influenced by compound urban structural and group dynamics. Ministry approaches that are insufficiently alert to contextual factors risk missing significant life-shaping details and particulars of the persons toward whom ministries are directed, sometimes remaining abstracted altogether from the daily realities of those persons' lives. The explorations and analysis of urban ministry in this volume are rooted in both theological and sociological perspectives and presuppositions that speak into these conceptual gaps.

The majority of the essays by the contributors to this volume focus on ministry contexts within the United States, but more than a third address ministry contexts in the Global South or Europe. Moreover, many of the essays in the volume make clear that urban ministries within each of these regions of the world encounter similarly global and globalizing populations, institutional influences, and socializing forces.

The case studies in this volume, then, provide windows into the dynamic process of ministry responses to newly forming contexts of urban social and religious life, drawing attention to circumstances and factors that make these contexts potentially unique in both the challenges and opportunities they present for Christian ministry.

Urban Framings

Urban has been defined by several factors, including by quantitative metrics, structural dynamics, and social cultures. Where urban has been defined along numerical lines, for example, the measurements have often differed from one nation to another. In the United States, the technical standard for an urban context is "an agglomeration of 2,500 or more inhabitants, generally living in densities of 1,000 or more per square mile." The technical standard in France is any context with 2,000 or more persons "living in contiguous houses or with not more than 200 metres between houses." Botswana and Zambia define urban as "localities of 5,000 or more inhabitants, the majority of whom all depend upon non-agricultural activities."[1] As this latter definition suggests, an urban designation may result from numerical formulas but also from the social and structural activities that have drawn persons into a collective existence—including production sectors that have served as organizing principles for

1. These definitions are charted in the *Demographic Yearbook*, 2005, table 6, http://unstats .un.org/unsd/demographic/sconcerns/densurb/Defintion_of%20Urban.pdf.

urban formation, as in the case of Detroit's auto industry, Johannesburg's mining industry, or the high-finance industries of London or New York.

These large cities epitomize key structural dimensions of urban formation, but such cities (along with much smaller contexts) also are embodiments of demographic, sociocultural, and institutional diversities characteristic more widely of urban spaces. When urban is defined (as one astute observer has) as "density with diversity," urban can be applied to many contexts—not only to New York and Johannesburg, but also to New York's Pleasantville suburb (population 7,055, population density 3,856 people/sq. mile) or Johannesburg's Rosebank suburb (population 10,000, population density 3,400 people/sq. mile).[2] In addition, the diversity of the contexts is evident from the fact that both of these suburbs are largely affluent while also possessing a mixture of economic classes, races, and ethnicities. Many contexts not immediately perceived as "urban," therefore, could accurately be accorded that designation.

Moreover, when measured by a standard of "density with diversity," urbanization has increased dramatically within the United States and elsewhere. Within the last two centuries, the percentage of the world's population living in urban areas has grown from 3 percent in 1800, to 14 percent in 1900, to 50 percent in 2008—with projections of reaching 70 percent by 2050. Increasingly, urban residents have been located in very large cities, with cities of one million or more residents multiplying from 12 in 1900, to 83 in 1950, to more than 400 in 2008—including 19 cities with 10 million or more inhabitants.[3] But as the Population Reference Bureau points out, "the bulk of urban population growth is likely to occur in smaller cities and towns of less than 500,000"—with the largest increases in urbanization taking place in Africa and Asia, which by 2030 will have cities accounting for "almost seven in every 10 urban inhabitants globally."[4] Therefore, urban residents globally will be increasingly people of color, not only in Africa and Asia, but throughout the Americas and in Europe. By 2030, the percentage of urban residents will reach 87 percent in North America, 84 percent in Latin America and the Caribbean, and 78 percent in Europe.[5]

2. Dhati Lewis, Quoted in D. A. Horton, "What 'Urban' Means Today," ReachLife Ministries, http://www.reachlife.org/uncategorized/what-urban-means-today/.
3. Population Reference Bureau, "Human Population: Urbanization," http://www.prb.org/Publications/Lesson-Plans/HumanPopulation/Urbanization.aspx.
4. Population Reference Bureau, "World Population Highlights 2007: Urbanization," http://www.prb.org/Publications/Articles/2007/623Urbanization.aspx.
5. Ibid.

Among the factors contributing to urban population diversity and growth have been population shifts within nations, but also between nations. In the United States, net outmigration from rural areas was roughly 75,000 persons per year between 2010 and 2013 and twice that amount during the mid-1980s.[6] In Europe, the outmigration from rural to urban areas has been so pronounced during the last century that it has been described as a "depopulation" of rural areas.[7] Sub-Saharan Africa has had the highest rate of urbanization in the world since the mid-twentieth century, ranging between 3 and 5 percent per year (or roughly twice the world average)—with a substantial amount of this urban growth resulting from rural to urban migration.[8]

Immigration from other countries also accounts for a significant amount of urban population growth, especially in the United States and Europe. Legal immigration to the United States has expanded from approximately 250,000 per year in 1950 to about 1 million per year in 2013, with 41.3 million immigrants residing legally in the United States in 2013.[9] Another 11.5 million immigrants are estimated to be residing within the United States illegally, roughly two-thirds of whom have come from Mexico. European nations received 3.6 million legal immigrants in 2015, the majority of whom were migrating from one European country to another.[10] Another 547,000 persons were present in European nations illegally in 2014, with an additional 464,000 migrants crossing into Europe by sea during the first nine months of 2015 (less than half of whom were granted legal asylum).[11] Immigration within

6. U.S. Department of Agriculture, "Rural America at a Glance: 2014 Edition," Washington: Department of Agriculture, 3–4, https://www.ers.usda.gov/webdocs/publications/42896/49474_eb26.pdf?v=42401.

7. Simon Tisdale, "Silent Blight in a Countryside of Empty Homes and Shut Shops," *The Guardian*, August 22, 2015.

8. Cecelia Tacoli et al., "World Migrations Report 2015: Urbanization, Rural-Urban Migration and Urban Poverty," London: International Institute for Environment and Development, 2015: 6, https://www.iom.int/sites/default/files/our_work/ICP/MPR/WMR-2015-Background-Paper-CTacoli-GMcGranahan-DSatterthwaite.pdf.

9. Migration Policy Institute, "Legal Immigration to the United States, 1820-Present," http://www.migrationpolicy.org/programs/data-hub/charts/Annual-Number-of-US-Legal-Permanent-Residents.

10. Eurostat, "Immigration by Citizenship," 2015, http://ec.europa.eu/eurostat/statistics-explained/index.php/File:Immigration_by_citizenship,_2013_YB15.png.

11. See Giulio Sabbati and Eva-Maria Poptcheva, "Irregular Immigration in the EU: Facts and Figures," European Parliamentary Research Service, April 27, 2015, http://epthinktank.eu/2015/04/27/irregular-immigration-in-the-eu-facts-and-figures/; Jeanne Park, "Europe's Migration Crisis," Council on Foreign Relations, September 23, 2015, http://www.cfr.org/migration/europes-migration-crisis/p32874; and BBC News, "Migrant Crisis: Migration to Europe Explained in Seven Charts," March 4, 2016, http://www.bbc.com/news/world-europe-34131911.

Sub-Saharan African countries has had a largely involuntary quality as well, with this region hosting about 2.6 million refugees in 2012, mostly in urban areas. South Africa, for example, was host to 153,500 refugees in 2012, about 82,000 of whom were asylum seekers (making South Africa the country receiving the greatest number of asylum seekers in the world at the time). It is also estimated that the number of illegal immigrants in South Africa has swerved between 3 and 8 million over the last two decades.

Urban spaces, therefore, are the primary connection points for a world that is "flattening" (to borrow a term from Thomas Friedman).[12] In this sense at least, they are places that facilitate a kind of demographic, cultural, and institutional integration across geographic boundaries, though not necessarily a smoothing out of the peaks and chasms of structural inequality that divide populations within and between urban spaces. Although urban contexts are where modes of economic growth and development are most concentrated and where many poor persons consequently can graduate out of poverty, urban contexts are also places where poverty is expanding and where disparities between richer and poorer populations are widening.

For example, in developing nations, the share of poverty located within urban areas grew from 17 percent in 2000 to 28 percent in 2010.[13] In European nations, the percentage of persons at risk of poverty or exclusion was 24 percent overall in 2014, with persons in cities more at risk than persons in rural areas (as least within western European nations).[14] In the United States, though the percentage of the overall population living below the poverty line decreased from 22 percent in 1960 to 14 percent in 2013, the percentage of the nation's poor living in the 20 most populous counties (such as Los Angeles, Cook [Chicago], Kings [Brooklyn], Maricopa [Phoenix], et al.) increased from 14 percent to 21 percent.[15] Also, within the United States urban contexts, poverty has become

12. Thomas Friedman, *The World Is Flat: A Brief History of the Twenty-First Century* (New York: Farrar, Strauss and Giroux, 2005).

13. Lawrence Haddad, "Poverty Is Urbanizing and Needs Different Thinking on Development," Bill and Melinda Gates Foundation, October 5, 2012, http://www.theguardian.com/global-development/poverty-matters/2012/oct/05/poverty-urbanising-different-thinking-development.

14. European Urban Knowledge Network, "The Inclusive City: Approaches to Combat Urban Poverty and Social Exclusion in Europe," 2014: 12 and 17; http://www.eukn.eu/fileadmin/Files/EUKN_Publications/EUKN_report_InclusiveCity_Final.pdf.

15. Jens M. Krogstad, "How the Geography of U.S. Poverty Has Shifted Since 1960," Pew Research Center, September 10, 2015, http://www.pewresearch.org/fact-tank/2015/09/10/how-the-geography-of-u-s-poverty-has-shifted-since-1960/.

more geographically concentrated, with the share of the poor who live in census tracts where 40 percent or more persons are below the poverty line increasing nationally from 9 percent in 2000 to 12 percent in 2012.[16]

To say that urban contexts are being reconfigured would be an understatement. Rapid and dramatic changes are taking place with respect to urban population demographics, human relations, and structural and technological connections—each with implications for individual and collective human prospects that are of social and theological significance. These intersections between urban contextual dimensions and their formative and normative impact on individual and collective life are at the heart of the present volume's urban ministry analysis.

The impact of urban expansion and escalation on the social, psychological, and spiritual formation of urban dwellers has been actively debated. On one side there have been those who have drawn attention to ways the mechanistic, materialistic, impersonal qualities of our industrially and commercially centered urban spaces have resulted in various forms of human alienation. Social theorists such as Karl Marx who viewed structural and psychological alienation of workers as symptomatic of modern industrial distortions, political novelists such as Upton Sinclair whose book *The Jungle* exposed inhumane conditions endured by urban laborers in the commercial meatpacking industry, and even contemporary television shows such as *Married with Children* with its parodying of unmeaningful employment, have pointed to a human estrangement from personal labor that leaves persons bereft of fulfillment.[17] Additionally, transcendentalist thinkers from Henry David Thoreau to Theodore Roszak (the former's "Walden Pond" juxtaposed to the latter's urban "wasteland"), and even wilderness retreat organizations such as Outward Bound, have sought to counter a modern materialist assault on human dreams, spirit, and connections to the natural realm.[18]

Similarly, some have connected a systematized urban depersonalization and human indifference to a substantial erosion of community connectedness, social purposefulness, and civic-mindedness. Social theorists from Richard Sennett (who laments the "fall" of public purpose in the

16. Elizabeth Kneebone, "The Growth and Spread of Concentrated Poverty, 2000 to 2008–2012," Brookings Institution, July 31, 2014, http://www.brookings.edu/research/interactives/2014/concentrated-poverty#/M10420.

17. Upton Sinclair, *The Jungle* (New York: Jungle, 1906).

18. Henry David Thoreau, *Walden* (Las Vegas, NV: Empire Books, 2013); Theodore Roszak, *Where the Wasteland Ends: Politics and Transcendence in Postindustrial Society* (New York: Doubleday, 1972).

modern metropolis), to Cornel West (who laments the loss of social meaningfulness among urban minority youth), and even cinematic depictions of street life such as *Boys in the Hood* or the South African film *Tsotsi*, all speak to a growing social disaffection on the part of urban dwellers.[19] Others have linked urban social disaffection more closely to urban systemic injustices and inequalities, as identified for example in Barbara Ehrenreich's critical analysis of social policies and business sector practices that trap the working poor in low-paying jobs without supplemental support systems, or Jonathan Kozol's denunciations of under-resourced public school systems that fail to adequately educate urban children and youth, or Michelle Alexander's condemnations of criminal justice approaches that ensure the over-incarceration of the black and brown poor through what are "school to prison pipelines."[20]

In other more explicitly theological readings of urbanization, as in the case of analysis by Robert Linthicum, the despoiling aspects of urban life are not tied necessarily to a jettisoning of spiritual sensibilities but actually to the active presence of a demonic spirituality manifesting in systems of injustice, dehumanization, and moral depravity.[21] Still others within theological circles, such as Francis Schaeffer, have argued that what has been most alarmingly sacrificed within the urbanization process has been theological intentionality itself, replaced by a celebration of human agency and achievement symbolized by urban development that has supplanted human reliance on divine agency and guidance.[22]

In contrast to these unfavorable readings of urbanization, some interpret the urban journey from simpler to more complex, from more religion-centered to more secular, from more anthropocentric to more mechanistic, and even from more consensual to more conflictual, as necessary (or at least unavoidable) dimensions of social progress. Though not minimizing the problematic nature of urban inequalities, injustices, and inhumanities, urbanists Sam Bass Warner and Harvey Cox, for example,

19. Richard Sennett, *The Fall of Public Man* (New York: Vintage Books, 1976); Cornel West, *Race Matters* (New York: Vintage Books, 1993).
20. Barbara Ehrenreich, *Nickel and Dimed: On Getting By in America* (New York: Henry Holt & Co., 2001); Jonathan Kozol, *Death at an Early Age: The Destruction of the Hearts and Minds of Negro Children in the Boston Public Schools* (Boston, MA: Houghton Mifflin, 1967); Michelle Alexander, *The New Jim Crow: Mass Incarceration in an Age of Colorblindness* (New York: The New Press, 2010).
21. Robert Linthicum, *City of God, City of Satan: A Biblical Theology of the Urban Church* (Grand Rapids, MI: Zondervan, 1991).
22. Francis A Schaeffer, *Death in the City* (Hants, UK: L'Abri Fellowship, 1969).

do not regard quintessential urban features such as individualism as leading necessarily to indifference, nor anonymity necessarily to alienation,
nor diversity (whether of thought, values, or lifestyles) necessarily to dis-
integration. Rather, urban attenuations of personal and societal norma-
tivity are viewed (at least when tracking toward constructive aims and
ambitions) as necessary components of independent thought and action
upon which a democratic and enterprising culture are premised. Whether
the relationship between urban life-worlds and Christian sensibilities are
viewed as complementary or in conflict, it is clear that Christianity (in its
ever-evolving formal and informal formations) is a factor that must be
accounted for within Western and Westernizing urban contexts.

Ministry Framings

Approximately one-third of the world's population identifies as Christian, and the vast majority of that Christianity is channeled through
denominational, interdenominational, or congregational institutional
frameworks, or through church-related civil society institutions such as
schools, hospitals, or social service organizations. Christianity, like much
of social life in westernized social contexts, plays out upon a highly institutionalized landscape.

Despite the expanded reach of institutions within societies, scholars
from many disciplinary vantage points have documented post-institutional
tendencies within contemporary life, noting the loosening grip of institutions ranging from governmental institutions, to civic and educational
institutions, to religious institutions.[23] It has been a movement away
from form to formlessness, away from permanence to impermanence,
away from rootedness to rootlessness. With respect to the black urban
poor, this also may be connected to deeper disaffections growing out of
longstanding race-based and class-based social antagonisms operative
within grossly unequal and highly racialized societies, such as the United
States and South Africa.[24] Moreover, ethnicity and national origin serve

---

23. Robert Wuthnow, *The Restructuring of American Religion* (Princeton, NJ: Princeton University Press, 1990); David Roozen and James Nieman, eds., *Church, Identity, and Change: Theology
and Denominational Structures in Unsettled Times* (Grand Rapids, MI: Eerdmans, 2005); John
Bibby, *Politics, Parties, and Elections in America* (Chicago: Nelson-Hall, 1987): 10–18; Mahmood
Mamdani, *Citizen and Subject: Contemporary Africa and the Legacy of Late Colonialism* (Kampala,
Uganda: Fountain Publishers, 1996); and Sennett, *The Fall of Public Man*.
24. R. Drew Smith, "Black Religious Nationalism and the Politics of Transcendence," *Jour-
nal of the American Academy of Religion* 66, no. 3 (1998): 533–47; Karin Chubb and Lutz Van
Dijk, *Between Anger and Hope: South Africa's Youth and the Truth and Reconciliation Commission*

as markers of social difference that may also potentially translate into social marginalization and distance within urban spaces, especially where these are impoverished population groups.

Nevertheless, the declining influence of religious, civic, and communal ideals that has accompanied movements away from societal normativities has been a matter of great consternation within institutional leadership circles—including among urban churches. Many churches within these urbanizing contexts have been reassessing and repositioning their ministries to revitalize their institutional life and their broader ministry influence. Many have engaged with contemporary urban contexts in innovative and relevant ways. Too often, however, ministry initiatives within contemporary urban settings have struggled with urban dynamics and circumstances they find unfamiliar, if not daunting.

Although not solely a result of urbanization, many global North countries have experienced steady and sometimes dramatic declines in formal religious involvement during the past fifty years or more. In the United States, for example, 23 percent of Americans over 18 years of age indicated having no religious affiliation according to a 2015 national survey by the Pew Research Center. This increased from 16 percent in a 2009 Pew survey and 8 percent in a 1990 Pew survey—which means that from 1990 to 2015 the percentage of religiously nonaffiliated Americans has tripled. One implication of these data is that while the vast majority of Americans continue to place importance on matters of faith, a growing number of Americans approach matters of faith informally rather than formally and individually rather than institutionally.[25]

This is especially true among poorer, more socially marginalized populations, who not only may not enjoy the same level of access to formal institutions but also who may regard those institutions as spiritually and culturally restrictive and exclusionary.[26] Either way, declining religious affiliation among the urban poor has become increasingly obvious since the 1960s (as urban poor populations became more geographically concentrated, culturally isolated, and pushed to the margins of social and institutional life). What may also contribute to declining religious

(Johannesburg: Witwatersrand University Press, 2001); Sharlene Swartz et al., "Ikasi Style and the Quiet Violence of Dreams: A Critique of Youth Belonging in Post-Apartheid South Africa," in Sharlene Swartz and Madeleine Arnot, eds., *Youth Citizenship and the Politics of Belonging* (New York: Routledge Press, 2013); and Cornel West, *Race Matters* (New York: Vintage Books, 1993).
25. Pew Research Center, "America's Changing Religious Landscape," May 12, 2015, http://www.pewforum.org/2015/05/12/americas-changing-religious-landscape/.
26. Frances Kunreuther and Patrick Corvington, *Next Shift: Beyond the Nonprofit Leadership Crisis* (Baltimore, MD: Annie E. Casey Foundation, 2006).

affiliation on the part of the urban poor is that these populations may be largely transient—driven from place to place through evictions for infractions (such as failure to pay), dislocations resulting from urban development schemes, or migratory pursuits of new opportunities (as in the case of migrants from other locales, or immigrants from other countries). These factors (whether taken separately or together) present significant challenges for ministries seeking to engage contemporary urban contests and challenges.

Structure and Focus of the Volume

A question central to the volume then is what does it mean to minister in urban spaces in ways that are intentionally responsive to ever-changing urban environments, conditions, and contexts? Asked another way, where ministries have been intentionally contextual in their approaches to urban challenges and complexities, how have they interpreted their mandate and framed their responses in these situations? For example, are ministries willing and able to grant their context a careful reading and adjust their ministries in relation to the potential and possibilities this reveals, or do they project or impose their institution-bound subjectivities and norms upon the context? When committed to forming open and fluid relations with their local community, what are the points of commonality and the procedures for relational bridge-building (e.g., do they look to meet the community inside the church walls, cultures, and operations, or outside all of these)? Additionally, are the necessary leaders and training opportunities in place to nurture and facilitate faith perspectives and innovation contributing to more robust and reciprocal church and community relations (e.g., are urban churches equipped for community organizing, policy advocacy, and cultural translation)? The essays in this volume wrestle in various ways with these concerns and considerations.

The volume is divided into four sections: Urban Conceptual Worldviews, Urban Community Formation, Urban Social Policy, and Urban Ministry Adaptations—each of which shed light on changes in urban landscapes and dynamics and on promising urban ministry practices and responses in the face of urban change. Essays in the Urban Conceptual Worldviews section explore transitions from earlier ministry frameworks largely informed by privileged Christian worldviews, to engagement in urban spaces increasingly characterized by a plurality of worldviews more cognizant of contemporary urban struggle and hope.

The Urban Community Formation section examines all too common patterns of eroded neighborhood economic conditions and social connectedness, the sometimes disruptive and/or enlivening influxes of newcomer populations and resources, and the diminishment of neighborhood "social capital" resulting from social separation and fragmentation in many of these contexts. Essays in this section outline ways congregations and their community-based ministries strengthen and sustain community in the face of countervailing forces.

The Urban Social Policy Section looks similarly at church-related community organizing, social service, and advocacy initiatives, but more in relation to specific urban policy concerns such as economic justice, gun violence, food security, and HIV/AIDS. Authors highlight ways urban churches pursue policy reforms and more effective frameworks to promote human flourishing. Responsiveness to evolving urban contexts and community formations are also the focus of the Urban Ministry Adaptations section, but with essays outlining details of ministry formations, practices, and methods suited to twenty-first-century urban circumstances. These ministry cases (and analysis throughout the volume) provide instructive contrasts to more traditional ministries that have not accounted as effectively for new social, cultural, and religious configurations and realities within urban contexts.

I

Urban Conceptual Worldviews

Chapter 1

Urban Conceptualizing in Historical Perspective

Ronald E. Peters

The city, among humankind's oldest social, economic, cultural, and political phenomena with origins dating back to the Paleolithic period, was also seedbed to human religious motivations.[1] In view of the fact twenty-first-century cities are larger than ever before, more numerous in quantity, and account for more than half the world's population, what are the role and function of religious engagement in these contexts?

In examining urban conceptual worldviews that inform twenty-first-century urban ministry approaches, it is helpful, first, to give some attention to the conceptual framework from which urban ministry, as we know it today, has originated. Conventional thought about urban ministry almost exclusively associates its roots with the old social gospel movement in the United States during the late nineteenth and early twentieth century. Scarcely more than a century ago religious narratives engaging urban wealth inequities, oppression, violence, poverty, and survival overwhelmingly were informed by comparatively privileged Christian worldviews. Accordingly, the origins of urban ministry are seen as having been primarily influenced by German idealists in philosophy and its liberal theology, interpreting the gospel primarily in response to social problems associated with industrial capitalism, its growth, and its influence on urbanization.[2] This post-Enlightenment thinking drew heavily

---

1. Lewis Mumford, *The City in History: Its Origins, Its Transformations, and Its Prospects* (Boston: Harcourt, 1961); Cheik Anta Diop, *Pre-Colonial Black Africa* (New York: Lawrence Hill Books, 1987); Robert C. Lithicum, *City of God / City of Satan* (Grand Rapids, MI: Zondervan, 1991); Bernard W. Anderson, *Understanding the Old Testament* (Englewood Cliffs, NJ: Prentice-Hall, 1966).

2. Ralph E. Luker, *The Social Gospel in Black and White* (Chapel Hill: University of North Carolina, 1991), 4–5; See also Kevin J. Christiano, William H. Swatos Jr., and Peter Kivisto, *Sociology*

on the rise of science along with faith in analysis of social challenges associated with the impact of industrial capitalism, its growth, and impact on urbanization.[3]

The writings of Émile Durkheim, Karl Marx, Max Weber, and Ernst Troeltsch are among those credited with providing critical analyses of the role of religion in society throughout this period. Marx, for example, outraged by the squalid living conditions of the urban poor working in industrial cities, became notable for his dialectical materialism, which interpreted religion as a negative factor in society ("the opium of the people"), contributing to the maintenance of systemic economic and social inequities. By contrast and more widely accepted were interpretations of Christianity's role represented by writers like Durkheim, Weber, and Troeltsch that interpreted religion as a catalyst for positive social functioning.[4]

During this period, the United States was focused on putting the ravages of the Civil War behind it and moved into the new century with unprecedented industrial growth and wealth. With crisp accuracy, J. Philip Wogaman described the era as one of rapid change that revealed critical social problems:

> The Civil War . . . had quickened the pace of the Industrial Revolution in the North, as industries grew up overnight to supply the Union war machine. Unlike the South, which was devastated, the North was stimulated economically. The following years were a

---

of Religion: Contemporary Developments (New York: Rowman & Littlefield, 2002), chaps. 1 and 4.

3. Kevin J. Christiano, William H. Swatos Jr., and Peter Kivisto, *Sociology of Religion: Contemporary Developments* (Lanham, MD: Rowman & Littlefield, 2002), 4–5.

4. Émile Durkheim saw the role of religion in society, including Christianity, in more positive light than the less complimentary views of Karl Marx or Sigmund Freud. In *The Elementary Forms of the Religious Life* (New York: Free Press, 1995), 44, Durkheim defined religion as "a unified system of beliefs and practices relative to sacred things, that is to say, things set apart and forbidden—beliefs and practices which unite into one single moral community called a Church, all those who adhere to them." Max Weber's classic sociological assessment of workings of religion in his *The Protestant Ethic and the Spirit of Capitalism* gave new religious blessing to the task of work and the accumulation of wealth: "Low wages fail even from a purely business point of view wherever it is a question of producing goods which require any sort of skilled labor. . . . Labor must, on the contrary, be performed as if it were an absolute end in itself, a calling. But such an attitude is by no means a product of nature. It cannot be evoked by low wages or high ones alone, but can only be the product of a long and arduous process of education" ([Lexington, KY: Renaissance Classics, 2012], 22). In *The Social Teaching of the Christian Churches*, the theologian Ernst Troeltsch sought to relate types of religious experience to the varieties of social teachings with which they might be correlated.

time of rapid expansion: new factories were developed to manufacture new products, railways were built spanning the continent, trade expanded. Wave after wave of new immigrants came to America to provide cheap labor. . . . It was a time of growing prosperity for many, and some became fabulously wealthy. . . . But many people . . . concentrated in the working-class sections of the industrial cities. . . . Industrialization meant backbreaking toil, long working hours, child labor, exploitation of women, adulterated food, periods of unemployment, vulnerability to industrial accidents and disease, little educational opportunity, inadequate medical attention, and general impoverishment.[5]

Against this backdrop, one of the preeminent personalities calling attention to this situation was Walter Rauschenbusch, a son of German immigrants, the nineteenth-century New York City urban pastor-turned-seminary professor. With the publication of his *Christianity and the Social Crisis* in 1907, Rauschenbusch became one of the principal articulators of the social gospel movement of the early twentieth century. As such, the motivational approaches of urban ministry were clearly influenced by liberal theology's socially progressive agenda, which sought to address these flagrant social injustices in the first half of the twentieth century.

These approaches included individualistic and direct-service elements, such as soup kitchens and settlement houses like Chicago's famous Hull House developed by Jane Addams, as well as more macro/systemic voices like the Congregationalist minister Washington Gladden.[6] As an example of this more systemic critique of the social injustices of the era, Gladden's 1886 volume titled *Applied Christianity* decried the widening chasm between the wealth of employers and their workers:

The hundreds of thousands of unemployed laborers, vainly asking for work; the rapid increase of pauperism, indicated by the fact that during the last Winter, in the chief cities of this rich commonwealth, nearly one tenth of the population sought charitable aid from the infirmary director or the benevolent societies; the strikes and lockouts reported every day in the newspapers . . .[7]

5. J. Philip Wogaman, *Christian Ethics: A Historical Introduction* (Louisville, KY: Westminster/John Knox Press, 1993), 194–95.

6. Ronald E. Peters, *Urban Ministry: An Introduction* (Nashville: Abingdon, 2007), 86.

7. Washington Gladden, *Applied Christianity* (Boston: Houghton Mifflin, 1886), 161.

Influential and urbane preachers and academicians of Christian Protestantism including Harry Emerson Fosdick, Henry Sloane Coffin, and George A. Buttrick articulated this social-emphasis agenda.[8]

Additionally, as successive generations of African Americans began to make their way north of the Mason-Dixon line in the United States to escape the ravages of post–Civil War social, political, and economic oppression in the South in search of better economic opportunity and living conditions, black churches in the North also focused on addressing the unabated racial hostilities that continued to define life for them "behind the veil" of race in America.[9] Meanwhile, the fifty-five-year period (1915–1970) of the Great Migration of blacks from southern cities to northern cities began its course.[10] In 1900, 90 percent of all African Americans lived in the South.[11] While racial segregation and circumscribed opportunities also defined northern life, southern blacks nonetheless were drawn to them as the United States became increasingly involved in events leading up to World War I and the supply of European immigrant labor rapidly declined.[12] Cities across the North, including Chicago, St. Louis, Detroit, Cleveland, Philadelphia, New York, Baltimore, and Washington were among those that saw substantial increases in the numbers of African Americans between the censuses of 1890 and 1920.

The new arrivals from the South often found themselves the victims of economic and social exploitation and were forced into squalid living conditions. Hostile whites often viewed blacks as intellectually and morally inferior and occasionally resorted to physical violence against the newcomers, whom they saw as competing for their jobs. Urban race riots in cities across America, North and South, erupted during this period in such places as New York City (1901), Springfield, Ohio (1904), Atlanta (1906), and East St. Louis, Illinois (1917).

8. See stories of the ministries and preaching of some of these leading figures during the early part of the twentieth century: Harry Emerson Fosdick, *A Preaching Ministry: Twenty-One Sermons Preached by Harry Emerson Fosdick at the First Presbyterian Church in the City of New York, 1918–1925* (New York: The First Presbyterian Church in the City of New York, 2000); for information on the ministries and preaching of Henry Sloane Coffin and George A. Buttrick during their successive pastorates at Madison Avenue Presbyterian Church in New York City, see: http://www.mapc.com/about-mapc/history/.

9. W. E. B. Du Bois, *Souls of Black Folk* (Mineola, NY: Dover Publications, 1903).

10. Isabel Wilkerson, *The Warmth of Other Suns: The Epic Story of America's Great Migration* (New York: Vintage, 2010).

11. Milton C. Sernett, *Bound for the Promised Land: African American Religion and the Great Migration* (Durham, NC: Duke University Press, 1997), 36.

12. Peters, *Urban Ministry*, 97.

The social gospel influences were manifested in ministry approaches of leaders like Charles A. Tindley of Philadelphia (1906, East Calvary United Methodist Church, later renamed Tindley Temple Church), Reverdy Ransom (pastor of Boston's Charles Street A.M.E. and Chicago's Bethel A.M.E. Churches), and Adam Clayton Powell Sr. (pastor of New York City's Abyssinian Baptist Church). The influence of the social gospel thinking and behaviorist agenda of this period clearly was a precursor to foundational paradigms for urban ministry approaches throughout the twentieth century. The conceptual worldviews that shaped ministry in these contexts and spaces overwhelmingly emerged from and engaged an urban arena with the language and values of Christianity.

By the mid-twentieth century, multiracial and multiethnic efforts from a variety of perspectives in ministry emerged, carving out broader religious approaches. Among them were the urban ministry perspectives and work of thought leaders and activists such as Harvey Conn, Manuel Ortiz, John Perkins, David Wilkerson, and Greg Boyle, whose faith-based approaches to remediating social inequities and injustices reflect the changed context of the post–civil rights era.[13] From various perspectives, these representatives engage challenges of poverty, socioeconomic disenfranchisement, the collusion of racial prejudice and profiling, dysfunctional educational systems, and politically defined housing patterns that feed warped policing and criminal adjudication in ways moving beyond racial constrictions of earlier periods. Moreover, they do so in ways that attempt to bridge common mistakes of the period that often established binaries between urban ministry's roots in social justice advocacy (ethical agency) and spiritual considerations (evangelistic emphasis).[14] Still, these perspectives all reflected worldviews largely engaging a social space and context influenced by values articulated from Christianity.

Within the twenty-first-century context, cyber technology has radically transformed global understanding of wealth inequities, violence, poverty, and oppression, yet without significantly engaging these realities helpfully. In 1968, Martin Luther King Jr. noted that in spite of

---

13. See Harvie M. Conn and Manuel Ortiz, *Urban Ministry: The Kingdom, the City and the People of God* (Downers Grove, IL: InterVarsity Press, 2001); Ronald E. Peters, *Urban Ministry: An Introduction* (Nashville: Abingdon, 2007); John Perkins, *Beyond Charity: The Call to Christian Community* (Grand Rapids: Baker Books, 1993); David Wilkerson, *The Cross and the Switchblade, and the Man Who Believed* (Grand Rapids: Zondervan, 2014); Celeste Fremon, *Father Greg and the Homeboys: The Extraordinary Journey of Father Boyle and His Work with the Latino Gangs of East L.A.* (New York: Hyperion, 1995).
14. See Conn and Ortiz, *Urban Ministry*, 25–26; and Perkins, *Beyond Charity*.

"technological advancements," society still had not demonstrated the ethical commitment to create a concomitant level of genuine "brotherhood." What is significantly different about this twenty-first-century context is the diminishing influence of Christianity in the urban public square, in all of its global dimensions, spaces, and virtual locales. Increasingly, the public role and function of organized religion within the city are increasingly suspect, increasingly viewed, at best, as cultural residue from past societies that unnecessarily complicates efforts to improve the quality of life going forward.

Without question, the role of religion in American society remains very strong in comparison to other advanced industrial counties, but it has declined significantly over the past decade at rates substantially higher than in prior years.[15] Ministry in urban contexts must necessarily transition from mid-twentieth-century approaches characterized by profound pain, fear, insecurity, and bereft of the ability to dream,[16] to a systemic uplifting of outcomes pregnant with new hope.

15. Pew Research Center. "America's Changing Religious Landscape," May 12, 2015, http://www.pewforum.org/2015/05/12/americas-changing-religious-landscape/pr_15-05-12_rls-00/.
16. Ta-Nehisi Coates, *Between the World and Me* (New York: Spiegel and Grau, 2015); Jonathan Kozol, *Amazing Grace* (New York: Crown, 1995); Cornel West, *Race Matters* (New York: Vintage, 1992).

Chapter 2

The New Urbanism and Its Challenge to the Church

Michael A. Mata

The New City

At the dawn of this new millennium humanity achieved a demographic milestone: for the first time in human history, more people were counted as living in cities than in rural areas. Explosive population growth and a torrent of migration from the countryside are creating cities that dwarf the great capitals of the past. During the 1900s people across the globe were moving to cities at a rate of nearly 200,000 per day, over 65 million each year.[1] The pace has slightly slowed; over 400 cities have more than 1 million residents. At least 28 "megacities" have populations of 10 million or more.[2] Of these, most will be in "majority world" nations, including some of the poorest countries on the globe. By 2045, the world's urban population is expected to exceed 6 billion and account for more than two-thirds of the world population.[3]

Meanwhile, Western culture cities, like New York, Los Angeles, London, Paris, and Berlin, have become worldwide symbols of the good life. Both well-advertised and underground travel routes have turned far-away cities into magnets for millions of people who leave their homelands in search of the more glamorous and exciting life. Cities have been

---

1. United Nations Human Settlement Programme, *State of the World's Cities Report 2008/9: Harmonious Cities* (Sterling, VA: Earthscan, 2008), https://unhabitat.org/books /state-of-the-worlds-cities-20082009-harmonious-cities-2/.

2. United Nations Department of Economic and Social Affairs, Population Division, *World Urbanization Prospects: The 2014 Revision* (United Nations, 2014), https://esa.un.org/Unpd /Wup/.

3. Wendell Cox, "What Is a Half-Urban World," The New Geography, 2012, http://www .newgeography.com/content/003249-what-a-half-urban-world.

transformed into vital links of a highly interconnected global village.[4] With this global transformation has come the emergence of a new cultural perspective that is decidedly framed by a plurality of interacting and interconnected ethnicities (though Western in orientation) and driven by technology and consumption. This is reshaping the consciousness of our global village's inhabitants and challenging our notion of "urban." It is also raising provocative questions about the mission or role of the church in this emergent global context.

The urban topography of Los Angeles (the paradigm of the global city, where I also live and minister) provides an excellent context for exploring emerging trends and the role of the faith community within these evolving twenty-first-century realities. In the heartland of Los Angeles (the "City of Angels") there is a dazzling constellation of global culture that simultaneously reaches out to every corner of the world and draws into the city an amazing array of once "exotic" but now ever-familiar influences. Its neighborhoods contain substantive microcosms of faraway and very different contexts, like the Republic of China, Indonesia, Bangladesh, and Thailand. There is a Little Tokyo and a vast Koreatown, a huge Mexican barrio with a sprinkling of maquiladora-type factories, and a Little Manila complete with remnants of pro-Marcos and anti-Marcos factions. There are Armenians periodically reviving their animosity with the Turks, and Jewish diaspora settlements from Iran, Russia, and Brooklyn debating Middle East politics. There are African marketplaces, discussing current events in Cape Town or Addis Ababa, along with purveyors of American-style *soul* food and Korea-style food from *Seoul*.

The multiethnic fusions and intersections of these varying societies are captured in such forms as kosher burritos, African tacos, and sushi pizza. There are more Samoans and Tongans in Los Angeles than there are in their respective Pacific homelands. There are mosques, temples, and religious centers for worshipers of every color and creed. There are also quite possibly the largest concentrations of Salvadorans, Guatemalans, and Belizeans outside of Central America. The kaleidoscopic landscape of Los Angeles, as is increasingly true of most major cities, reflects a world atlas, and neither we as a society nor our churches are close to grasping the significance of what this means and portends. This essay wrestles with several dimensions of these changing urban circumstances and with some of their implications for Christian ministry.

---

4. Parag Khanna, *Connectography: Mapping the Future of Global Civilization* (New York: Random House, 2016).

Global Communications

Cultural annexation is not new. It has been with us at least since Alexander the Great spread Hellenism from the Nile to the Ganges. Where new ideas once advanced at the foot pace of advancing armies or merchant caravans, they are now spread instantly by satellites bringing Hollywood's fantasies and Madison Avenue's commercials to places as widely separated and isolated as the Alaskan tundra, Guatemalan villages, and the Kenyan bush. The formation of culture is the process of the telling of stories. Today's far-reaching signals have new tales to tell of affluence, freedom, and power.[5]

The acceleration of information technology has facilitated the promotion of these new stories or retelling of stories ("going viral" being the new nomenclature). Throughout the village people are using the same electronic devices to watch or listen to the same commercially or privately produced songs, stories, and soap operas, in the same real-time instant. Alaskan children watch *Teletubbies* cartoons, and Muslim viewers of *Baywatch* in Arab countries compare its glamour and turmoil with their conservative family-centered culture.[6] Traditional ways of life are challenged under the spell of advanced communication technologies. At one time films, television, radio, music, periodicals, clothing, board games, toys, and theme parks had been the media for disseminating Western ideas and international images and for spreading global dreams. Now the World Wide Web has shrunk the globe to human scale, with cyberspace creating nodes of connections and exchange at nanosecond speed.

The Spiritual Dimension of the New Urban Landscape

Most people, from all parts of society, desire to build new and better lives for themselves. Whether they move to a new land or city they carry with them their hopes and dreams as well as their beliefs, ideals, and understanding of the sacred. It should not then be too surprising to find, even in the most prosaic of neighborhoods, transplanted expressions of world religions and sects. Asian architectural design may reveal a Buddhist

5. Ann T. Jordon, "The Critical Incident: Story Creation and Culture Formation in a Self-Directed Work Team," *Journal of Organizational Change Management* 9, no. 5 (1996): 27–35.

6. *Teletubbies* is a commercially successful and internationally recognized British preschool children's television series featuring a mythological species named for television screens implanted in their abdomens and inhabiting a commonly shared, earth-like environment. *Baywatch* is a now syndicated U.S.A.-television action drama series produced for more than a decade between 1989 and 1999. Its plot focused on the social lives and intrigues of lifeguards who patrolled the beaches of Los Angeles County, California.

temple in the new community. The presence of a mosque may testify to the growing global presence of Islamic practitioners within the city.

There was a time when virtually all of America's European ancestors and missionaries could imagine no substitute for the church. Now the church must compete for attention with a host of alternative religious pursuits, not to mention the social forces creating the new urban world. Certainly, traditional and established Judeo-Christian forms of religion are still quite present in the physical landscape, although the activities inside increasingly lack cross-generational appeal and are often disconnected from the changing demographic and socioeconomic contexts in which they are located.

New religious expressions proliferate in the city. They may be as controversial as, for example, the Church of Scientology or as provocative as New Age and spiritualist movements. In many Latino communities the ubiquitous herbal medicinal shop, the Botanica, sells religious artifacts which are often affiliated with spiritualism or with Santeria, one of the syncretistic religions that arrived from the Caribbean via Central America. Within the same neighborhood, one would find Charismatic or Pentecostal groups aggressively competing with Santeria, vying for the loyalty of those same Central Americans.

These religious expressions in the urban terrain point to the irreducible fact of the vitality of religious pluralism and other sources of cultural diversity that greatly feed questions about the locus of Christianity within these contexts. The fourth-century ascendency to power of Constantine as emperor of the Roman Empire, and his attendant support for and political legalization of the Christian faith, reframed the proclamation of faith in line with values and traditions informed by the European societies that were part of the former empire. For over one thousand years, this representation of Christianity furnished the overarching worldview and moral ethos for Western civilization. Over successive epochs of Western civilization, however (including throughout the rising influence of scientific thinking), Christendom's cultural predominance has diminished profoundly. Given these global religious and cultural transformations, Christianity struggles to understand where it fits within a post-Christendom, rapidly urbanizing world.

Back to the Future

The postmodern, conflicted, and kaleidoscopic nature of urban contexts, indeed, poses difficult questions for the Christian community. How are we to be defined (e.g., denominational affiliation, values, mission)? Do we stand for exclusivity and privilege or do we engender acceptance and invitation (not just in attitude but reflected in the design and aesthetics of our worship centers)? Do we foster class distinctions or reconciliation? Do we look toward ethnic affirmation and acculturation or rote forms of ethnic segregation and marginalization? Do we truly embody an ethic of service and caring? Do we bring a moral dimension to public life? Do we represent justice and mercy? Do we promote a deeper relationship with God? Do we reflect anything more than cultural ethnocentrism? Do we encourage economic and environmental responsibility? Are these values evident in the facilities that we build or renovate and the physical environment that we control? These questions might not be new but the context is.

That the ministry of the church must be realigned to take into account the global changes that are occurring is no longer optional. I suggest here a few crucial components of that ministry and focus.

Global Alertness: Andrew Davey, former resident urbanologist to the Church of England's Council of Bishops, suggests that meeting the pastoral needs of ordinary people and struggling for social justice in our urban communities will inevitably take us into global territory.[7] Addressing the concerns of an unemployed parishioner means considering the effects of the shifting global economy that forces the closure or relocation of factories and work. Financial quakes in Asia and Eastern Europe are quickly felt in both Madrid and Manhattan.

Broad Community Builders: The global dimensions of the contemporary urban world set new challenges as new technologies and communications (including social media) alter the way we live and relate to one another and make the quest for community increasingly difficult. Certainly the rise of self-help groups and the ever-accessible Alcoholics Anonymous groups reflect the need for community. So do youth gangs and Internet chat rooms. But while Internet social networks may be dominant, they are no substitute for the kind of community to which Christians are called.

Christian-based communities or cell groups have already challenged the conventional concepts of "church," and point to the fact that community building is still an important function of the church. Yet the role of the church may well go beyond community building among believers. Admittedly, it may be tough going within a diverse and fluid urban population but in the long run more rewarding for the Christian Church to

7. Andrew P. Davey, "Globalization as Challenge and Opportunity in Urban Mission: An Outlook from London," *International Review of Missions* (October 1999).

effect coalitions with neighborhood groups, civic associations, and non-profit entities to work for broad objectives of economic, environmental, social, and cultural justice. More importantly, community building may prove to be one of the best ways to articulate the message of the gospel within emerging urban contexts.

Peacebuilders: The church will be faced with much more than the task of bridging individuals, groups, and organizations. If there is one distinct feature of the emerging urban reality, it is the increasing diversity of the city's residents. Immigration adds ethnic diversity and often contributes to the creation of ethnic enclaves. Regional migration creates geographic subcultures, and divisions along color lines reinforce their own kind of diversity. Communities forged along the lines of generational or sexual orientation have emerged and will continue to be important.

Ideological and identity battles are now waged on numerous fronts, challenging religious leaders to rethink their roles in these conflicts—and specifically, whether they should be aligned with a particular camp or serve as ministers of reconciliation. Moreover, the church is being challenged to give attention to less vocal communities overshadowed within such conflicts. Persons aligned with dominant cultures have much to learn from persons on the periphery; in fact, the main stimulus for rethinking the mission of the church may come from "bottom and edge" sectors of the world. The marginalized Christian faithful may be in places inhabited by the poor, by Christian minorities surrounded by non-Christian cultures, by communities of faith living under political oppression, by communities of color, and by women struggling within institutional structures that perpetuate patriarchy. These are the "voices from the margins," and their struggles and hopes may offer a vision for the church that proves liberating.

Midwives to a New People: In the same sense that old-line denominations have much to learn from newly emerging denominations and non-denominational faith communities, the white minority has much to learn from the "People of Color" majority. The fact of the matter is that we are embarking on a global path that challenges notions of race and ethnicity as anthropological categories. Biracial and multiethnic families are no longer an anomaly within human interactions but rather are becoming more of the norm. Our global cities have become incubators of a bold new mix of humanity, exemplified by a global youth consumer class. This new urban demographic tends not to define themselves along the lines of existing races or ethnic groups but, instead, have created new social classifications for themselves such as "white chocolate," "funky Aztecs," and "honorary homegirls." Such definitions wreak havoc on stubborn conventional stereotypes and archaic notions about what it is to be African,

Asian, or Caucasian within an ever-transfiguring urban world. This rejection of older identity frameworks is an honest, eyes-wide-open embrace of the new urban realities older generations find confounding. Churches can stay locked in older social frameworks or embrace opportunities available to them for helping birth this new sense of peoplehood.

Messengers of Hope: In addition to being a context defined by ethnic diversity and religious pluralism, the global village appears to be characterized increasingly by consumerism. In part a pursuit of hope, the consumer culture so evident in nearly every billboard or corner-mall of the city is driving people to work harder to fulfill their need for material amenities of a comfortable life. People have confused standard of living for quality of life, and ultimately these material dreams will reveal themselves to be an illusion for most people.[8]

As we move further into the twenty-first century, old questions about God and mammon, wealth and injustice, development and stewardship likely will resurface with more vigor. The Christian faith has included a central message of a hope that transcends our social and material circumstances—something learned from those who have struggled on the margins. As the world is being reshaped, that message needs to be presented more clearly than ever before.

Concluding Thoughts

Now well into the twenty-first century, every aspect of what we call the urban context is indelibly marked by the powerful changes emanating from the globalization of our world and the advances in technology. The profound transformations in peoples, institutions, demography, and geography are physically evident in the new urban reality. Continuous class and ethnic conflicts, internal social disorder (communal, familial, and individual), spiritual movements, and patterns of geographic mobility and economic stress have become part of our multicultural urban terrain.

The Christian faith has never had a greater opportunity or a more urgent responsibility to live and proclaim eternal truths. While pulled in two directions—to remain faithful to its roots while relevant to a kaleidoscopic world—the church's fundamental challenge is to discern the action of God in new ways, which likely means finding ways to carry out faithful and bold ministry within forms yet to be conceived.

---

8. Pew Research Center, "America's Shrinking Middle-Class: A Close Look at Changes within Metropolitan Areas," May 11, 2016, http://assets.pewresearch.org/wp-content/uploads/sites/3/2016/05/Middle-Class-Metro-Areas-FINAL.pdf.

Chapter 3

The City's Grace

Peter Choi

A vision of the city as a place where grace abounds has largely been absent from the Christian imagination of recent years. Urban ministry approaches have tended to view cities as places marked by compromised good at best and unchecked evil at worst. For those who have eyes to see, however, the city is also a site of boundless human ingenuity and possibility. So long as we are blind to the city's dignity and grace, Christian witness in urban contexts will fall short. This chapter argues for the city's grace even in the face of much that is wrong about cities. It begins by examining the shortcomings of Western missiology's dualistic approach to urban ministry, proposes a new way of thinking about incarnational ministry that aspires toward intersectional intimacy, and concludes with a story of hope in the Tenderloin, San Francisco.

Urban Ministry and the Tragedy of Western Missionary Theology

Because Christian mission in the modern Western world has long been inextricably linked to the expansionist agenda of European nations, any reframing of urban ministry must grapple with this checkered past.[1] Wil-

---

1. According to Dana Robert, "The spread of Christianity to Africa, Asia, and the Americas occurred within the colonial framework in which European peoples poured into other parts of the world." Dana L. Robert, *Christian Mission: How Christianity Became a World Religion* (Malden, MA: Wiley-Blackwell, 2009), 51. For an excellent study of the symbiotic relationship between British imperial officials and missionary leaders forged by powerful mutual interests, see Andrew Porter, *Religion versus Empire?: British Protestant Missionaries and Overseas Expansion, 1700–1914* (Manchester: Manchester University Press, 2004). For a more forceful critique of conversion as a process of colonialism that demeaned indigenous converts, see Jean Comaroff and John L. Comaroff, *Of Revelation and Revolution*, vol. 1, *Christianity, Colonialism, and Consciousness in*

lie James Jennings's identification of "a reductive theological vision in which the world's people become perpetual students" is a mistake urban ministers have been especially prone to make.[2] Marked by spiritual conceit and based on a legacy of cultural imperialism, the missiological perspective of Western Christendom focused primarily on a teaching project designed to improve the lives of specially targeted, unreached groups. It is an ideological starting point that has had far-reaching ripple effects. Confident of theological and cultural advantage, such attitudes generally denied the dignity of those who failed to believe or live the way of Jesus as narrowly defined by European missionaries.

As a consequence, the Western Christendom approach to cities conceptualized urban ministry in the impersonal terms of research-based strategy that held the city at arm's length as a problem to be solved. From Donald McGavran's call for the empirical study of church growth to Alan Tippett's delineation of "winnable" people groups to Harvie Conn's mandate for "urban church research," the default position of urban missiologists inclined toward a project-based view of the city.[3] With this bias, the overall message tilted negative in the majority of urban missiological writings, decrying the "moral malignancy" of "postfall cities" that are "human-centered, often violent, and rife with friction, greed, and carnality." Notwithstanding the obligatory lip service to common grace, cities represented "visible ramifications of the curse."[4]

While recognition of the brokenness of cities may be biblically and theologically accurate, a crucial misstep occurred. Urban ministry became a rescue operation and urban missionaries saw themselves as the primary chosen agents of redemptive work in the city. A sense of theological and spiritual superiority tarnished urban missiological rhetoric,

South Africa (Chicago: University of Chicago Press, 1991), and vol. 2, *The Dialectics of Modernity on a South African Frontier* (Chicago: University of Chicago Press, 1997). See also Elizabeth Elbourne, "Review Essays: Colonialism and the Possibilities of Historical Anthropology—Word Made Flesh: Christianity, Modernity, and Cultural Colonialism in the Work of Jean and John Comaroff," *American Historical Review* 108, no. 2 (2003).

2. Willie James Jennings, *The Christian Imagination: Theology and the Origins of Race* (New Haven, CT: Yale University Press, 2010), 112.

3. Donald MacGavran, *Bridges of God: A Study in the Strategy of Missions* (Eugene, OR: Wipf & Stock, 2005). Alan Tippett, *Ways of the People: A Reader in Missionary Anthropology* (Pasadena, CA: William Carey Library Publishers, 2013). The influence of leaders in the Church Growth School—like MacGavran and Tippett—on developments in the theology of urban ministry as well as Conn's application of their findings are described in Harvie M. Conn, *Planting and Growing Urban Churches: From Dream to Reality* (Grand Rapids: Baker Academic, 1997), 26–28.

4. Roger S. Greenway and Timothy M. Monsma, *Cities: Missions' New Frontier* (Grand Rapids: Baker Academic, 2000), 5–6.

leading to statements like: "We Christians are the only people on this earth who have the integrated worldview of matter and spirit that enables us to tackle sewer system development and the salvation of souls with equal gusto."[5] Alongside pessimism toward cities grew a triumphalistic overestimation of the church's ability to turn things around.

Despite the fact that we live in a post-Christendom world, this old way of engaging in urban ministry continues to proliferate as Christians increasingly fix cities in the crosshairs of their missional vision. Evangelistic zeal of this sort that rides roughshod over the dignity of so-called target groups represents a failure of biblical, Christlike humility as well as careful theological reflection. The shortcomings of a Christendom approach to Christian witness are epitomized by a false supersessionist ecclesiology of Western Protestant evangelicalism as the crowning achievement of Christian history. David Bosch's compelling message has gone unheeded: "[The church] has no monopoly on God's reign, may not claim it for itself, may not present itself as the realized kingdom of God over against the world. The kingdom will never be fully present in the church."[6] By conceiving of their particular expression of the church as the city upon a hill Jesus spoke about in Matthew 5, Western Christians mistook themselves as the light.

One of the consequences of this slide into theological, spiritual, and cultural hubris has been the propensity of Western Christians to see themselves as teachers and everyone else as students. In this worldview, there is the Christian responsibility to teach and a lost world whose only hope resides in their willingness to learn. One need not look far into our past to see how such a view of the world has led to harsh, coercive measures of theological hegemony. The elevation of Christian witnesses to a spiritual pedestal, as God's messengers, will need to be reconsidered and revised if we are to move beyond the deleterious effects of Christendom missiology.[7]

The Hope of Post-Christendom Missional Theology: Duality without Dualism

The life and ministry of Jesus show us another way, a model for ministry to which we can all aspire. The call to incarnational living in the way of

5. Ray Bakke, "The Challenge of World Evangelization to Mission Strategy," in Greenway and Monsma, *Cities*, 80.

6. David J. Bosch, *Transforming Mission: Paradigm Shifts in Theology of Mission* (Maryknoll, NY: Orbis Books, 1998), 517. For a more recent argument along the same lines, see Graham Tomlin, *The Provocative Church: Fourth Edition* (London: SPCK Publishing, 2014), 55.

7. Michael W. Stroope, *Transcending Mission: The Eclipse of a Modern Tradition* (Downers Grove, IL: IVP Academic Press, 2017).

Jesus, as we will see, involves cultivating a love for the city that results in an embrace of intimacy in the face of mystery.

In this endeavor, however, no blind fetishizing of the city will do. Faithful Christian witnesses will ask hard questions of what motivates our hope and ardor for cities. Being sanguine about all that is wrong in the city represents an important part of public and civic duty as well as spiritual calling.[8] At the same time, an informed appreciation of the inherent dignity of the city is an indispensable part of the call to urban ministry. The city is a place of contradictions and paradoxes. The sweet aroma of a bakery mingled with the stench of garbage in the city, melodious music wafting down the street and the noise pollution of traffic, architectural wonders overlooking rundown housing projects—these are the cacophonies of the city that remind us of the messiness of human life together. What's more, Christian spirituality with its sacramental, Trinitarian, and incarnational dimensions of mystery is well poised to encounter the city's myriad dualities without devolving into a rigid dualism.[9] A robust biblical view of humanity that affirms people made in the image of God, while at the same time remembering they are from the dust of the earth, will lead to more commodious missiological frameworks. Rather than offering quick and tidy solutions, we might roll up our sleeves and join others in the work of peace already happening in the city.

A posture of listening and learning flows from genuine esteem toward other people rooted in an appreciation of their multilayered, intersectional identities. It is not an attitude that comes naturally for ministers who feel duty-bound to teach others the way to truth without stopping to question their own inherited viewpoints. But resisting the knee-jerk tendency to presume the role of teacher can open the way to finding our rightful place as fellow learners in the process of translating the Christian message. In this way we can avoid the mistake—described with penetrating depth by Willie Jennings—of supposing others "theologically infantile"

8. A popular work that encapsulates recent trends in new urbanism and the celebration of the city's virtues is Edward Glaeser, *Triumph of the City: How Our Greatest Invention Makes Us Richer, Smarter, Greener, Healthier, and Happier* (New York: Penguin Books, 2012). A countervailing perspective and sober critique of new urbanist enthusiasm can be found in Joel Kotkin, *The Human City: Urbanism for the Rest of Us* (Chicago: Agate B2 Books, 2016). Both kinds of works need to be held in tension as we build a missional theology that embraces both common grace and the reality of the fall.

9. With respect to living with mysteries that defy explanation while continually engendering reflection, Mark Noll's description of the Chalcedonian definition as an invitation to a rigorous life of the mind may serve as a helpful model for the potential of faithful Christian engagement with culture. Mark A. Noll, *Jesus Christ and the Life of the Mind* (Grand Rapids: Eerdmans, 2013), 19–21.

while thinking of ourselves as theologically superior. His concerns over a disembodied, overly didactic approach to missions are rooted in his analysis of the conflation of incarnation and translation in Western theology.[10] Likewise, his critique of the "vernacularization thesis that isolates the gospel message into its essential components" opens the way toward "a new form of communion with the possibility of a new kind of cultural intimacy between peoples."[11] This vision of mutual learning has the potential to radically alter the labor of Christian ministry in cities. It would move us past our preoccupations with the transmission of information and the transformation of others into our own image. Christians would more and more enter urban contexts not with the goal of teaching non-Christians but rather with the intention of together seeking the common good. The aim of Christian mission would then become the flourishing of all rather than the salvation of atomized individuals and their disembodied souls.

Seeing the city as a place of grace abounding means that we embrace the consubstantiality of the city as home and far country in the same moment. Rather than the work of translation that too easily devolves into a one-way transaction, we can recover the explicitly two-way process of language learning as a new metaphor for imagining Christian ministry. In this journey as pilgrims, the arduous activity of gaining fluency in another tongue becomes a path to deeper life together. More than instructing others, the vocation of Christian witness might cultivate the greater aspiration of friendship with others. It is a vision in which the *telos* of missions is nothing less than a living community of followers of Jesus growing and learning from one another. Together they embody the radical new possibilities of a God who has always been full of surprises in redrawing boundary markers.

City Hope in the Tenderloin, San Francisco

The story of City Church San Francisco and its City Hope Community Center presents a helpful picture of the kind of post-Christendom approach to loving the city we have been describing in this chapter. As senior pastor Fred Harrell puts it, the earliest commitment of the church from its founding was "to discover and join what God was already doing

10. For the vernacularization thesis, see Lamin O. Sanneh, *Translating the Message: The Missionary Impact on Culture* (Maryknoll, NY: Orbis Books, 2009). For Andrew Walls on translation as incarnation, see Andrew F. Walls, *The Missionary Movement in Christian History: Studies in the Transmission of Faith* (Maryknoll, NY: Orbis Books, 1996). For Jennings's critical response to Sanneh and Walls, see Jennings, *The Christian Imagination*, 155–61.
11. Jennings, *The Christian Imagination*, 265.

in the city."[12] The imperative was to listen, learn, and apply what the city had to teach. In keeping with this value, a key mantra in the early days was, "Let's build a church that's not just for ourselves." The work of ministry following this statement consisted primarily of listening to neighbors without proposing ideas or solutions. In other words, the church deliberately took steps to resist the supersessionist fallacy of assuming theological superiority, choosing instead to walk alongside and learn from neighbors.

Paul Trudeau came to City Church as an intern and later became the director of City Hope Community Center in the Tenderloin—one of the most densely populated neighborhoods in San Francisco, with high rates of poverty, addiction, and mental illness, but also people on the road to recovery, reentering society after jail, and soaring numbers of children. He recalls the challenge of grappling with ministry in a city that disarmed and overwhelmed him at seemingly every turn. As he saw his whole conception of ministry upended, the city was teaching him to focus less on changing or improving people's lives and to be more concerned about listening to their stories. Paul's eyes light up as he talks about this shift: "When you listen to people, you stop looking for answers and solutions, and you start saying things like, 'It's amazing that you're alive!' and 'You're a walking miracle!'"[13] This movement involves eschewing the common critical spirit missionaries have toward their target cultures along with any underlying judgment that the person we are talking with might have had a better life had they met us earlier. Instead, there is glad recognition of the opportunity to discover light in the midst of darkness, to revel in our shared humanity rather than wallow in prejudice based upon shallow caricatures and condemnations.

Since those early forays into the city, a new clarity of vision has emerged for the ministry of City Hope. "The goal is not to fix thy neighbor, it's love thy neighbor," says Trudeau. Jesus' words lead us to a recognition of our own limited ability to help or save others, which then lead us to a deeper, truer love of neighbor. Following this principle led church volunteers through City Hope to the county jail, where they heard the desire for regular worship services. At present there are twelve worship services a month facilitated by City Hope in the San Francisco County Jail facilities. In addition, the relationships built there led to many volunteers walking alongside people who left jail only to commence the long road to recovery. Painful firsthand encounters with relapse and recidivism gave

---

12. Fred Harrell (pastor) in an informal interview with author, April 19, 2017.
13. Paul Trudeau (director of City Hope) in an informal interview with author, May 2, 2017.

birth to the idea of a community center focused not only on providing relief but also a "safe, sober, and social" space for people on a journey that led through the valleys of SRO territory (short for "single room occupancy") that is the Tenderloin. In a neighborhood filled with dwellings that lack living rooms, bathrooms, and kitchens, City Hope set out to become a "living space" for all. Sit-down dinners, cooking lessons with chefs from popular local restaurants, talent shows, and karaoke nights are some of the most popular events for people who have few opportunities for letting their gifts shine or to cultivate new ones. In a neighborhood where people fight daily to maintain their dignity, there is a place where they can belt out tunes to the cheers of adoring fans, a place where they are known by name, where community develops not only through relief but the hard road of reforming life, neighborhood, and the city together. In other words, people are finding grace and intimacy together not by standing above one another but walking alongside one another.

Conclusion

When we smell what's for dinner next door, overhear lovers quarreling, and know more than we'd care to about the sleep habits of a newborn neighbor, there is an intimacy to urban living that feels almost effortless. And yet the city is full of strangers living quite apart from each other. Given the frenetic pace of life and the variability of schedules, it's possible that neighbors who have lived for years next door to each other have never met or stopped for conversation. The intimacy of the city is often marked by closeness but not connection. In this context, what would it look like for Christian ministry to focus on the intimacy of urban life? To celebrate the persistence of the human desire for deep, meaningful connection?

A vision of incarnational, intersectional community marked by deep intimacy begins by recognizing the inherent worth of city dwellers as people who bear God's indelible image despite persistent reminders to the contrary. Establishing the starting point of our missional engagement as a conversation between equals will have wide-ranging implications. It will also provide a helpful corrective for past missionary actions that often devolved into the worst aspects of cultural imperialism, where missionaries saw themselves as the bringers of light to blind and benighted primitives. The urban context represents both fallen humanity in need of redemption and the triumph of human achievements. It is in this beautiful cacophony of the city that brings such complex people together that we might discover grace in a new way.

Chapter 4

Toward a Missiological Turn
in Urban Ministry

Scott Hagley

I noticed the unkempt man the first time I visited Midtown Baptist Church as well as on subsequent visits.[1] He was standing in the back with the ushers—dressed notably different from the sober, business-casual crowd. After he helped with the offering, I watched him return to his seat in the back corner of the sanctuary, a halo of empty seats on all sides. The man sometimes came into the sanctuary, apparently having had no shower, with the stench of life on the streets; but on other Sundays he appeared clean and showered. For many urban congregations, such a man presents a problem: the obvious difference he represents from congregational norms culturally and socioeconomically. The problem involves economic inequality, injustice, failing mental health systems, homelessness, and mixing suburban commuters and affluent re-gentrified urbanites with the urban poor in worship, namely, "the street" arising unbeckoned in the sanctuary.

As Christians in the urban-influenced culture of the twenty-first century, can we move, like Midtown, from *problem to possibility*? Is it possible that this man's arrival presents a *revelatory* moment for the congregation? Is it possible that this unshowered, unkempt body in the midst of washed, pampered, smartly dressed bodies reveals the Living God?

These are not unreasonable questions. The Jerusalem church in Acts 11 also discovers the problems from the street in its sanctuary. After Peter returns to the Jerusalem church from an extended stay with Cornelius, the community wonders aloud about Peter's contamination. Why did

1. Midtown Baptist Church is a pseudonym for an actual congregation located in a downtown neighborhood of a large American city. I studied this congregation in 2009–2010.

35

Peter go into the house of a Gentile and eat at an unclean table?[2] Rather than offer a defense or appeal to a deontological principle, Peter responds by telling a story of God's guidance and Cornelius's surprising insistence. Peter did not go looking for contamination, it found him in such a way that challenged every notion he had about the clean and unclean.[3] The world, the "streets," suddenly interrupted the emerging church's sense of "sanctuary." Peter insisted that this interruption was the work of God revealing a clearer vision of the gospel it proclaims.[4]

Theological education for urban ministry must learn from Midtown Baptist and Acts 11, to respond in faith and hope to the ways "the streets" impose themselves on the sanctuary. In what follows, I explore the pedagogical and theological implications of this possibility by considering the missiological dimensions of urban ministry and the urban ministry dimensions of missional theology. Missional theology, I suggest, can offer a robust vision for theological discernment in the context of urban ministry. Urban ministry offers missional theology as an interesting form of attentiveness to bodies and the critical social sciences.

The Intentional Embodied Attentiveness of Urban Ministry

The profound diversity and fluidity of urban environments demand contextual attentiveness for urban ministers. Nancy Ammerman's memorable *Congregation and Community* studies different congregations in changing urban contexts across the United States.[5] Some congregations

---

2. Acts 10–11 records the same story twice. In Acts 10, the story narrates Peter's experience with Cornelius. Acts 11 begins back in Jerusalem. News of Gentile conversion had reached Jerusalem. The question they had for Peter was with regard to his ritual uncleanliness with regard to food: "Why did you go to uncircumcised men and eat with them?" (Acts 11:3).

3. The challenge for Peter and the Jerusalem church, it seems, is not Gentile acceptance of the gospel but the fact that God accepts Gentiles as Gentiles. It is the experience of God's surprising acceptance—of the Gentile as gift to the Christian community rather than moral reclamation project—that calls into question notions of purity and impurity. Mission, in this instance, acts back upon the Jerusalem community; it marks *their* conversion as well as Cornelius's. See Lamin O. Sanneh, *Translating the Message: The Missionary Impact on Culture*, 2nd ed. (Maryknoll, NY: Orbis Books, 2009), 324. For a reading of Luke-Acts as a text tracing the discernment and fluid identity of the Christian community, see Luke Timothy Johnson, *Scripture and Discernment: Decision-Making in the Church* (Nashville: Abingdon Press, 1996), 166.

4. Richard Beck argues something close to this, tying together the phenomena of disgust and the historical experience of the church in mission. See Richard Allan Beck, *Unclean: Meditations on Purity, Hospitality, and Mortality* (Eugene, OR: Cascade Books, 2011), 201.

5. Nancy Tatom Ammerman, *Congregation and Community* (New Brunswick, NJ: Rutgers University Press, 1997).

discover means for survival or even thriving. Others struggle to keep the doors open. Ammerman's research suggests a complex urban social ecology, where the "spiritual energies" of congregations shape the political, moral, and social spaces of neighborhoods while a host of sociopolitical and socioeconomic forces "govern" congregational shape and vitality.[6] Congregations shape their environment even as they depend upon it for their well-being.

Those writing and teaching urban ministry knew this before Ammerman's study. Ministry longevity in urban contexts requires attentiveness and adaptability to social, religious, political, and economic realities. Truthfully, congregations and ministries in suburban or rural contexts must also remain attentive to such realities, but the density of urban spaces, coupled with fluid socioeconomic, racial-ethnic, and religious diversities heightens the demand for adaptability. Most of Ammerman's congregations were located in urban neighborhoods that had changed in unpredictable ways; she discovered that adaptability increases the likelihood of congregational survival. Thus, while the adjective "urban" can sometimes function as a "code word" implying benevolence for "those [often non-White] people" or as displaying a preference for social justice over evangelism, it is, in practice, a holistic expression of Christian ministry.[7] As such, the unique pressures of urban contexts have given urban ministry practitioners and teachers particular gifts that may be lacking in other settings. Specifically, urban ministry teaching and practice works at the intersection between theology, social theory, and the social sciences for the sake of imagining and participating in *shalom*.[8] As such, urban ministry begins with bodies.

First, urban ministry begins with the social body (or, better yet, social embodiment), for we cannot understand the "urban" apart from social theory.[9] In cities, political and economic "mega-systems" shape congre-

---

6. Ibid., 2–3.

7. Ronald Edward Peters, *Urban Ministry: An Introduction* (Nashville: Abingdon Press, 2007), 25–28.

8. Mark R. Gornik, *To Live in Peace: Biblical Faith and the Changing Inner City* (Grand Rapids: Eerdmans, 2002).

9. Books on urban ministry often begin with a discussion of the "urban," seeking to both define it and retrieve it from negative stereotypes. It is one of the few approaches to ministry that begin with some use of social theory, identifying urbanization and a ministry in urban contexts with demographics, economic patterns, and governmental policy. See, for example, Peters, *Urban Ministry*, 197; Harvie M. Conn and Manuel Ortiz, *Urban Ministry: The Kingdom, the City, and the People of God* (Downers Grove, IL: InterVarsity Press, 2001).

gational life in significant, yet imprecise ways.[10] For example, a congregation might experience the cross-pressures of gentrification when the built space and cultural world of the neighborhood suddenly shift. While this creates certain social or cultural demands on the congregation, it points toward the confluence of political and economic factors, working beyond the control of any one agency. Where does such a congregation turn? City hall? Local developers? The business community? Because gentrifying forces are diffuse and systemic, urban ministers lean upon social theory to discern action, learning the importance of civil society and its deliberative and collective agency in relationship to political and economic systems.[11] While this engagement is not always theorized, it is certainly actualized in partnerships cultivated by organizations like the Christian Community Development Association (CCDA), among others.[12]

Attention to the social body, however, stems from the attention urban ministry gives to persons in its neighborhood and community. Our concern for actual bodies—for general well-being, community, healing, education, opportunity, discipleship, renewal in worship—leads urban ministers, secondly, to consider social scientific tools in the course of ministry.[13] For residents, gentrification does not express itself in abstract data sets or the play of symbols but discloses itself through embodied interactions. The symbolic significance of a neighborhood diner turning into a high-priced restaurant or "flipped" rental properties is experienced on the street and in neighborhood interactions as alternately exclusion or opportunity, loss or gain. Holistic ministry in such a setting will need to draw upon a wide variety of tools both to make sense of neighborhood

10. Jürgen Habermas's theory of civil society suggests a three-tiered understanding of Western society. At the human level, we live in a "lifeworld" constituted by our family ties, traditions, and sense of personal meaning. At the impersonal level, modern life is shaped in profound ways by the two mega-"systems" of the economy and the state. In between the systems and the lifeworld remains the public, communicative space of civil society where nonprofits, neighborhood groups, and congregations flourish. As urban ministries build partnerships with other agencies to address needs or concerns in a neighborhood, they are naturally drawn into civil society partnerships aimed at understanding and influencing the impersonal systems that (sometimes) threaten the "lifeworld." See Gary M. Simpson, *Critical Social Theory: Prophetic Reason, Civil Society, and Christian Imagination* (Minneapolis: Fortress Press, 2002).

11. Gary Simpson suggests the metaphor of "civil society companion" to describe such congregations. This is the natural way for urban ministries to operate. Ibid., 141–45.

12. "About: Christian Community Development Association," http://www.ccda.org/about.

13. Urban ministry texts tend to begin with an analysis of the "urban" and then to suggest methods for understanding, narrating, studying, and paying attention to one's context through the use of various social science methods. See Peters, *Urban Ministry: An Introduction*, 197.

dynamics and to address the whole person in the name and hope of Christ. Christian ministry in such a context requires an answer to the question, What is going on? In a more stable or even homogenous social context, we might be able to make certain assumptions about context and the cultivation of spaces for healing, wholeness, or *shalom*. But the potential and fluidity of urban neighborhoods demand robust contextual attentiveness to the realities, injustices, anxieties, and opportunities of the neighborhood.

Thus, urban ministry draws upon a wide variety of social science tools. Those trained in urban ministry are often better equipped than their suburban or rural colleagues in the use of demographics, interviews, ethnography, and asset-based community development. These tools are imagined not as the work of urban ministry but as a critical voice for shaping the work of such ministry. They are a means for attending to the complex interactions of persons in their ministry context who can inform the minister as to the possibilities and needs in the neighborhood. As such, social sciences provide a particular "bottom-up" approach to the ministry and theology of the urban worker; they are a necessary element for participating in the urban ecology.[14]

The use of social theory and social sciences in urban ministry cultivates the possibility for a more *lively* or *lived* approach to theology and theological education, where the particularities of place and body and experience become a *generative site* for theological understanding rather than its application. Despite our collective awareness that all theology is contextual, old habits of practice and institution die hard. Our "contextual" theologies still tend to be produced from academics and written for other academics. While these works necessarily subvert the pretensions of universality and the hegemony of the Western theological tradition, they can be difficult to enact on the ground. Despite our protests to the contrary, our "contextual" theological education remains mired in a theory-praxis dichotomy; for even a "contextual theology" course within the seminary is unlikely to involve interviewing neighbors or an ethnographic study of a neighborhood.[15] When doing theology we make context conveniently abstract. When engaging context we "apply" the theology learned in classrooms. Thus, we struggle to reflect theologically

14. Ibid., 84.
15. For all the gains we have made in declaring the cultural locatedness of theology, we struggle to connect cultural studies and sociological methods with theological research. Where we do, the conversation remains relatively abstract and at the meta-theological level. See, for example, Kathryn Tanner, *Theories of Culture: A New Agenda for Theology* (Minneapolis: Fortress Press, 1997).

on the unkempt man in the sanctuary. Our social scientific tools can help us to attend to the man and meet his needs, but our struggle to practice "context" and "theology" simultaneously reflects an impoverished approach to theological work and urban ministry.

Here the teaching of urban ministry can benefit from a "turn" toward missional theology, where the social scientific and socially attentive practice of urban ministry can fruitfully enact contextual, theological practice. Similarly, the present concern in missiological circles for a "missional church" will do well to draw upon the grounded, neighborhood-focused attentiveness of urban ministry.

Missional Theology: Discovering God in God's World

The Latin term *missio Dei*, which means mission of God, came into popular use after the Willingen meeting of the International Missionary Council in 1952.[16] The council report drew upon Trinitarian theology and postcolonial missiology to redefine mission according to God.[17] *Missio Dei* provides not only a renewal and subversion of missions, but also room for reimagining the task of theology. If mission describes the triune God, then missions can no longer be imagined as a strategic expansion of the gospel entrusted to the church. Rather, *missio Dei* offers mission as a gift and invitation for the church to participate in the fellowship of Father, Son, and Spirit in, for, and with God's world. The ecclesiological implications of this shift are significant, leading to works like J. C. Hoekendijk's *The Church Inside Out*, David Bosch's *Transforming Mission*, Lesslie Newbigin's formation of the "Gospel and Our Culture Network," and our current conversation regarding the "missional church."[18]

---

16. Lesslie Newbigin drafted the conference document "The Missionary Calling of the Church" published in *Missions under the Cross*, where Norman Goodall writes, "the missionary movement of which we are a part has its source in the Triune God himself . . . . There is no participation in Christ without participation in His mission in the world. That by which the Church receives its existence is that by which it is also given its world-mission. 'As the Father has sent me, even so I send you.'" See Norman Goodall, *Missions under the Cross* (Richmond, VA: International Mission Council, 1953), 189–90.

17. Craig Van Gelder, "How Missiology Can Help Inform the Conversation about the Missional Church in Context," in *The Missional Church in Context: Helping Congregations Develop Contextual Ministry*, ed. Craig Van Gelder (Grand Rapids: Eerdmans, 2007), 20.

18. Each of these texts represents different manifestations of the *missio Dei* insight. Hoekendijk imagines a decentering or even diffusion of the church into God's work in the world. Newbigin and "missional church" folks imagine a much more central role of the church as a sign of God's reign in the world. See Johannes Christiaan Hoekendijk, *The Church Inside Out* (Philadelphia:

The upshot of all these attempts to think differently about mission and church is that now *world* or even *neighborhood* constitutes some aspect of ecclesial identity. The shift from mission as a project to participation in God's mission, coupled with a renewed awareness of the world as the site and horizon for this mission, means that our understanding of faithfulness to God must make sense of the places and the communities where God has called us. God's mission shapes congregations in patterns of responsiveness as they establish trustworthy relationships within their neighborhoods and communities.

Practically, this frames mission theology as a process of discovery cultivated by practices of discernment. The church, in responding to and cultivating trustworthy relationships within its neighborhood, does so as a means of discovering the Living God. Like Peter responding to Cornelius's request, the church discovers God even as it seeks to live its faith outwardly in community. In this way, missional theology is not unique. Other theological approaches make similar claims, recognizing the theological importance of experience or praxis or social location. The gift of mission for theology, however, is that this experience in the world is claimed theologically before we consider the social sciences or social location or praxis. Put another way: God's mission, *because it is the giving of God's life*, compels us to attend to God's world with great care. This means we should draw upon the tools available to us—social sciences, social theory, community praxis, or critical theory. Lesslie Newbigin, concerned to connect worldly, historical experience and revelation of the living God, asks: "Is [your] relationship with God something separate from your involvement in the ongoing life of the world, your family, your neighborhood, your nation in the family of nations? . . . Is your relationship with God necessarily bound up with your acceptance of the part God assigns for you in his purpose for this world?"[19] Practically, this means that missional theology invites *discernment* as a means for doing theology. Like Peter with the Jerusalem church, missional theology calls the congregation to reflect on its experiences in the world in order to discover the *missio Dei* among them.

Westminster Press, 1966), 212; Bosch, *Transforming Mission: Paradigm Shifts in Theology of Mission*, 587; Lesslie Newbigin, *The Gospel in a Pluralist Society* (Grand Rapids: Eerdmans, 1989), 244; Darrell L. Guder, *Missional Church: A Vision for the Sending of the Church in North America* (Grand Rapids: Eerdmans, 1998), 280.
19. Newbigin, *The Gospel in a Pluralist Society*, 67.

Urban Ministry as Missional Discernment, Missional Discernment as Urban Ministry

Imagining the theological work of congregations as discovery in partnership with neighbors and strangers through practices of discernment offers rich possibilities to the practice of urban ministry, for missiology provides an open-ended theological rationale for urban ministry's attentiveness to bodies and its use of social theory and the social sciences. With missiological expectation regarding the triune God's commitment to the world, the use of social sciences becomes an "interested" use, not only because they provide sociological analysis but also because they can provide new insights about God's world. But the arrows do not flow only one way. The grounded, embodied emphases of urban ministry provide an important corrective and gift for missional theology. Despite the rhetoric within the missional church regarding the importance of the world for understanding God's mission, old theological habits die hard. Academic work in this area has tended to avoid engagement with the social sciences and the close attention to bodies, neighborhoods, and communities.[20] More popular works in this area might attend to the particularities of place, but not in a theologically disciplined way. We still seem to imagine that we can teach missional theology without embodying it. We talk about discovery and discernment but struggle to help congregations and seminarians to participate in such practices with discipline and care.

It is time to recognize that mission cannot be taught or engaged in general or universal terms. It must be discovered in its concrete particularity as an encounter with the living God in real places and communities.[21] Here missional theology needs an urban "turn" in our classrooms and in our congregations along with the use of missional theology within urban ministry.

Midtown Baptist Church recognized the work of God, the presence of Christ, in the man from the streets. He was received not as a problem to be solved but as a gift to be received, so they invited him to serve as the congregation continued its homeless ministry. He served as an usher on

20. Except for *Treasure in Clay Jars*, studies of actual congregations or communities has not featured in "missional church" literature. See Lois Barrett, *Treasure in Clay Jars: Patterns in Missional Faithfulness* (Grand Rapids: Eerdmans, 2004).
21. Patrick Keifert has suggested, along with David Kelsey, a "return" to congregations as central participants in theological education. This, I think, is right for both urban ministry and missiology. See Patrick R. Keifert, "The Return of the Congregation: Missional Warrants," *Word and World* 20, no. 4 (Fall 2000): 368–78; David H. Kelsey, *To Understand God Truly: What's Theological about a Theological School*, 1st ed. (Louisville, KY: Westminster/John Knox Press, 1992).

Sundays, and his bodily presence in the sanctuary created opportunity to reconsider the identity of the congregation in relationship to upwardly mobile, middle-class values. In recognizing the work of Christ in the man from the street, Midtown learned a new posture toward its neighbors and its context, recognizing diverse expressions of discipleship and faithfulness.[22] Its urban ministry informed its theological identity. Its practice of missiological discernment shaped its urban ministry. As we consider the formational strategies for urban ministers, a context like Midtown where street meets sanctuary will invite students to connect attentiveness to context with the ambiguities and uncertainties of theological discernment, cultivating urban and missiological formation.

22. Midtown had established a reputation as a "come as you are" kind of place, even though it had historically been a congregation of middle-class professionals. This transition in identity, of course, was not due only to the man from the street, but through a host of such encounters where people from many different walks of life could gather to worship together on a Sunday and serve together throughout the week.

Chapter 5

Urban Ministry as the New Frontier?

Felicia Howell LaBoy

With the explosion of missional and new monasticism movements, urban communities across America became new sites for evangelical mission outreach. Moving beyond traditional partnerships with black and other racial ethnic congregations in blighted communities, suburban, mostly white, churches began to see these urban communities as the "new frontier." Contending that they knew better than their black counterparts, and blinded by their own racial and economic privilege, these churches purchased buildings, set up staff and, in some cases, even "divided up" urban areas as territories in their quest to "save the city." While many of these initiatives seem successful (based upon number of members, or facilitation of housing development projects, etc.), few of these do much to address systemic issues of injustice affecting persons in these communities. Sometimes described as "urban church plantations," these missional outposts often show a lack of diversity in their leadership teams, even though they boast of growing diversity within their membership and with regard to those served.

This essay explores the phenomenon of urban church "plantations" and principles of the "missional" and "new monastic" movements and offers insights into the challenges and opportunities they pose to black urban churches.

Urban Church Plants/Plantations

The term "urban church plant/plantations" was first defined in a March 2014 blog post by author Christena Cleveland to describe the way in which some suburban, mainly white, congregations are mimicking imperialistic and colonialistic practices with regard to urban ministry. Seeking to "save the city," these congregations set up "missional outposts" often with little to no diversity in their leadership teams and with little disregard for the indigenous churches that have been working in these urban communities. Cleveland further asserts that not only are these new "urban church missionaries" oblivious to "their own privilege and cultural incompetency," many, fueled by ideas of colorblind liberalism that standardize "white ways" of ministry and being, believe that the lack of any real change to the urban core is solely due to the incompetence of indigenous black church leaders, and can be remedied by the "successful" pastor's entrance into the community.[1]

Although Cleveland's post was shared throughout missional and new monastic networks, as well as through popular evangelical blog posts, little of it filtered down to black or other racial-ethnic, urban congregations. However, another description of urban church plantations had. Just a few months earlier, Gloria Ann Wesley of Urban Intellectuals posted her blog on urban church plantations, titled "Is the Black Church the New Plantation?" This post accused predominantly black churches, especially black megachurches, of adopting a highly capitalistic and individualistic worldview as the central theme of the gospel, with scarce attention to the black church's once unparalleled role of "serving as the voice for equality and justice and functioning as a service institution for spirituality, emotional support and social improvements."[2] Furthermore, the essay compared contemporary black churches solely focused on congregational prosperity, as exemplified in personal wealth and church buildings, to a slave master "profiting from the work of its slaves, the congregation,"[3] while failing to effect systemic social change as their predecessors once had.

Although many urban black congregations provide social services and fight against injustices in urban communities, too many black churches understand the gospel to be primarily contractual rather than covenantal and often treat the poor and disenfranchised surrounding their congregations no better than society treats them in general. In many of the instances in which urban black churches engage in outreach to the community, these

---

1. See Christena Cleveland, "Urban Church Plant/Plantations," blog, March 21, 2014, http://www.christenacleveland.com/blogarchive/2014/03/urban-church-plantations.

2. Gloria Ann Wesley, "Is the Black Church the New Plantation?" Urban Intellectuals blog post, January 10, 2014, http://urbanintellectuals.com/2014/01/10/black-church-new-plantation/.

3. Ibid.

outreach activities are designed such that those served have little to no interaction with the often commuter memberships of these congregations.

White suburban congregations involved in urban ministry or in partnerships with urban churches tend to bring an even more glaring patron/client dynamic. White suburban congregations supply urban churches primarily with money, food, and clothing, and urban churches supply white suburban churches with photos and letters of the impact of those helped. Even in those instances in which suburban churches send volunteers to urban communities, the relationship and service are rarely seen as mutually beneficial; and in many cases the value to the urban congregation can be deemed detrimental.[4] At issue are colonialistic ideas of outreach that typically lack an understanding of systemic social privilege and the need for mutually inclusive and beneficial relationships.[5] These approaches to outreach and missions also tend to convey a cultural superiority on the part of patrons, believing themselves to be better than the persons they are assisting, and that the recipients of their patronage have nothing to teach them.

In light of these socioreligious impositions upon urban communities by urban missionaries, let us explore steps urban black churches can take to meet these challenges head on.

Shift from Need-Based Understandings of Ministry to Asset-Based Approaches

From my almost twenty years as an urban church pastor, community developer, and scholar, I have learned that one of the key factors with regard to the community "clout" an urban black church possesses, especially when a small-sized congregation, has to do with whether that congregation is able to determine the full range of assets available to it in its efforts to confront challenges within its community. According to John P. Kretzmann and John McKnight, this "asset-based community development" approach reads contexts in terms of the existing capacities and collaborative possibilities within contexts, where "your organization's assets connected to (+) community assets produced (=) strong-based community projects."[6] If an urban black congregation (or any other

---

4. For more on this concept, see Robert C. Linthicum, *Toxic Charity: How Churches and Charities Hurt Those They Help (And How to Reverse It)* (New York: HarperCollins, 2011).

5. Joerg Rieger. "Theology and Mission between Neocolonialism and Postcolonialism," *Mission Studies* 21, no. 2 (2004): 201–27.

6. John P. Kretzmann et al., *Discovering Community Power: A Guide to Mobilizing Local Assets*

church or organization) sees only its needs, it limits how it understands its gifts, engaging instead in unproductive comparisons of itself to larger entities. Its mantra will be continually, "If only we had . . ."

When focused primarily on what they need rather than on what they have, congregations are then susceptible to patron-client relationships with larger congregations which in many instances have been white and suburban congregations. In this manner, urban black "client" churches become mostly recipients of food, clothing, and money, with no real relationships developed between the patron and client congregations that would lead to deeper engagements on systemic issues such as racial reconciliation or economic justice. Each simply extracts from the other a "good" without fundamentally altering the social equation within or between their respective communities.

For urban black churches that function as the client in patron-client relationships, several dangers are eminent. First, when the resources of the patron dry up, these urban black client congregations are finding that their dependency has rendered them vulnerable by effectively causing their outreach, as well as many core ministries, to decrease or even cease. Second, these client congregations often find themselves unable to critique or hold these patrons accountable in addressing systemic issues of racism, classism, and poverty. In essence, patron-client relationships between suburban white and urban black churches leave both the patron and the client congregation complicit with a system of philanthropy that causes "the philanthropist to overlook the circumstances of economic injustice which make philanthropy necessary."[7] Third, many of these urban client congregations tend to replicate the patron-client relationship and become as guilty as their patrons of engaging in colonialistic practices of ministry *to* persons surrounding their churches rather than being in ministry with them. Fourth, these urban client congregations, habituated in practices that privilege white ways of doing and being, imitate practices that undermine their indigenous ways of doing and being and distance them further from their surrounding communities.

Meanwhile, what is also emerging is that suburban churches with access to resources and connections are seeing that they can be more "efficient" in addressing urban community needs by cutting out the "middle man"

---

and Your Organization's Capacity: A Community-Building Workbook (Evanston, IL: Northwestern University, Asset-Based Community Development Institute, 2005), 3. Also see https://resources .depaul.edu/abcd-institute/publications/Documents/Workbooks/Asset-BasedStrategiesFaith Communities.pdf.

7. Martin Luther King Jr., *Strength to Love* (Minneapolis: Fortress Press, 2010), 25.

(i.e., the urban black client church). Simultaneously, many of these suburban white congregations and their leaders, having been exposed to twenty or more years of practical wisdom and research on the success of "missional" and "new monastic movements" (discussed below), have leveled, often correctly, critiques against many urban black congregations pertaining to the failure of many black churches to adjust their ministries to the current post-Christendom era. Many urban black congregations, client or not, have not made revisions to their worship, administrative, or evangelistic practices necessary for reaching the communities surrounding them. Therefore, due to the purportedly spiritual and financial insufficiency of urban black churches, many of these suburban-based "urban church planters" are moving in to do the work they believe urban churches have neglected or are ill-prepared and ill-equipped to do.

Contrast this with alternative inner-city black churches' understanding of themselves as partners and "yoke-fellows" with urban ministry–oriented suburban churches as opposed to those who operate as client congregations. Irrespective of their size, urban black churches in these instances engage in asset-based analysis of themselves and their communities. They conduct an honest assessment of their congregations' strengths, weaknesses, opportunities, and threats. They investigate ministries that are similar to them in terms of size, culture, and surrounding community to glean lessons for community engagement, revitalization, and discipleship that are not colonialistic or based on business models of growth. They also engage the community to determine the community's potential and its social "assets" (e.g., human capacities, buildings, businesses, empty lots, etc.). These congregations are careful about who they partner with and demand of their partners equal and mutually beneficial relationships.

Simply put, these black urban congregations start with what they and the community have, believing God will provide the right people and assets for them to continue the ministry. In this way, these churches are not only transforming their communities and those partnering with them, but the engagement is also transforming those engaged in the work. Because of this confidence in their assets, no matter the size, they operate from an abundance rather than a scarcity mentality. They are comfortable holding their partners accountable on issues of systemic racism and classism and countering so-called best-in-class practices promoted by suburban congregations or organizations. They are also less likely to be manipulated or strong-armed by governmental agencies or commercial interests, instead of approaching them out of the same asset-based analysis they have used elsewhere.[8] Notable examples of these kinds of churches are Windsor Village United Methodist Church in Houston; First Presbyterian Church of Jamaica in Jamaica, Queens, New York; Emory United Methodist Church in Washington, DC; and St. James United Methodist Church in Houston.[9]

Having a more asset-based mentality and moving beyond patron-client relationships with suburban white congregations and organizations addresses only part of the imbalance between suburban-based urban church planters and urban black congregations—meaning mainly, the lack of financial or human capital to address the needs of communities surrounding their congregations. If black urban churches are going to more effectively counter the socioeconomic, political, commercial, and spiritual colonization of their communities, then they are also going to have to address the charge that they are not accounting sufficiently for the post-Christendom context into which we have entered. Black urban churches will have to contend with the criticism that their current forms of worship, evangelism, and mission are no longer productive in the urban core, especially among post–civil-rights-era generations.[10] To this end, I suggest they take a page from those who are coming to their communities and learn to be both missional and monastic in relating to their congregations and to the communities surrounding their churches.

Be Missional and Monastic

Two key evangelistic movements of the last fifteen to twenty years that have been driving this expansion into inner cities have been the missional church and new monastic movements. The missional church movement maintained that in light of a post-Christendom society, North American churches had become so accommodated to American life that discipleship had been reduced to citizenship or club membership, making it "no longer obvious what justifies their [church] existence as particular communities."[11] Therefore, to survive in this post-Christendom context,

8. For more information, see R. Drew Smith and Fredrick Harris, *Black Churches and Local Politics: Clergy Influence, Organizational Partnerships, and Civic Involvement* (Lanham, MD: Rowman and Littlefield, 2005).

9. Ibid.

10. F. Douglas Powe Jr., *New Wine, New Wineskins: How African American Congregations Can Reach New Generations* (Nashville: Abingdon, 2012).

11. Darrell L. Guder, ed., *Missional Church: A Vision for Sending the Church to North America* (Grand Rapids: Eerdmans, 1998), 78.

North American churches now had to reevaluate their understanding and practice of outreach and mission. Shifting from an *ecclesiocentric* (church-centered) to a *theocentric* (God-centered) understanding of church mission also required that the global church reorient its understanding of church mission as something with "an aim to extend the church or plant it in all of its cultural norms in new places," to something whose orientation instead is toward "a community spawned by the mission of God and gathered up into that mission."[12] In this way, mission is not what the church does; instead mission, as in the mission of God (*missio Dei*), is the essence of who the church is.[13]

With this new sense of mission and purpose, and armed with a multiplicity of resources and networks, North American, predominantly white suburban, churches focused on being missional with their sights on urban communities. While a missional mindset is easily theologically defensible, the issue has been to equate missions and missional without again investigating race, gender, and socioeconomic privilege and systems of injustice that seem to be commonsense ways of being.[14] Black churches that have modeled themselves from white denominations are also prone to conflating *missions* with *missional*, with very little understanding of their own participation in systems of privilege. Many black congregations are also stuck on earlier forms of outreach and evangelism where the church is seen as a physical place, not a people, and where everything the people do in terms of ministry must lead people back to the physical location of "the church."

To be missional, urban black congregations must begin to dismantle the idea of church as place and reorient their members to an understanding of church as a people. These churches must move from club and volunteer models of membership to helping persons engage in the idea of being called to a particular body, the congregation. An understanding of themselves as a sent-out people will mean urban black churches, especially those with primarily commuter memberships, will have to reorient themselves to engage relationally with persons beyond their walls. This should not be done in colonialistic ways, or in ways that could be described as patron-client relationships but rather in ways that seek to meet people where they are and to learn from them.

12. Ibid., 81–82. Also see Alan Roxburgh, *Missional Map-Making: Skills for Leading in Times of Transition* (San Francisco: John Wiley and Sons, 2010).
13. Timothy C. Tennent, *Invitation to World Missions: A Trinitarian Missiology for the Twenty-First Century* (Grand Rapids: Kregel Publications, 2010), 58–59.
14. Powe, *New Wine.*

This means that urban black churches will not only have to learn how to be missional toward those who are economically disadvantaged, but also they will need to begin to forge strategies of outreach with their new, and often white, neighbors who are moving to their neighborhoods as urban communities become increasingly gentrified. The challenge here will be whether urban black churches can learn to be more multicultural in ways that do not disempower blacks within their churches or silence them from speaking out against racial and socioeconomic injustice and oppression.

Although academic advocates and early adherents of the missional movement contend that a missional understanding of the church is centered in relationality through its embeddedness in Trinitarian theology and participation in the sacraments, they critique newcomers as remaining tied to forms of ministry praxis focused on capitalistic notions of success more than the gospel and failing to move beyond individual piety, tithing, volunteerism, and Bible study. These critics contend that what is needed is a model of discipleship that produces radical Christians who are in love with God and who exist in mutually accountable communities whose justice work in the world flows from their life with God and with their neighbors.[15] What is viewed then as lacking in the missional movement is the kind of discipleship pointed to by new monasticism.

New monasticism is an evangelical Christian movement begun in the late 1990s that contended, similar to missional theologies, that evangelical Christianity as typically practiced by modern North American evangelical Christians has been little more than a "Christian spin on the American Dream." New monastics contended that to live an authentic Christian life, disciples must forsake all and follow Christ, while taking seriously how their positions of privilege have created distorted readings of Scripture leading to distorted worship, evangelistic, and ethical church practices. They take seriously that personal holiness is only possible through intentional and mutually accountable and beneficial communities and that Jesus is most often found by engaging, interacting, and developing friendship and fellowship with the least of these.[16]

15. Mike Breen, "Why the Missional Church Will Fail," part 1, Verge Network website, September 14, 2011, http://www.vergenetwork.org/2011/09/14/mike-breen-why-the-missional-movement-will-fail/.

16. Shane Claiborne, *The Irresistible Revolution: Living as an Ordinary Radical* (Grand Rapids: Zondervan, 2006).

More interesting is that a good number of these new monastics are doing a few things that their suburban colleagues have never dreamed of. First, they are immersing themselves in the history, theology, and ethics of the historical black church to understand and build a relationship with black urban churches in the neighborhoods in which they find themselves. Second, they are submitting themselves to the leadership and mentoring of black and other racial ethnic urban pastors who have been long engaged in the work of justice and outreach with the residents of the community. New monastics are also becoming advocates and yoke-fellows in movements such as Moral Mondays and Black Lives Matter, laying down their privilege and reputation and taking equal risks with racial ethnic communities and congregations. A most recent example of this is the partnership of Jonathan Wilson-Hartgrove and Rev. William Barber II in the Moral Monday Movement fighting against the recent North Carolina legislation limiting voting rights.[17] In addition, new monastics are opening their doors widely becoming radically welcoming communities that model the diversity and complexity of the reign and people of God, embracing persons across boundaries of race, socioeconomic location, gender, sexual orientation, and even faith tradition. Simply put, new monastic communities understand that the triune God is radically welcoming to all persons and that all persons have gifts (i.e., assets) to bring to bear within the life of the church and its ministry.

The work by new monastics challenges urban black churches to gauge where they are in terms of discipleship and in terms of being prophetic witnesses in their communities. If the challenge is a discipleship that is both prophetic to the unjust powers of this world and priestly to those caught in the grip of the injustice, then urban black churches are going to need to be more welcoming in terms of their membership and their leadership. Urban black churches concerned with the threat of these new urban church planters are going to have to examine their own biases with regard to race, gender, socioeconomic status, and sexual orientation and act accordingly. They are going to have to learn how to "walk across the aisle" and make friends beyond their denominations, race, and faith traditions to effect the common good within their communities.

17. William J. Barber II and Jonathan Wilson-Hartgrove, *The Third Reconstruction: How a Moral Movement Is Overcoming the Politics of Division and Fear* (Boston: Beacon Press, 2016).

Concluding Thoughts

As long as it is trendy to come to the city to do ministry or move to the city as part of waves of new gentrification, urban black churches are going to have to contend with possible by-products of modern-day social and religious colonization. Rather than seeing these new influxes solely as threats, this essay proposes that urban churches see the arrival of suburban urban church planters as an opportunity to reassess their own ministries. As urban black churches critique the intent and effect of these newly arriving ministries, these can also be occasions for determining whether urban black churches themselves are engaged in asset-based or patron-client ministries, and in theological orientations emphasizing bringing about the reign of God on earth rather than focusing primarily on getting persons "saved" for heaven. Finally, not only do these newcomers offer the opportunity to assess mission and outreach practices of urban black congregations, but they also provide opportunities for urban black churches and their leaders to assess the kind of discipleship being facilitated among their members and how radically welcoming they are in embracing others and in being changed by them. Otherwise, urban black churches will find themselves poorly positioned in their responses to these ministry newcomers arriving in urban communities.

Chapter 6

Urban Ministry as Incarnational

Kang-Yup Na

As I write this essay, I am thinking gratefully and fondly of a scholar friend, Father Phillip J. Linden Jr., whose life of urban ministry inspired me because of the sometimes dangerous urban setting in which he has lived for many years. On the theology faculty of Xavier University of Louisiana, Father Linden has embodied a life of urban ministry simply by living in his urban neighborhood *among* those who sometimes live without hope or with only very little hope. Father Linden's life among the urban poor reflects two major considerations for urban ministry studies. The first concerns an *ideological-methodological critique* of assumptions that may limit the way we approach urban ministry and live in a sociologically plural world (with particular attention here to the impact on Asian communities but also beyond). A second concern is with culturally and historically conscious, conscientious, and conscientized approaches to forming and living together in urban communities: what I'm referring to as a *biblical-incarnational perspective* on urban ministry. Each of these are explored from my vantage point as a theological educator of Asian descent.

Matters Asian: Cultural and Definitional

Born in South Korea, I moved to Tennessee just before turning ten. As a "naturalized" American, my worldview has been shaped by my idiosyncratic experiences in various Korean diaspora communities where I have lived, worked, studied, taught, and served churches in Trenton, New Jersey, Atlanta, and New York City, as well as in Göttingen, Germany. A person born and raised in Los Angeles whose great-grandparents emigrated from Korea would probably have experiences of American urban life palpably different from mine. Yet, my experiences as an American may still be interpreted by casual observation or assumption to seem very similar to others of Korean ancestry. It is worth asking, therefore, whether I or any human being can represent experiences of or offer reflections on behalf of a larger group in a fair way that lends integrity to the diversity of urban experiences among the various ethnic groups we categorize as Korean or even more broadly as Asian. Clearly, the experiences of one Korean cannot be used to surmise that all Koreans share the same experiences or as is often generalized more broadly, that all multigenerational Asian immigrants or naturalized citizens throughout U.S. history share similar realities.[1] This point should keep us analytically sober and honest when making claims about significant features or patterns of Korean or, more broadly, Asian urban life in the United States. What we ordinarily assume to be Asian or Asian American reflects, as far as I am aware, our stereotyping deficiencies, even among the most conscientized of scholars and critics.[2]

Asia is a continent comprising about 60 percent of the world's population. And although for many, if not most—not just in the Western Hemisphere—the word *Asia* evokes countries like China, India, and Japan, it actually consists of forty-eight countries, including some of the less-than-Asian-seeming countries, like Armenia and Azerbaijan, Iran and Israel, Tajikistan and Turkey, to name a few.[3] Various peoples of Asia have been

---

1. It would help to remember the ancient Greek philosophical question of the one and the many. As soon as we focus on the particularities of Asian urban ministry we must consider what universals constitute or underlie that particularity—what *one* is manifested in the *many*. Asia is a large continent, and there is hardly one culture or ethnic identity, one history or ethical norm. We must ask of any particularity, my own experiences in this case: For *all* Asians? For *all* urban ministries? To think of *one* and *unity* may compromise the realities of particularities; at the same time, an emphasis on particularities may expose what we habitually assume to be universal.

2. To *conscientize* is "to make (a person, group, etc.) aware of social and political conditions, esp. as a precursor to challenging inequalities of treatment or opportunity"; *conscientization* as "the action or process of making others aware of political and social conditions, esp. as a precursor to challenging inequalities of treatment or opportunity; the fact of being aware of these conditions" *Oxford English Dictionary*, 7th ed. (Oxford: Oxford University Press, 2013).

3. Melissa McDaniel, Erin Sprout, Diane Boudreau and Andrew Turgeon, "Asia: Resources," last modified January 4, 2012, https://www.nationalgeographic.org/encyclopedia/asia-resources/. The complete list by National Geographic listed on its website is as follows: Afghanistan, Armenia, Azerbaijan, Bahrain, Bangladesh, Bhutan, Brunei, Cambodia, China, Cyprus, Georgia, India, Indonesia, Iran, Iraq, Israel, Japan, Jordan, Kazakhstan, North Korea, South Korea, Kuwait, Kyrgyzstan, Laos, Lebanon, Macau, Malaysia, Maldives, Mongolia, Myanmar, Nepal, Oman, Pakistan, Papua New Guinea, Philippines, Qatar, Saudi Arabia, Singapore, Sri Lanka, Syria, Tajikistan, Thailand, Turkey, Turkmenistan, United Arab Emirates, Uzbekistan, Vietnam, and Yemen, https://www.britannica.com/topic-browse/Countries-of-the-World/Countries-of-Asia.

colonized by others, both from within Asia and from outside of Asia. It would be a daunting task indeed to say anything that represents all the ethnic groups and cultures originating from such a wide variety of histories, languages, and worldviews. One of the ways we should reframe urban ministry in and for the twenty-first century is to recognize the complex reality behind what we assume to constitute ethnic categories like "Asian."[4]

Moreover, what does it mean to speak of the cultural relevance of urban ministry in the sense of a Christian culture that spans two millennia and multiple ethno-geographic contexts? How could our self-critical enlightenment be enabled by a perspective that recognizes that Moses, Jesus, and Mohammed were all Asians and that Christianity began as an Asian religion? One hope from such a methodological reorientation would be that we could learn from studying the ethnocultural dynamics of urban settings to challenge what we may have assumed about ethnic boundaries and definitions in the very process of conducting our study.[5]

Biblical Preparations for Theological Pedagogy

As odd as it may seem, I would suggest turning to the biblical narrative about Job to orient us toward wisdom about urban ministry and a sound critique of the ways we think about it. The story of Job in Job 2:11–13 can teach us how we may (re)form the fundamental character of Christian ministry and mission—a Christian culture—urban or otherwise, and for Asian or any other communities.

When Job is utterly devastated and hopeless, his three friends learn of his plight, in response to which each "set out from his home . . . to go

---

4. This problematization of concepts, like "Asian," should extend to other concepts in need of critical assessment, e.g., "Asian American," "African American." Here are some possible questions of cultural definition or conception: What is Asia? What is an Asian? What is an Asian American? Because I was born in Korea, am I an Asian in America? Because I have a U.S. passport, am I an American of Asian descent (or ascent)? Why is it that many in the United States assume that Asian American means, more often than not, Far East Asian American? Why does the concept of "model minority" refer stereotypically to those from Far East Asia? What about U.S.-born Asians? Is a second-generation Japanese in Peru an Asian American? Is a fourth-generation Dutch family in South Africa an African? And if that family immigrated to Mexico, could that family, looking so pale and speaking Afrikaans, eventually fit in our mind's imagination as African American? Can we speak of U.S.-born European Americans?

5. For a good place to begin considering the complexities of ethnic relations and cross-cultural interaction in urban culture see Elijah Anderson, *The Cosmopolitan Canopy: Race and Civility in Everyday Life* (New York: W.W. Norton, 2012).

and console and comfort him" (Job 2:11).[6] What is remarkable is Job's friends' response: "They sat with him on the ground seven days and seven nights, and no one spoke a word to him, for they saw that his suffering was very great" (Job 2:13). What they *do for* Job is in a sense nothing; what they "do" is *be with him* silently in his suffering. They understood the depths of Job's suffering to know that the only authentic response would be silent compassion.

Derived from Latin, *compassion* means to suffer *with* (*com* = with; *passion* = suffering). It is basically the same as the word *sympathy*, which is derived from Greek (*syn* = with; *pathos* = suffering, experience).[7] When examined etymologically, *compassion* and *sympathy*, although ordinary words in English, bear great Christian truth and mission. Compassion, "suffering with," is precisely what Job's friends do so impressively when they "raised their voices and wept aloud" and "tore their robes and threw dust in the air upon their heads" (Job 2:12). When Job's life was destroyed beyond words, his friends knew to be silent and just to sit *with* him.

The reason for pointing to this brief portion of Job is that the friends, unable to do anything *for* Job, did the one thing that was needed: that is, to be present and *with* him in his misery. Here arises a biblical, peculiarly Christian insight into ministry, urban or otherwise. Christian ministry ought to (con)form itself according to the witness of the Old and New Testament in which *with-ness* constitutes the fundamental character of compassion, which has to do with relating or connecting *with* someone. Even as Israelites and Jews knew God to be Immanuel, God-*with*-us, Christians came to know that same God as incarnate in Jesus Christ, who according to John 1:14 was the eternal *logos* that "became flesh and lived among us"—the ultimate experience and expression of divine-human "withness."

This *withness* we see in the case of Job provides a model of human fellowship or community that is germane for the urban ministry discussion

---

6. We see here the first lesson for ministry and Christian culture: we must move when moved by the suffering of others. We can see this fundamental biblical pattern in Exodus when God "comes down" in response to God's people's misery and sufferings in Egypt (Exod. 3:7–8); we see it also in the Gospels where Jesus reaches out in compassion to people's suffering (e.g., Matt. 9:35–36).

7. Compassion and sympathy are deceptively different in English. Even if we recognize the similarity in meaning, we use them differently depending on the context. For example, we send our sympathies to people who experience the loss of a loved one. We are more likely to send a sympathy card than a compassion card; an image search for both of these on the web generates intriguing results.

at hand. Equally significant is the strong parallel tradition of divine *presence* among the Israelites in the Old Testament. Most significant for Christians is the way in which both the human and divine dimensions converge in the integrity, that is, wholeness, of incarnation. In John's claim that the divine *logos* (John 1:1–3) "pitched a tent among us" (John 1:14, author's translation), the verb that is translated "lived" or "dwelt" means to "settle down" or "take up residence" and evokes the Mosaic tabernacle that re-presented the presence of God among Israelites.[8] As *The Message* puts it, "The Word became flesh and blood, and moved into the neighborhood."

Alluding to the nomadic, tent-dwelling language of the Exodus and Sinai traditions, the incarnation invites us to at least two paths of meditation through biblical history and theology that can inform, form, and reform any authentic ministry: (1) the Jewish and Christian understanding of the presence of God among us and (2) the Christian notion that God has "moved into the neighborhood" (John 1:14). With this theo-christological orientation from the sacred Scriptures along with the human model of pastoral ministry from Job 2:11–13 we turn now to the main hermeneutical-practical matters, which I have proposed above, to cover in a way that is transcultural and not according to the various assumed stereotypes or sociological patterns people generally perceive or assume to be "Asian," whether in general or specific to the United States.

From Insufficient (Doing-For) to Incarnational (Being-With) Ministry

Urban ministry approaches and pedagogies ought to be mindful of the general pitfalls in secular analyses of and responses to urban realities. Even if we go beyond the needs of urban settings, for which we as a society sense an obligation to do something to help, we tend to adopt implicitly a *doing-for* mentality, particularly in the marginalized or minoritized segments of urban geography or of the socioeconomic spectrum.[9] That is to say, we generally tend to address urban issues in order to *fix* problems

---

8. If not for the constraints of this essay, we should engage in biblical-theological reflection on understanding the Mosaic tabernacle as a proto-incarnational sacrament, a visible sign of YHWH's holy presence among the people of Israel, an understanding that provides the biblical precedent for the container used in some churches for the "reserved Eucharist."

9. Samuel Wells, the vicar of St. Martin-in-the-Fields, argued well in 2013 what I had long believed and what the Bible even longer taught in his article "Rethinking Service," *The Cresset* 76 (2013): 6–14, http://thecresset.org/2013/Easter/Wells_E2013.html.

rather than by living among and sharing the experiences of those whom we try to help—regrettably altogether in an objectifying way; we *study* a "them."[10] This is true not only for those who lack social conscientization but also for those whose cause is the conscientization of society. In fact, I would argue that precisely because of our *conscientization about* urban life, we try to do things *for* others rather than sharing communal life by being and living *with* them to become a *we*.[11]

Martin Luther King Jr. dreamed that "one day little black boys and girls will be holding hands with little white boys and girls."[12] At least in most urban settings, we as a society have achieved this in various degrees: for example, schools, higher education, social institutions, political processes.[13] Some may consider the presidency of Barack Obama as a milestone in the cause of King's dream. There is no doubt there have been welcome changes in the structures of American life that have enabled the urban landscape to move beyond our days of segregation. That improvement notwithstanding, today's inner-city black neighborhoods, Chinatowns, and other innocuous and even intentional ghettos in American society stand as witnesses to the fact that governments and even churches have been *doing things for* the needs of urban life while coming very short of King's dream, at least in the sense that ethno-economic groups hardly live with each other. Genuinely integrated neighborhoods and communities are difficult to find.[14]

We expend a lot of energy trying to figure out what we can *do for*

10. I mean *objectifying* in the sense of viewing people and their experiences as the objects of our scholarly investigation and the beneficiaries of our sociopolitical and even ecclesial efforts and programs, in which case the fundamental concern is not how we ought to live and relate with each other but how to procure and allocate money and resources that have alternative uses, including human capital.

11. Consider Heidegger's discussion in *Sein und Zeit* (*Being and Time*) on human beings as *Dasein* (= there-being = human being), *Mitsein* (with-being), *Mitdasein* (= with-there-being = human-being-with-others), and *Miteinandersein* (with-one-another-being).

12. Martin Luther King Jr., "I Have a Dream" (speech, Washington, D.C., National Mall, August 28, 1963), Government Archives, p. 5, https://www.archives.gov/files/press/exhibits/dream-speech.pdf.

13. Cf. the concept of "the cosmopolitan canopy" in Elijah Anderson's *The Cosmopolitan Canopy: Race and Civility in Everyday Life* (New York: W.W. Norton & Company, 2011), which refers to public settings in which urban people of diverse backgrounds interact across ethnic lines comfortably.

14. Nearly unimaginable are socio-econo-ethno-culturally mixed communities in which no one notices such differences. The nearly impossible dream would be to cultivate intentional communities that become no longer conscious of their intentions or their diversities, or no longer find their differences significant (cf. Gal. 3:28).

people; we tend to fail at *being with* others, especially as we objectify them as targets of study or ministry. This is not altogether negative since we are striving to care for people in their particular contexts, improve relationships with them, and make the world a better place by *doing things for* others. But how different would politics and ministry be if we who theorize and write *about* urban realities were actually to *be with* urban people, living in their communities and embodying compassion in the way Job's friends did and as Christ's incarnation represents? Admittedly, *doing-for* can sometimes evolve toward *being-with*. As to how that relexicalization of our concepts and practical efforts should take place is the challenge set before everyone with a heart for urban ministry and a desire to reenvision it.

Concluding Thoughts: Matters Cultural and Hermeneutical

Contextual(ized) hermeneutics—culturally and historically conscious, conscientious, and conscientized approaches—are broadly accepted as being essential to any task of thinking about and understanding life together or life in community. With the best of hermeneutical and pedagogical intentions, ours is nonetheless an apparently invariable pattern of theory and praxis that is near- or shortsighted, *not* due to our lack of honest enlightenment but precisely *because of* the enlightenment that comes from contextualized conscientization. Most approaches of ministry and pedagogy, typically (d)evolve into realpolitik, disclosing our pragmatic longing for visible, tangible ways of *doing something for others*, that is, to minister to or serve others. While effective quantitatively, this pragmatic end of analyzing issues and (ad)ministering justice falls short of what we (should) know from the dominant pattern in biblical and church traditions: namely, not doing something for others but being there with others.

Transforming *our* approach in urban ministry from doing-for to being-with could transform our critical and ideological methodology in practical and spiritually strengthening ways. One wisdom we might recall from the biblical expressions of unity (as opposed to uniformity or sameness) is that the covenantal identity in baptism relegates all significant identity markers ultimately to insignificance, no matter how significant they may be for sociological analysis. Paul argued it quite well: "There *is no longer* Jew or Greek, there is no longer slave or free, there is no longer male and female; for all of you *are one* in Christ Jesus" (Gal. 3:28; emphasis added). Being-with in a community of love is fundamental to Christian mission and ministry; being-with is much more profound and more transformative than doing things for someone.

Like Paul, we should be very clear about the actual significance of the ethno-religious, socioeconomic, gender-sexual, and any other descriptions by which we identify human beings. But we should be equally clear that even with conscientization and the best of our intentions toward justice for people populating urban sprawls, Christian ministry should know and proclaim the transcendent, transforming the power of baptismal identity (e.g., Gal. 3:27–28), which is the true character of all Christian ministry. It is this unifying power of Christian baptismal identity that *unites* us to Christ and one another as spiritual siblings that can (in)form the foundations for a Christian being-with-one-another and thereby a being-with-all-others—without disregarding the particularities of anyone's identity.

The authenticity of urban ministry should be tested, like all other contexts of ministry, by the incarnational standard of *withness*. Urban ministry is most effective and transformative when it is able to move beyond the "we-they" ideological conscientization of people's social location toward actual lived-out collocation and (re)formative "being with" experiences that expand from the often blind tendency to *do things for* others rather than *being with* them in community. In this way, as in the case of Job's friends, the reality of "being with," even when empirically little can be "done for," allows for establishment of a context whereby mutual transformation is possible, a greater awareness of God's presence can be perceived, and the Christian gospel is proclaimed by its living in community.

Chapter 7

Religion and Race in Urban Spaces across Africa and the Diaspora

William Ackah

I am a child of the African Diaspora. I was born and raised in North East London after my parents migrated to the United Kingdom from Ghana West Africa in the 1960s. I spent much of my formative years living in a high-rise tower block. My family and I lived on the sixteenth floor of a twenty-story building. It was a horrible place to live, with its often broken elevators and its tight, dank stairwell with danger lurking around each corner. To use the title of a Bob Marley classic, it was a "concrete jungle." At that age, I was too young to understand the complex intersections of postcolonial labor migration, race, and religion, which resulted in my being in this space. I simply knew I did not like it.

It was in this inhospitable environment however that I found God, after members of the local church ventured one day to the sixteenth floor and knocked on our door to invite us to church. That knock and the invitation eventually opened the door to new urban landscapes. Since then I have been privileged to travel around the globe interacting with African-descendant people of faith in urban contexts and witnessing, firsthand, how religious faith operates in the bleakest of urban environments, profoundly impacting and changing the lives of people and communities.

In reflecting on the kinds of urban ministry I have experienced and researched over the last forty years traversing across Africa and the African Diaspora, I have been impressed by churches and individuals engaged in heroic efforts to keep hope and faith alive in environments where black lives were disadvantaged and marginalized. Yet, going forward, I sense the need for multilevel urban engagement by churches in the urban environment. Heroic individualism needs to be supplemented or replaced by approaches to urban ministry that address structural inequalities and seek justice for disadvantaged communities.

United Kingdom:
Building Kingdoms within Kingdoms in the Urban Landscape

London has a long history of diversity and migration where religion and race have intersected leading to the establishment of communities that have left a distinctive mark on the city.[1] One thinks of the East End of London and the influence there of the Jewish community at the beginning of the twentieth century.[2] The worship spaces they inhabited and the businesses that were established meant a rich cultural, religious, and diverse urban landscape was created in a very poor part of the city. The establishment of these religious and cultural spaces assisted the community in their struggles against racism and provided a platform from which they could develop and make positive inroads into the wider society, eventually enabling them to move to other parts of the city. After the Second World War, that same space was synonymous with Bangladeshi and Pakistani immigrants who also established places of worship and established businesses that afforded a livelihood but also created linkages between themselves and the wider community.[3] This process also contributed to the multicultural and multireligious mix of the urban landscape.[4] In similar ways, the creation of this space also provided a bulwark against racism that has enabled these communities to develop organizations and ways of being which gave and continue to give them a sense of place in London's urban landscape.[5] At times in the wider society where Muslim presence and acceptance by the nation are contested, these spaces which they have carved out become important symbols of presence and belonging.[6]

---

1. John Eade, *Placing London: From Imperial Capital to Global City* (New York: Berghahn, 2000).

2. David Feldman, *Englishmen and Jews: Social Relations and Political Culture, 1840–1914* (New Haven: Yale University Press, 1994).

3. Delwar Hussain, "God and Galloway: The Islamization of Bangladeshi Communities in London," *Journal of Creative Communications* 2, no. 1–2 (2007): 189–217.

4. Gregg Smith, "East London Is No Longer Secular: Religion as a Source of Social Capital in the Regeneration of East London," *Rising East* 4, no. 3 (2001): 124–53.

5. Claire Alexander, *The Asian Gang: Ethnicity, Identity, Masculinity* (Oxford: Berg, 2000).

6. Tariq Modood, *Multicultural Politics: Ethnicity, Racism, and Muslims in Britain* (Minneapolis: University of Minnesota Press, 2005).

Likewise, people of African descent brought their religions and cultures to the London urban context. Yet, unlike Jewish people who brought Judaism (which largely framed their self-contained religious and ethnic experience), or Pakistani and Bangladeshi migrants who brought Islam (which, while a universal faith, was closely identified with particular ethnic groups within the context), continental Africans and African-descendant persons from the Caribbean primarily brought their Christianity to the city (in all of its variety and diversity).[7] As such, these African-descended groups brought religious traditions with African roots, but which included religious traditions inherited as part of their encounter with British colonialism.[8]

Given the closely intertwined religious heritage African descendants living in the United Kingdom shared with their white British counterparts, one would think their urban experience would be different from that of their Jewish and Pakistani and Bangladeshi counterparts with respect to being accepted more readily into the wider society. This, however, has not been the case. African descendants have been racialized as black, and black has a negative value in British society, including black religious expression. So even though many African descendants in the United Kingdom are members of mainline British denominations (e.g., Methodism, Anglicanism, and Catholicism), racialized hostility and a broader lack of acceptance of the value of African religious expression has led to the creation of distinctive (and largely segregated) religious traditions emerging in urban contexts.

One consequence of these immigrant influxes has been that a context long considered devoid of religious life and energy has been reenergized by the presence of religious migrants that have come from all faiths and all parts of the world. Former pubs (now converted into worship spaces) are now filled with people producing a different kind of spirit; old cinemas are telling new stories; former shops are selling new religious products; and old office blocks and warehouses are now producing and reproducing the merchandise of faith, hope, and love in the urban environment. In some cases, African-descendant migrants have bought or are renting old church buildings, providing income to previously struggling churches (characterized by reduced numbers of members

---

7. Mark Sturge, *Look What the Lord Has Done! An Exploration of Black Christian Faith in Britain* (Milton Keynes: Scripture Union, 2005).

8. Robert Beckford, *Jesus Is Dread: Black Theology and Black Culture in Britain* (London: Dartman, Longman & Todd, 1998).

and resources). Given the rise in the number of immigrant communities needing worship space, churches formerly open only on Sunday mornings are now open Sunday afternoons, Saturdays, and several evenings during the week.

This religious transformation has not come about due to the efforts of traditional clergy, but rather it has been fostered by lay leaders: working people who have given up their career or trade (including doctors, engineers, and other professionals) to establish churches and bring the gospel to people of the United Kingdom. It has been a remarkable story of religious and racial urban revitalization, but it is a confined revitalization.[9] Urban spaces have been changed socially—but it has been primarily in places characterized by poverty, criminality, and poor housing located on the margins of the city. Where in instances these places have changed economically and the racial demographics of these neighborhoods have altered, the churches that brought new life to the area are now regarded as an inconvenience.

Despite the international outlook of many African-descendant churches, their congregations have mainly comprised African immigrant members and their families. The reach and influence into the wider urban community have been very limited, including the reach among white British persons, nonwhite immigrant populations, or people of other faiths or no faith. The challenge is to broaden the appeal while ensuring all persons feel represented in their social particularities as part of the urban landscape.[10]

Haiti and Ghana: Signs of God Everywhere, but the Power?

I lived in Haiti for almost a year and visited Ghana on several occasions, and what struck me in the cities of Port-au-Prince, Accra, Cap Haitien, and Kumasi was the ubiquity of the presence of God in the public spaces.[11] Not that the presence of God is not in London or other European capitals, with their huge cathedrals and religious-inspired civic spaces. Yet in these European contexts, this religious presence often feels muted,

---

9. Babatunde Adedibu, *Coat of Many Colours: The Origin, Growth, Distinctiveness, and Contributions of Black Majority Churches to British Christianity* (London: Wisdom Summit, 2012).

10. David Leong, *Race and Place: How Urban Geography Shapes the Journey to Reconciliation* (Downers Grove, IL: InterVarsity Press, 2017).

11. For background reading on these places, see, for example, Laurent Dubois, *Haiti: The Aftershocks of History* (New York: Metropolitan, 2012); and Steven Salm and Toyin Falola, *Culture and Customs of Ghana* (Westport: Greenwood, 2002).

like a historical relic of a bygone age. Clearly, the real spaces of authority are the secular office buildings, the theaters, cinemas, restaurants, and bars, along with the new technology companies, medical complexes, and higher education institutions. The insertion of African spiritual presence into these spaces has been on the margins of the city.

In Haiti and Ghana, however, the visible sign of belief in God is every-where—painted onto the side of the buses in Port-au-Prince, or boldly spelled out on shop fronts in Kumasi and Cap Haitien. In these spaces God's name is called upon and spoken in the everyday and is in the midst of the people. If you are sick, you call on God. If you need resources, you call on God. If you want to give thanks, you call on God. On several occasions on the coach from Accra to Kumasi I have witnessed the driver allow a traveling preacher to board the bus and preach to the passengers and sell religious items. In these urban contexts, there is no shame in knowing and believing in a personal God who intervenes to shape and change the course of your life.

A belief in God in the everyday of these urban environments makes the spaces livable. Among the dirt, sweat, congestion, and lack of amenities, the bright manifestations of the signs and symbols of God give hope and meaning to many people.[12] Nevertheless, it has occurred to me in my travels within these spaces that the God so evident in the personal lives of people is not necessarily so evident in the structural affairs of these nations. Where is God's presence in shaping the corridors of power? Where is the power of God in moving the economic and political powers toward greater mindfulness of justice and the poor? Why aren't more believers in Ghana, Haiti, and similar spaces who believe in the power of the Spirit in their personal lives as fervent about seeking spiritual intervention at the structural levels of society?

There have been fleeting examples of attempts to bring spiritual power to bear upon structural concerns within these contexts. One prominent example was the priest who became president in Haiti, Jean-Bertrand Aristide. His presidency engendered hope among many as an erstwhile "savior" of a socially troubled Haiti and as an advocate for the poor.[13] Sadly, the hope was short lived, and Haiti continues to stagger from disaster to tragedy to disaster. Although Haiti and Ghana have been important beacons of Pan African identity and hope for African-descendant people

12. J. Kwabena Asamoah-Gyadu, *Contemporary Pentecostal Christianity: Interpretations from an African Context* (Eugene: Wipf & Stock, 2013).
13. Jean-Bertrand Aristide, *In the Parish of the Poor: Writings from Haiti* (New York: Orbis, 1990).

and places of deep and fervent spirituality, they also deserve to be spaces of economic and political flourishing. That means spiritual fervency needs to confront structural and systemic challenges in a sustained and systematic manner.[14]

Trinidad and South Africa: Ministry in the Ugly Spaces

As part of my global travels, I have visited places where poverty and crime have been especially pronounced and life extremely precarious. Two such places were Laventille in Port of Spain, Trinidad, and Diepsloot, an "informal settlement" in the Johannesburg region of South Africa. In Laventille (at a meeting between local ministers and an international gathering of academics and faith leaders), local pastors described horrendous living conditions in the neighborhood, including lack of running water for some residents, high crime rates, mass poverty, and the stigma and psychological trauma associated with coming from this neighborhood. Thousands of miles away on another continent, the stories in Diepsloot were similar, with the added dimensions of widespread HIV/AIDS infection and addictions to dangerous locally made drugs.

These poorer areas are proximate to relatively affluent contexts, but the isolation, neglect, and deprivation felt within these poor areas make them feel light years away from healthier and more privileged landscapes. In these brutally neglected spaces, church ministers as well as community activists stand in the gap as people of faith engaged in frontline ministry, providing food and clothes while advocating and challenging civil authorities to provide better living conditions for residents. In these ways, they reveal God's presence in spaces and places where people otherwise seem forgotten while undertaking ministry that is not glamorous and is sometimes dangerous.

Pittsburgh U.S.A.: Ministry in the Face of Urban Change

I write this essay from the city of Pittsburgh where I have spent the past year assessing the impact of urban revitalization policies on the African American church in two local neighborhoods. Pittsburgh is a city on an upward trajectory, rising from the ashes of a devastated coal and steel

---

14. William Ackah, "Back to Black or Diversity in the Diaspora? Re-imagining Pan-African Christian Identity in the Twenty-First Century," *Black Theology: An International Journal* 8, no. 3 (2010): 341–56.

industry and reinventing itself as a high-technology, medical, and education hub. Pittsburgh's renaissance has been impressive but uneven, with tightly bounded neighborhoods characterized by high rates of underdevelopment and poverty, in some instances, alongside wealth and revitalization in other instances.

African American neighborhoods have been largely on the wrong side of this equation, with profound effects on communities and churches. Once full at the seams and at the forefront of the social, political, and cultural lives of the community, many congregations in African American neighborhoods now find themselves struggling to maintain members and remain viable.[15] Given declining numbers of African Americans within Pittsburgh, this trend will continue unless African Americans become more integrally part of Pittsburgh's urban renaissance, rather than its victims.

As these urban changes are taking place, there have been notable examples of positive urban ministry. One such example is a faith-based ministry that supports African American renters in transitioning toward home ownership which, among other things, increases the number of African Americans in possession of appreciating assets in these changing neighborhoods. The program provides full wraparound services of support to these families to ensure their home ownership is self-sustaining. It does this within a context of engaging in racial justice and reconciliation work between white Christians and the broader African American community. Another faith-based initiative focuses on the psychological and physical trauma of living in an impoverished and racist environment and provides block-level wraparound health and support services within neighborhoods to promote community revitalization one step at a time.

Pittsburgh communities are not short of ministries in the urban environment. There are a plethora of ministries that focus on meeting people's basic needs and engaging in economic and policy development on a neighborhood scale. Despite the range and depth of ministries in operation, the bulldozers (both physical and metaphorical) remain intent on upending traditional African American neighborhoods perceived to be ripe for urban revitalization. Can the faith-based communities of these neighborhoods protect the core values of these communities while enabling them to develop and flourish?

15. Joe W. Trotter and Jared N. Day, *Race and Renaissance: African Americans in Pittsburgh since World War II* (Pittsburgh: University of Pittsburgh Press, 2010), 16.

Concluding Reflections

There is a perception that Christian faith in African-descendant urban contexts has moved away from a focus on people to an emphasis on the size, resources, and grandeur of church ministries. This is one aspect of religious life, but it is not the only aspect. There are forms of urban ministry where people of faith have been willing to take risks and to innovate in order to bring about positive change in their urban locales. What is also evident from the present sketch is that as impressive as some of these ministries have been, they are not changing the underlying nature of structural racialized inequalities that manifest themselves in diverse ways around the globe. At their core, these inadequate faith responses to structural inequality result in people of African descent being amongst the most marginalized and dispossessed people in the spaces and places they occupy.

Churches and faith-based entities within Africa and the Diaspora tend to operate in a piecemeal manner when the nature of the problem demands working together on a comprehensive agenda of economic transformation and social justice.[16] Dealing more effectively with the social difficulties that blacks face in urban contexts will require ministry responses that are international, multilayered, and concerned about structural inequalities.

Ministries in African-descendant communities possess the necessary capacities (especially when working collaboratively) to help constructively guide the transformations taking place in urban spaces. Now is the time for them to work collaboratively and across social and geographic boundaries on behalf of their people.

---

16. See examples of this comprehensive approach in the work of entities like the Samuel DeWitt Proctor Conference and the Transatlantic Roundtable on Religion and Race reflected on their websites: sdpconference.info and www.religionandrace.org.

Chapter 8

Wholeness and Human Flourishing as Guideposts for Urban Ministry

Lisa Slayton and Herb Kolbe

Too often urban ministry has been shaped by a view of redemption expressed through an emphasis on addressing the practical needs of individuals, or doing so only to open doors for the verbal proclamation of an individualistic, "soul-saving" gospel message. Throughout both the Old and New Testaments, the impact of sin and the power of redemption are portrayed as broad and comprehensive, touching every aspect of God's creation. Sin is presented as a corrosive that undermines and corrupts God's plan not only for humans but also for the entire creation that God loves. Redemption in Jesus Christ brings transforming power to "all things": individuals, families, communities, institutions, businesses, education, health care, art, recreation, etc. In his inaugural message regarding the kingdom of God, Jesus quoted the prophet Isaiah: "The Spirit of the Lord is upon me, because he has anointed me to bring good news to the poor. He has sent me to proclaim release to the captives and recovery of sight to the blind, to let the oppressed go free, to proclaim the year of the Lord's favor."[1]

As this passage suggests, Christians are called to be agents in the process of transforming communities into places filled with truth, beauty, justice, goodness, and human flourishing. This high calling, however, is complex and fraught with challenge, and it requires people of courage, compassion, and commitment who are able to adjust to a constantly changing environment. It also requires leadership that can be both humble and fiercely resolved to seek the "welfare"—the *shalom*—of that community. Healthy leaders need to be willing to check our assumptions and to examine our context.

1. Luke 4:18.

70

Four focus areas, or "frames," are essential for being agents of full redemption and for addressing the daunting challenges that so many communities face: stewardship, work, place, and relationships. These four frames are explicated below and are referenced to create perspectives that can be leveraged for needed paradigm shifts capable of changing structures and processes that serve the needs of urban communities. The Pittsburgh Leadership Foundation incorporates these frames into every aspect of our work, starting with the development of our staff, and then out into our collaborative cohorts and consulting work as we respond to underlying systemic blind spots inhibiting effectiveness. Our focus on these frames here reflects their importance within our work as guideposts for helping people and organizations to learn, grow, and willingly embrace needed change in the pursuit of human flourishing.

Stewardship

Stewardship is not just about financial resources but also about all the resources God has entrusted to us, starting with the fact we are created in God's image (*imago Dei*), and through the resource of our humanity, we are to create value in the world. As suggested by the Greek term *oikonomia*, we are all given stewardship over God's divine economy, and we all have a responsibility to manage our small piece of that economy with wisdom and prudence. We may steward a household, a church, or a business. We also steward ourselves and our personal resources, those gifts and talents God has placed in us. Our stewardship in any of these instances is part of our Christian vocation and calling. Amy Sherman, in her book titled *Kingdom Calling*, refers to what she calls "vocational stewardship" and defines it as "the intentional and strategic deployment of our vocational power—knowledge, platform, networks, position, influence, skills and reputation—to advance foretastes of God's kingdom."[2]

In urban environments, false assumptions related to stewardship tend to undermine our effectiveness and warrant corrective attention. One false assumption is, we don't have what we need to accomplish our mission. In 2015, the Pittsburgh Leadership Foundation (PLF), where the two of us are based, launched a new initiative called the Urban Leaders Project (ULP), whose purpose is to help nonprofit leadership rethink their understanding of what they need to achieve their mission. Many

---

2. Amy L. Sherman. *Kingdom Calling: Vocational Stewardship for the Common Good* (Downers Grove, IL: InterVarsity Press, 2011).

urban ministries emerge out of a passion for responding to an important need within their ministry context. The next steps are usually to start providing the service and seeking funding sources, often without evaluating existing resources that can be stewarded well in the launch of the ministry. These resources start first with the leaders themselves and then with other pre-existing resources within the context. At PLF we believe that the fundamental resource God has given us to steward is not what we have in our pockets but who God created us uniquely to be. Leaders must not only steward themselves well but also the people who have been entrusted to our care and ministry, including conditions in which decisions get made and how people interact with one another. Creating a vibrant culture where people's gifts can flourish is an important stewardship we possess in the work we have been called to do.

Therefore, it is important to properly assess opportunities placed in front of us and not overlook these opportunities because they do not fit our narrow paradigm of ministry. Perhaps God is already blessing something we should join rather than starting something new and then asking God or anyone else to bless it. Stewardship is about making wise decisions that ultimately create value, provide opportunities for meaningful work and contributions that lift people out of poverty, affirm the dignity of the human person, and bring productivity back to the communities.

Work

We are created in God's image to work and to contribute to the flourishing of the human community. Nonetheless, there are three common assumptions about the nature of work that typically undermine the health and effectiveness of our ministry in urban contexts.

One assumption is that only certain types of work matter to God. A bifurcated understanding of work has crept into Christian theology that goes something like this: "As a Christian, I work to take care of my personal and family needs and to be able to contribute to the *real* work of the church that happens through my local congregation and various mission and charitable agencies." This is a false narrative that we must counter with the truth of Scripture. In the words of pastor and author Tom Nelson, "Being made in God's image, we have been designed to work, to be fellow workers with God. . . . In our work we are to show off God's excellence, creativity, and glory to the world. We work because we bear the image of One who works."[3]

3. Tom Nelson, *Work Matters* (Wheaton, IL: Crossway, 2011), 22.

The implication of this perspective is that our work is how we partner with God to create value and meaning for ourselves and the good of others. We should therefore understand that "real Christian work" is part of every vocation, every calling.

A second false assumption about work is that its primary purpose is to make money. Although Scriptures teach us we must engage in productive work and fruitful economic exchange, this often translates into the idea that we work to make money. We work first and foremost to create value, which is the economic term for well-being.[4] When people have the opportunity to contribute meaningfully to value creation for the good of the community, something remarkable happens. The dignity that God has placed in each of us, as God's image bearers, is affirmed. The flourishing of the community occurs when its members are able to contribute to the welfare of others.

Pastor Chris Brooks of Evangel Ministries in Detroit has challenged his congregation's understandings of "real" work (including the work of ministry) by asking his congregation to determine whether its programs and ministries empowered the people it served by promoting a view of work wherein all persons were seen as image-bearers of God who had something of value to contribute to the world. For Evangel, every program run by the congregation should facilitate the sharing of each person's skills and gifts and encourage self-reliance and meaningful involvement by all concerned and wholeness within the community.

A third incorrect assumption about work is that it indicates our value. Although facilitating movement toward self-reliance and economic flourishing is vitally important, it can cause us to overlook work that many within our communities must do that may not be *paid* work. A stay-at-home parent may not be remunerated, but she or he makes a vital contribution to both family and community life. With respect to the latter, parents whose primary place of work is in the home often contribute in ways that reach well beyond that home. They volunteer in schools and serve in their community and church. Some families can make this choice without economic consideration, but for most it requires sacrifice and careful financial stewardship.

Urban ministry must have an ultimate purpose in affirming the *imago Dei* in each person it serves and be a part of that person's journey to create value and contribution to the community. We must respond to the

---

4. The Economic Wisdom Project, A Christian Vision for Flourishing Communities (Deerfield, IL: Oikonomia Network, 2013), 8, https://oikonomianetwork.org/wp-content/uploads/2014/02/EWP-NewVersion.pdf.

many and often urgent needs of our neighborhoods; but if we are not affirming all persons in their work and their ability to contribute and bear God's image brightly, then we have missed the mark.

Place

God cares about places and cities. As those called to urban communities, we must take the time to exegete those places and understand contexts well in all the richness with which they are imbued. God's ultimate vision for the kingdom is reflected in the interconnections of a city.[5]

In Pittsburgh, we have a great deal of city pride. Our "Stillers, Buccos, and Pens" (i.e., Steelers, Pirates, and Penguins sports teams) are often what come first to mind. But there is also Pittsburgh's great industrial history and then its resilience as those industries faded and new economies emerged and strengthened. Pittsburgh is often described as a city of neighborhoods, separated by hills, tunnels, and rivers. While there is one Pittsburgh, there are many faces and shapes to our beloved city. Wherever we are placed, we must do the hard work of understanding that part of the city in context with the broader culture of the region.

Once again, false assumptions can interfere with bringing wholeness to the cities in which we live and work. One false assumption interfering with the wholeness of our cities is that the only persons capable of doing effective ministry within a given urban context are persons who live within that context. This is a noble idea that has motivated many passionate people to move into neighborhoods where needs are great as acts of genuine solidarity with those within the contexts. For example, one of the truly great urban ministry organizations, the Christian Community Development Association (CCDA), emphasizes three operational principles: Relocation, Reconciliation, and Redistribution. As a result of the good work of CCDA and ministry organizations inspired by its model, many vulnerable neighborhoods in cities around the country and the world have experienced positive change. Nevertheless, more people than those living in urban neighborhoods are needed to bring flourishing to all areas of our cities.

According to the New International Version of Proverbs 11:10, "when the righteous prosper, the city rejoices." This passage suggests that there are persons with a heart for the city whose prosperity will benefit the city. These persons are not identified in the passage by where they live but by the fact that they are persons with a heart for the city. The "righteous"

5. Revelation 21.

in this instance then may not all live in the community they are called to serve, but they nevertheless participate in creating value, wealth, and meaningful work for many and understand their stewardship responsibility to invest into the community. The righteous may be persons in the business sector but can just as well be persons in the justice system who understand that prosperity in their sphere of influence is to be leveraged for the well-being of all; or the righteous may be persons in government responsible for systems serving the most vulnerable.

Moreover, if stewardship is our guiding principle, we all (including churches) must steward our power, influence, and resources in pursuit of a broad common good. Our global population has become too urbanized for anyone to think they can ignore the well-being of our cities—and similarly, persons residing in cities must appreciate interconnections to their contexts by persons living outside their city or neighborhood spaces. Urban ministries or urban social programs undertaken only by the people in the target community, without partnerships with other ministries, businesses, or governmental and non-profit leaders outside of their community will likely not reach their full potential.

Relationships

God hardwired people for relationships. It is easy to lose sight of this in our highly individualistic culture. The coming of the kingdom will not be through the individual but through the community—the body of Christ—in action. We need each other.

The primary example of relational health and connection comes to us in our theology of the Trinity. The apostle Paul speaks in 2 Corinthians 13:14 of the triune nature of God, where the grace of Jesus, the love of God, and the fellowship of the Holy Spirit dance in submission and service to one another. We too are to seek clarity on our own gifts, talents, and strengths while learning to work in collaboration with others to accomplish a shared outcome or set of goals.

However, we must avoid temptations to believe that we alone are capable of meeting the needs we encounter. Often we see individuals and churches launching ministries to serve a need, perhaps without sufficient resources, while a similar ministry may already exist nearby. Why is partnering not our first thought and response in these instances? The reality is that we must learn to seek collaboration in urban ministry. We must be willing to set ego aside and join what God may already be doing through others.

Related to this is that we often assume no one will care about the work as much as we do. This can be a self-fulfilling prophecy, for the tighter we cling to control and ownership, the fewer the number of people who will join us. We must find people who can come alongside and bring complementary gifts for creating ministries and programs of excellence and fruitfulness. Finding likeminded companions for the journey is essential to a broad-based empowerment and wholeness of urban communities.

II

Urban Community Formation

Low-Income Residents and Religious In-Betweenness in the United States and South Africa*

R. Drew Smith

According to recent U.S. survey data, one-third of religiously unaffiliated American adults characterize themselves as "spiritual" but not "religious," with Americans born between the early 1980s and early 2000s (the so-called millennial generation) especially likely to characterize themselves in this way.[1] This points to a twenty-first-century religious liminality (a state of in-betweenness), suggestive of ways religious content can be embraced without embracing fully or at all its larger ideological and institutional packaging.

Liminal encounters with religious life—this embrace of precepts but not packaging, of ideals but not forms—is descriptive of ways urban poor populations in the United States and beyond sometimes experience Christianity. This can be seen in instances where low-income urban Americans who have had little or no interaction with churches have nonetheless placed a high priority on their personal religious devotional life. This liminality is evident as well where the urban poor have enjoyed some degree of formal interaction with congregations, but in ways that proved quite selective and utilitarian. In these cases, low-income participants acquired what they could of spiritual or social value from the interactions without ever fully entering into the community of congregants or subjecting themselves to its authority or broader influences. Here, religious participants may have *passed through* religious institutions temporarily and superficially without the individual or the institution being

---

*A longer version of this essay was previously published as "Urban Marginality, Religious Liminality, and the Black Poor," *HTS Theological Studies*, 71, no. 3 (2015).

1. Pew Research Center, "'Nones' on the Rise," October 9, 2012, http://www.pewforum .org/2012/10/09/nones-on-the-rise/.

affected by the encounter in deep or enduring ways. Liminal, informal religious engagement is evidenced increasingly (though not exclusively) within black urban poor contexts across the United States and in the transitory urban landscapes of countries such as South Africa, where internal dislocations of the urban poor and the geographical instabilities of migrating and immigrating populations have contributed to a persistent unsettledness.

Attempts to construct normative institutional bridges across cultural and structural divides within these contexts (including the racial, ethnic, and class dimensions of these divides) have been meeting with less and less success within urban America and South Africa.[2] Increasingly, churches and faith-based institutions have been looked to within these contexts as strategic resources for community bridge-building due to their geographic positioning on the front lines of impoverished neighborhoods.[3] Nevertheless, despite a greater social services emphasis by urban churches (and the more favorable humanitarian light in which these churches are potentially cast as a result), many urban congregations especially in the poorest neighborhoods appear to be quantitatively and qualitatively weakening as sources of community.[4]

But as experiences discussed here of the stationary and migratory poor in urban America and urban South Africa make clear, institutional church life may be of far less importance to Christian formation and religious community-building among the poor than the formational steps they take from their own spaces and on their own terms. I explore this through research I conducted via a four-city study of interactions between churches and the poor in U.S. neighborhoods, and a study of interactions

2. See, for example, Benjamin E. Mays and Joseph Nicholson, *The Negro's Church* (New York: Greenwood Publishing, 1933); Goran Hyden, *Beyond Ujamaa in Tanzania: Underdevelopment of an Uncaptured Peasantry* (Berkeley: University of California Press, 1980); Danielle Resnick, *Urban Poverty and Party Populism in African Democracies* (Cambridge: Cambridge University Press, 2013); R. Drew Smith, *Beyond the Boundaries: Low-Income Residents, Faith-Based Organizations, and Neighborhood Coalition Building* (Baltimore: The Annie E. Casey Foundation, 2003); and E. Wayne Nafziger, *Inequality in Africa: Political Elites, Proletariat, Peasants and the Poor* (New York: Cambridge University Press), 1988.

3. See, for example, Mark Chaves and William Tsitsos, "Congregations and Social Services: What They Do, How They Do It, and with Whom?" *Nonprofit and Voluntary Sector Quarterly* 30 (2001): 660–83; Ram Cnaan and Stephanie C. Boddie, *Black Church Outreach: Comparing How Black and Other Congregations Serve Their Needy Neighbors*, Center for Research on Religion and Urban Civil Society, University of Pennsylvania, 2001; and Marian Burchardt, "Faith-Based Humanitarianism: Organizational Change and Everyday Meanings in South Africa," *Sociology of Religion* 74, no. 1 (2013): 30–55.

4. Smith, *Beyond the Boundaries.*

between churches and recently arrived migrants and immigrants in the Sunnyside neighborhood of Pretoria, South Africa.

Comparisons of Informal Religious Formation in the United States and South Africa

The four U.S. cities where the study took place are Camden, New Jersey; Hartford, Connecticut; Indianapolis, Indiana; and Denver, Colorado—cities that varied by size, overall demographics, and region of the country. The research neighborhoods were predominantly African American, although a number of the research neighborhoods contained sizeable white and Latino low-income populations as well. Researchers conducted a door-to-door survey in two or more low-income housing complexes in each of the four cities. The surveys yielded responses from 1,206 residents about their interactions with local congregations and their involvement in other aspects of community life. Researchers also conducted telephone interviews with churches within one mile of the housing complexes, asking official representatives of 136 churches about their community outreach initiatives and other aspects of their congregational ministries. Nine out of ten church respondents were clergy.[5]

The survey and interview research showed that churches, although a significant institutional presence in most urban communities and an important spiritual and social resource for some low-income families, have had limited impact on the lives of families living in the poorest urban neighborhoods. This was demonstrated to have resulted, in part, from limited interaction between congregations and their low-income neighbors—an observation amplifying related scholarly findings on this matter.[6] What this makes clear is that physical proximity between congregations and the urban poor is not necessarily a sufficient basis for meaningful interaction and engagement between the two.

Among the evidence of weak connections between congregations and residents in these neighborhoods was that two-thirds of the survey

5. Housing complex residents surveyed included 401 in Denver, 401 in Indianapolis, 225 in Camden, and 179 in Hartford. Churches surveyed included 40 in Indianapolis, 33 in Denver, 33 in Hartford, and 30 in Camden.

6. William J. Wilson, *The Truly Disadvantaged* (Chicago: University of Chicago Press, 1987); Loic Wacquant and William J. Wilson, "The Cost of Racial and Class Exclusion in the Inner City," *Annals of the American Academy of Political and Social Science* 501, no. 22 (1989): 8–25; and Lowell Livezey, ed., *Public Religion and Urban Transformation: Faith in the City* (New York: New York University Press, 2000), 83–106.

respondents indicated they were not members of any religious congregation, and roughly the same percentage indicated they had not attended religious services at a congregation more than a few times the previous year. Approximately two-thirds of the respondents also stated that they had not been contacted by churches through any means the previous year. Even where respondents had participated at some level in religious worship activities or in a church-based social service program, the respondents appear not to have formed strong connections with the congregation or developed a sense of community with fellow churchgoers—due both to the low frequency of participation by these residents in congregation-based activities and to the low interpersonal and relational level of those interactions.

Relationship-building and community-building possibilities were impeded in these contexts by cultural barriers between low-income populations and what were largely working-class and middle-class congregants—with low-income residents expressing a lack of comfort interacting with congregants whose expectations pertaining to church attire, cultural bearings, institutional protocols, and religious pieties might be hard for residents to satisfy. Substantive interactions between low-income residents and congregants were also impeded by the often transient quality of residential life in these low-income neighborhoods. Almost 70 percent of the residents had lived at their present address five years or less, 59 percent actually lived at their current address three years or less, and 23 percent had lived at their address one year or less. The fact that so many of the residents had not lived in these neighborhoods long was suggestive as well that they may not remain there for long either.

Low-income residents relocate for a variety of personal reasons, but they are sometimes forced to relocate en masse as a result of governmental public housing policies. This was the case for residents at several of the public housing complexes in Denver and Indianapolis, whose complexes were targeted by a public housing policy initiative called Hope VI aimed at deconcentrating urban poverty by demolishing low-income housing complexes and replacing them (sometimes) with mixed-income housing. Whether or not mixed-income housing was actually built in place of the demolished low-income housing, the residents of the low-income housing complexes were dispersed during the process and only occasionally able to return to these neighborhoods as occupants of any newly constructed mixed-income housing. This residential transience decidedly reduces resident prospects for long-term relationship-building and community connections within these neighborhoods, including aspects bearing on church life.

Residential impermanence and cultural incompatibilities with church life represent two of the more prominent reasons low-income residents who pursue involvement with congregations may achieve little more than a cursory relationship with their respective congregation. As a result, these congregations tend to serve as temporary church homes at best but more often simply as stop-over or pass-through activities. Low-income residents may derive lasting spiritual resources from these interactions, but far less may result in enduring social or cultural bridge-building value for these individuals or institutions.

An equally important finding of the four-city study is that limitations impacting low-income residents' religious formation via formal channels are countered by informal steps residents take on their own behalf to facilitate their religious formation. For example, 73 percent of low-income residents said they felt it was important they spend time in prayer, with 57 percent indicating they pray every day, and another 8 percent stating they pray at least once per week. When asked about their habits related to reading the Bible, 64 percent of the residents said they felt it was important they read the Bible on a regular basis, with 16 percent indicating they read the Bible every day, and another 15 percent stating they read it at least once a week. Residents were also asked whether they watch religious television programs or listen to religious radio programs and 42 percent indicated they turned to such programs, with 10 percent stating they turn to these religious programs at least once a day, and another 17 percent stating they turn to these programs at least once a week.[7]

Contrary then to presumptions of widespread religious disinterest and disinclination among the urban poor, these data reveal instead that the urban poor are strongly disposed toward spiritual matters but weakly committed (in theory and in practice) to formal church institutions as effective contexts in which to pursue these spiritual interests and inclinations. Instead, the urban poor are more likely to pursue spiritual formation through more readily available and personally facilitated means.

Urban South Africa provides an important comparative window on the relationship between social and religious transience and ways formal

---

7. Data from the Pew Forum's 2015 American Religious Landscape Survey provides similar findings about the importance of informal processes of religious formation in instances where religious formation is not necessarily being pursued via formal channels. At least with respect to the data specific on African Americans who are not affiliated with any religious group, the Pew data show that 48 percent of these unaffiliated African Americans pray daily. See Pew Research Center, "A Religious Portrait of African Americans," 2009, http://www.pewforum.org/2009/01/30/a-religious-portrait-of-african-americans/.

religious formation is supplemented and countered by informal religious formation. Survey and interview research I conducted in Sunnyside, a central Pretoria neighborhood, sheds light on this dynamic through the experience of newly arriving black and mostly impoverished migrants and immigrants within what had been a historically white, working-class context of residential and congregational life.

Sunnyside, a roughly four-kilometer area comprised mainly of high-rise apartment flats and approximately 30,000 residents, is one of six neighborhoods located in the area referred to as Pretoria Central.[8] Sunny-side has been a gateway neighborhood where civil servants and tertiary students have resided (primarily whites until recently) while pursuing governmental jobs or tertiary studies at the University of Pretoria or University of South Africa. Once these residents became more economi-cally mobile, secured employment elsewhere, or ended their studies, they frequently relocated to other neighborhoods. Nevertheless, the neigh-borhood maintained its predominantly white, largely Afrikaans-speaking character until South Africa's democratic transformation was well under way in the early 1990s. Since the early 1990s, Pretoria Central neighbor-hoods have undergone as rapid and extensive a demographic transfor-mation as any place within post-apartheid South Africa. Migrants from across the country relocated there from rural areas and black and colored townships, and there has also been a post-apartheid immigrant influx from other African countries. In 1996, the white population within the ward comprising most of Sunnyside was 15,230, while the black popu-lation numbered 4,432. By 2001, the white population had declined to 9,009 and the black population had increased to 16,125.

These recent neighborhood in-migrations and out-migrations are part of the generally transient nature of post-apartheid South African life, characterized as it is by institutional and organizational flux and a physi-cal and cultural unsettledness. In large numbers, beginning in the early 1990s, blacks began moving into higher-income neighborhoods from which they were once excluded, whites began seeking neighborhoods further removed from central urban areas or else moving out of South Africa altogether, and black migrants and immigrants from elsewhere in the country and elsewhere in the continent began arriving in urban core

---

8. Pretoria Central includes the Arcadia, Clydesdale, Hatfield, Marabastad, Sunnyside, and Pretoria Central Business District neighborhoods. This area conforms to parts of what were electoral wards 56, 58, 59, and 60 (as of the 2001 Census), but what as of 2011 are electoral wards 56, 58, 59, 60, 80, 81, and 92.

neighborhoods such as Sunnyside. This movement was captured in 1996 Census data which showed approximately 59 percent of South African–born persons ages 20 to 55 had migrated to their residential district.[9]

This amount of residential flux and unsettledness no doubt poses significant challenges to an effective process of community formation and belongingness, especially in a national context where there have been such strong legacies of resistance to social and geographic boundary-crossing. Certainly, as the resident population of neighborhoods such as Sunnyside changed during the 1990s, its community life and institutions (including its churches) were also transformed. It therefore is important to ask whether this resulted in communities and institutions that gained new strength and vitality as a result of culturally diverse population influxes, or whether these in-migrations (and out-migrations) resulted in a weakening and fragmenting of these institutions and communities.

In exploring these matters, in 2005 I interviewed pastors of nine of Sunnyside's ten well-established congregations and surveyed 975 worshipers from eight of those congregations. Eight of the nine congregations were founded in the 1970s or earlier (with half of those founded in the 1940s or earlier). Although the racial composition of these longstanding congregations transitioned from predominantly (if not exclusively) white to predominantly persons of color, as of 2005 the denominational identity, doctrinal priorities, and (often) leadership teams within the congregations had remained the same in most instances. Six of the congregations had white pastors, four of whom had served in that capacity six years or more. Two of the congregations had "colored"[10] pastors who had served five years or less. The approach several of these congregations had taken in attempting to maintain their historical identity while accommodating their new demographic realities had been to facilitate parallel congregations via multiple worship services each Sunday. Typically this meant holding an early morning service that maintained continuity with the congregation's historical worship culture and constituency—which is to say a service that conformed liturgically and linguistically to mostly elderly, white, Afrikaans-speaking or English-speaking members. A second service later in the morning was often contemporary in worship style, youthful in orientation, and conducted in

9. Tukufu Zuberi and Amson Sibanda, "Migration and Employment," in Tukufu Zuberi et al., eds., *The Demography of South Africa* (London: M. E. Sharpe, 2005), 267.
10. "Colored" is a designation used historically in South Africa to refer to mixed-race persons of one or another combination of African, white, and Malay ancestry.

English (often interspersed with African languages). The primary continuity between the two worship contexts was that the white pastor generally presided over both services.

The surveys were conducted during the English-speaking services of the respective congregations, which meant the respondents tended to be recent migrant and immigrant arrivals to the neighborhood. Only 8 percent of these respondents had lived in the neighborhood longer than ten years, with another 10 percent indicating residency in the neighborhood between six and ten years. A full 40 percent of the respondents had lived in the neighborhood less than a year, and another 26 percent had lived there between one and three years. Also, two-thirds of the respondents said they lived two kilometers (1.24 miles) or less from the congregation they were attending, while only 14 percent lived more than 10 kilometers (6.21 miles) from their respective congregation. In fact, very few of these recently arrived migrants or immigrants possessed vehicles, so it is understandable that those interested in attending church would choose a congregation within walking distance.

Attempting to integrate black migrants and immigrants into previously white congregations through separate worship tracks for distinct constituencies certainly facilitated black-white coexistence within these newly diversifying congregational contexts, but this did not necessarily translate into a sense of community and relationality across racial and ethnic boundaries. The distinct worshiping constituencies seemed weakly connected to one another, and within several of the congregations where the leadership and authority structures remained under white control, the congregation appeared weakly connected institutionally to its now predominantly black neighborhood environs, and the black worshipers within these congregations appeared weakly connected to the institutional life of the congregation beyond the worship experience.

These congregations seemed to function as pass-through worship experiences for many of these black migrants and immigrants, where they were content to gather for worship on Sunday morning (and felt very welcomed in doing so), but where relatively little was gained in some instances from their congregational involvement that provided them with social footing and social structuring of their lives beyond Sunday worship. There is certainly some urgency to assisting persons with gaining social footing within a national context characterized by large numbers of refugees and asylum seekers (153,300 in 2012 according to the United Nations High Commissioner for Refugees (UNHCR) and a considerably larger number of undocumented immigrants (2 to 8 million in 1996 by

South African Police estimates and possibly as many as 12 million in 2004 according to Seafarers Assistance Program). This population would not be able to exercise a vote within South African elections and would be positioned even less favorably than most South African citizens already are in efforts for acquiring limited employment opportunities or bursary support for tertiary studies.

Responses to the Sunnyside congregational survey make clear the relative disconnectedness of Sunnyside's largely migrant and immigrant population from South African mainstream culture and institutions—and the disconnectedness of the congregational ministries from the social needs of these parishioners. First of all, only 46 percent of these churchgoers were employed, and 33 percent of these survey respondents indicated having no income whatsoever. Another 8 percent earned less than 20,000 rand (or $3,300 at 2005 exchange rates). But when asked how helpful their congregation had been in assisting them with job skill training and employment matters, only 22 percent of the respondents considered their congregation as having been "very helpful." Additionally, although the large immigrant populations would be especially susceptible to isolation from South African civic affairs given their voter ineligibility and potential estrangement from local and national political life, only 34 percent of the respondents felt their congregation had been very helpful in encouraging civic participation and only 43 percent said the congregation was very helpful in encouraging awareness about national current events.

Although these congregations serve as anchor institutions within the Sunnyside neighborhood (at least in the sense of their enduring institutional and religious presence), they have not provided especially strong social anchoring within a local context where so many of the new residents hail from and retain strong connections to faraway contexts, and where the encounters and intersections between the cultural worlds of Sunnyside's residents and local congregations are not as organic or compatible as those existing within the context prior to the transitions of the 1990s. This engagement between congregations and newly arriving residents reflects an increasing breadth, but not necessarily depth, with residents and congregations coming together on Sunday mornings in vibrant worship portrayals of cultural pluralism. Nevertheless, migrant and immigrant residents in large numbers will pass through Sunnyside congregations on Sunday mornings, perhaps for several years, then likely move on to new contexts or to the one from which they came—often without any acknowledgment from their host congregation that they were ever there, or that it even mattered they were there (beyond the optics).

This is not to suggest these encounters did not provide significant benefits to the migrants and immigrants moving through these congregational contexts. The Sunday worship experiences served as religious and cultural wells from which migrants and immigrants drank deeply, although often in the kind of impersonal and disconnected way persons viewing religious television programs or listening to religious radio programs drink from those wells. Congregational platforms, in the same sense as television and radio platforms, serve simply as delivery vehicles to which there is a momentary and primarily utilitarian connection and toward which migrants and immigrants hold no longer-term attachment than many of these congregations appear to hold toward them as a population of worshipers. In short, the encounter and interaction between many of these congregations and worshipers lack formalization—it remains informal.

Concluding Thoughts

Self-determined and informal approaches to religious formation feature prominently within contemporary Christianity—as illustrated in the experiences of the black poor in Sunnyside and the four U.S. cities. But this also points to a broadening stream within Western Christianity in general, increasingly characterized by a consumerist approach to church engagement. Churchgoers constantly shop for the next best iteration in Christian worship and programming and concern themselves decreasingly with congregational life as a source of community to which they might belong or as a pathway into community affairs. Nevertheless, in this growing tendency to uncouple faith formation from formal faith structures, at least one conclusion can be reached about situations where faith formation takes place separately from formal church structures: mainly, that there are a variety of encounters between people and the gospel that are not impeded by formal church walls and boundaries.

Chapter 10

Racial Equity and Faith-Based Organizing at Community Renewal Society

Curtiss Paul DeYoung

In 1882, six lay leaders and one clergy from the Congregational Church (now the United Church of Christ) launched the Chicago City Missionary Society, now the Community Renewal Society (CRS), as an independent nonprofit organization. The mission from the beginning was twofold: "to serve the poor (and) serve the organized church" in Chicago.[1] The Society's purpose was to encourage Congregational churches to serve in urban neighborhoods and to do it in partnership with other Christian churches. These goals were often in tension. At times the Society was the de facto outreach arm of the Congregational Church denomination. At other moments they acted more as a catalyst for ecumenical urban ministry in Chicago.

The needs of those at the margins of urban society in Chicago defined the focus of the Society's social service work. In the early years the Chicago City Missionary Society served European immigrants—Germans and Bohemians in particular. While the Society was connected to the few black Congregationalists in Chicago, their work with African Americans only became significant after 1910. In the 1930s, they published two pamphlets to create racial understanding, *The Negro in Chicago* (1930) and *The Mexican in Chicago* (1931).[2] By the mid-1950s the Society initiated work with Puerto Ricans in Chicago through their Casa Central program.[3]

From the inception of the Chicago City Missionary Society in 1882

---

1. David Lee Smith, *Community Renewal Society: 100 Years of Service* (Chicago: Chicago Review Press, 1982), 21.
2. Ibid., 60.
3. Ibid., 77. Casa Central became an independent program in 1965.

until the midpoint of the twentieth century, the programs were primarily charitable in nature with a social service or church mission focus. The Society developed new congregations, Sunday schools, community centers, neighborhood missions, cooking classes, sports programs, day cares, youth programs, job training, and the like. They also financially resourced the construction of urban church buildings.

A Civil Rights Movement Reframe

In the 1950s and 1960s the fervor of the civil rights movement emerged in Chicago culminating in 1966 with the Chicago Freedom Movement—a partnership of Chicago activists and organizations working for civil rights with Martin Luther King Jr.'s Southern Christian Leadership Conference (SCLC). Many historians have undervalued the impact of the Chicago movement. Others have considered it a failure. These notions have been challenged or corrected by a book released in 2016, at the fiftieth anniversary, written by activists from the time and historians: *The Chicago Freedom Movement: Martin Luther King Jr. and Civil Rights Activism in the North*.[4] The editors and contributors of this volume note many accomplishments for the Chicago Freedom Movement. They show how the networks built in the 1966 movement led to the subsequent elections of the first black mayor of Chicago, Harold Washington, and the election of then Chicagoan Barack Obama as the first black U.S. president.

The civil rights movement in Chicago inspired a shift at the Society from a focus that was primarily on the work of charity to one that addressed the structures in society that caused economic and racial injustice. This shift was best illustrated by the formation of the West Side Christian Parish in 1952 with help from leaders of the East Harlem Protestant Parish in New York City. The West Side Christian Parish provided "a 'militant form of Christianity,' it combined the Christian Gospel with the everyday practical concerns of the people and embraced both liturgy and community social action."[5] The Parish program brought together congregations on the West Side of Chicago to address community issues.

Civil rights activist James Bevel and his wife, Diane Nash (a Chicago native), moved to Chicago in 1965 after the success of the Selma voting

---

4. Mary Lou Finley, Bernard Lafayette Jr., James R. Ralph Jr., and Pam Smith, eds., *The Chicago Freedom Movement: Martin Luther King Jr. and Civil Rights Activism in the North* (Lexington: University Press of Kentucky, 2016).

5. Ibid., 74.

rights campaign. Bevel was a key strategist for the Southern Christian Leadership Conference (SCLC) and was laying the groundwork in Chicago for Dr. King's move to the North. He took a job as program director with the Society's West Side Christian Parish. Historian James Ralph notes, "The West Side Christian Parish desperately sought Bevel. . . . No one in America seemed better equipped to galvanize a southern-style movement in a northern city."[6] The selection of James Bevel by the Society was a choice for the "prophetic tradition of organizing" rather than that of Chicago-based Saul Alinsky. Ralph continues, "Bevel was not simply a community organizer but a manufacturer of movements infused with Christian brotherhood and nonviolent spirit [and an] organizing philosophy, based on nonviolence and Christian love and with universal redemption as its fundamental goal."[7]

Shortly after James Bevel took the job with the Society's program, "a dozen or so members of Dr. Martin Luther King Jr.'s southern field staff moved into the West Side Christian Parish's Project House in the heart of Chicago's Near West Side."[8] So Bevel became both the program director of the West Side Christian Parish and in charge of SCLC's project in Chicago. Historian Ralph notes, "As so often happened in the civil rights movement, organizational lines blended [and] much of the parish's staff merged with SCLC's staff under Bevel's leadership."[9] This intermingling of the staffs and resources of the Society and SCLC influenced the future direction of the Chicago City Missionary Society.

The Society's connection to the civil rights movement continued to expand. A program of the Society, the Urban Training Center for Christian Mission, hired former SCLC staffer C. T. Vivian. The Urban Training Center trained hundreds of people in nonviolence for the Chicago Freedom Movement. Jesse Jackson Sr. notes, "With C. T. Vivian at the Urban Training Center and James Bevel joining the West Side Christian Parish to work on Chicago's West Side, there was a confluence of forces and timing in 1966."[10]

The engagement with SCLC and the civil rights movement transformed and reframed the Society. In 1967 the Chicago City Missionary Society changed its name to Community Renewal Society (CRS) to

6. James R. Ralph Jr., *Northern Protest: Martin Luther King, Jr., Chicago, and the Civil Rights Movement* (Cambridge, MA: Harvard University Press, 1993), 41.

7. Ibid., 58–59, 60.

8. Finley et al., *The Chicago Freedom Movement*, 1.

9. Ralph, *Northern Protest*, 44.

10. Finley et al., *The Chicago Freedom Movement*, 241.

reflect this new frame for operation. A stronger focus on racism in Chicago was observed in CRS programs. John McDermott, a key leader in the Chicago Freedom Movement with the Chicago Catholic Interracial Council, joined the staff of CRS. He launched *The Chicago Reporter* at CRS as an investigative journal focused on the unfinished racial and economic justice agenda of the Chicago Freedom Movement.

Beginning with Donald Benedict's tenure from the 1950s to the early 1980s, Community Renewal Society had four executive directors who were shaped by the civil rights movement era. The other three were Paul Sherry, Yvonne Delk, and Calvin Morris. Paul Sherry left CRS to lead the United Church of Christ denomination. Following seven white males since 1882, Yvonne Delk became the first African American and first woman executive director of CRS. Calvin Morris, also African American, led CRS in the first decade of the twenty-first century. He was a member of King's Chicago SCLC staff in the late 1960s and in many ways brought to completion the reframing of CRS through a civil rights movement lens. Morris retired in 2012.

A Postcolonial Reframe

In the second decade of the twenty-first century, Community Renewal Society is an urban faith-based organization committed to racial and economic justice working for structural change through church-based community organizing, policy advocacy, and investigative journalism. CRS moved from a charitable (or missions) approach in its work to a strong focus on social change (or community renewal). CRS expanded its work to confront unjust social structures imbedded in the city of Chicago, Cook and Lake Counties, and the state of Illinois that inhibit racial and economic justice.

In 2014, CRS was a majority-white organization with a stated mission of racial justice in a city where whites were only one-third of the population. Following the retirement of Calvin Morris and nearly twenty-five years of black leadership at the executive level, I was the new white male executive director arriving in Chicago from Minneapolis with limited knowledge of the history of Community Renewal Society. I had assumed that as a racial justice organization in Chicago the organization would reflect the demographic reality of the city. I was trained at a historically black colleges and universities (HBCU) seminary, Howard University School of Divinity, and studied with Calvin Morris. I spent years addressing issues of racism. Immediately I knew that this internal racial reality at CRS and my hiring posed a serious question of integrity.

This was further illuminated by events that interrupted the second decade of the twenty-first century in Ferguson, Missouri, and other cities, as well as the emergence of the Black Lives Matter movement. But the social eruption in Ferguson and the Black Lives Matter movement were not only about policing in the United States. They also brought to the center of public discourse that organizational integrity around issues of race was considered essential for authentic social change. Soon I began to contemplate the length of my tenure.

Older organizations like CRS were confronted with a reframing challenge. It was not enough for the Community Renewal Society to have black leadership at the executive director level (as was the case with Delk and Morris). The organization must fully express internally its commitment to racial and economic justice. Addressing institutional racism cannot just be the organization's work in society. This is challenging work for a 135-year-old organization like CRS. Organizational integrity calls for institutions to transform into entities that are fully inclusive (gender and LGBT as well) and with leadership by persons of color at all levels of staff and board. This is particularly important at the board level. While a black executive director or black board chair may signify that the organization is "black led," a board that is over 50 percent African American demonstrates that the organization is black owned. For an organization with congregational members like CRS, this must also be true for its base of member congregations. Congregations located in the communities most affected by racial injustice must have lead roles.

Liberation movements from the 1950s and 1960s offer a framework for the present. Postcolonialist theorists and writers from the same period contemplated what was needed to reverse the effects of colonialism as many colonial societies seemed to be collapsing. With Black Lives Matter, Ferguson, and other urban interruptions, we are in a postcolonial moment in the United States. Allan Boesak noted that blacks in South Africa under apartheid experienced a "'colonializing' of our humanity." They were classified as "non-white," as nonpersons.[11] The cry of "black lives matter" is a call for U.S. society to rediscover the humanity, dignity, and power of black people (and other people of color)—a decolonizing of people of color. Social justice organizations like CRS must show evidence of this awareness and process in how they operate.

---

11. Allan A. Boesak, *Black and Reformed: Apartheid, Liberation, and the Calvinist Tradition* (Maryknoll, NY: Orbis Books, 1984), 4.

The Community Renewal Society needed to be decolonized. I noticed during the executive director interview process that the board of directors was majority white. In my first year at CRS, I asked white board members to make room for persons of color at the table. Within a year and a half, the board became majority black. The board that was 52 percent white when I arrived was 64 percent African American and 73 percent persons of color in 2017. The leadership of the board (executive committee) shifted from 83 percent white to 60 percent African American and 80 percent persons of color. This transformation completely changed the conversation at the "ownership" level.

With a black-led board of directors, CRS began the transformation of the staff. With my departure in June 2017, the leadership staff that was 70 percent white in 2014, was 87 percent African American and 100 percent persons of color. The full staff that was 52 percent white, was 69 percent persons of color (48 percent African American, 14 percent Latino, 7 percent Asian) when I left. The board approved a strategic plan in April 2017 that called for CRS to be black-led. In 2017 the board and staff were majority black and black-led (which would be finalized with the hire of an executive director who was black).[12]

A postcolonial critique rejects the usually unstated expectation of assimilation into whiteness. Paulo Freire wrote that people who are oppressed often exhibit "an attitude of adhesion to the oppressor."[13] Historically people of color in the United States have been pressured to assimilate into whiteness—to assume the posture and perspective of whites. This happens even in racial justice organizations. Franz Fanon reflected on the overwhelming power of whiteness when he said, "Then I will quite simply try to make myself white: that is, I will compel the white man to acknowledge that I am human."[14] The power of whiteness must be deconstructed and defanged.

Although CRS has gone through a dramatic racial demographic change in its leadership, a black-led organization can still assimilate into the ways and culture of whiteness. An organization that has been dominated by a white internal culture for its 135-year history needs to be analyzed and transformed. CRS has committed to antiracism training, racial audits, and culture change to remove the whiteness frame.

---

12. The demographic statistics noted here and subsequently come from an unpublished final executive director report to the board at CRS by Curtiss Paul DeYoung, June 27, 2017.
13. Paulo Freire, *Pedagogy of the Oppressed* (New York: The Seabury Press, 1970), 45.
14. Frantz Fanon, *Black Skin, White Masks* (New York: Grove Press, 1967), 98.

For organizations such as CRS to reframe how race operates internally, a postcolonial critique further suggests that whites must accept that their role historically and still presently has been as a "non-legitimate privileged person."[15] Whites must reject this non-legitimate identity of superiority and let go of the privileges that go with that position. This is not easy given that unjust systems and non-legitimate privileges often appear normal to whites. Freire noted that even when white people "cease to be exploiters or indifferent spectators or simply the heirs of exploitation and move to the side of the exploited, they almost always bring with them the marks of their origin . . . Because of their background they believe that they must be the executors of the transformation."[16]

During apartheid in South Africa, Steve Biko noted there were whites who wanted social change and claimed they were "black souls wrapped in white skins." Yet they believed that they "always knew what was good for the blacks and told them so."[17] Letting go of the levers of power is not easy for whites, even when the intention is positive social change. For CRS to become black-led, the white executive director had to leave. After three years I resigned to make room for full transformation.

I believe that for CRS to fully live into its faith-rooted call and its mission to build power for social transformation, a broader multiracial future is on the horizon. The process has begun by transforming the historical white/black multiracial reality to one where black congregations and leaders take leadership roles, and white congregations and leaders stay in strong relationship with CRS as allies and accomplices for racial justice. The white-over-black racial binary has been flipped, placing blacks in leadership. The design of a multiracial future must be led by those most affected by racism among the CRS membership—African Americans. Next, CRS needs to break the white/black racial binary and create a more racially inclusive future by building relationships in Latino, Asian, Arab, and other racial and cultural communities. Both the gospel and the required needs for power and continued relevance in Chicago call forth such a future.

Older organizations like Community Renewal Society must welcome opportunities to reframe their urban ministry to remain relevant and effective. Whereas the civil rights movement reframe reconfigured the

---

15. Albert Memmi, *The Colonizer and the Colonized* (Boston: Beacon Press, 1965), 52.
16. Freire, *Pedagogy of the Oppressed*, 46–47.
17. Steve Biko, *I Write What I Like: Selected Writings* (Chicago: University of Chicago Press, 2002), 20.

external racial justice work and focus of CRS, this present reframe decol-onizes and reorients the very identity of CRS. A postcolonial reframing challenges the inequities of power and answers the question of identity for the future. This is especially true for those who are accustomed to being in charge. Albert Memmi warned that whites often do not recog-nize the "deep transformation of [their] own situation and of [their] own personality" that is required.[18] Reframing urban ministry around racial equity is the next phase of organizational change for faith-based entities.

18. Memmi, *The Colonizer and the Colonized*, 40.

Chapter 11

Ferguson Lessons about Church Solidarity with Communities of Struggle

Michael McBride

As people of deep moral conviction informed by the faith of our ancestors, how do we respond to the twenty-first-century daily reality of human suffering of those Howard Thurman described as those "whose backs are against the wall"?[1]

When I arrived in Ferguson, Missouri, just days after the August 9, 2014, murder of Michael Brown, the community's pain was palpable, tension thick, and the trauma was real. This small and multiracial but predominantly black neighborhood had been militarily occupied, terrorized, and attacked by rogue and unaccountable law enforcement agencies from the region. Moreover, the level of distrust and suspicion between the most distressed in the streets and the faith community was just as real as the disconnect between community members and law enforcement. For me, this context revealed a divine opportunity for the church, religious institutions, and people of faith and good will to be baptized by this fire of rage, pain, and fractured relationship.

Among the clergy colleagues who joined me in Ferguson was Michael-Ray Mathews, and he has raised a pivotal question regarding the stakes for the church at this time. Ray asked, as church leaders, "will [we] be chaplain[s] to the empire, or prophet[s] of the resistance?"[2] In short, will Christian believers be "maintainers" or "disruptors" of an unjust status quo? Martin Luther King Jr. referred to the choice before the church as

---

1. Howard Thurman, *Jesus and the Disinherited* (Nashville: Abingdon-Cokesbury Press, 1949), 11.
2. Michael-Ray Mathews, "Will You Be Chaplain to the Empire or Prophet of the Resistance?" *Sojourners*, February 16, 2017, https://sojo.net/articles/faith-action/will-you-be-chaplain-empire-or-prophet-resistance.

being either "adjusted or maladjusted" to social injustice.[3] This is the question before a church living in a twenty-first-century, post-Ferguson age. It requires our deepest reflection and struggle, because unless our churches can be infused with fresh capacity to helpfully engage this new socioeconomic, cultural, and political context of resistance to oppression, they will increasingly become what King warned of long ago: a church that has become "an irrelevant social club without moral or spiritual authority" because it has failed "to recapture its prophetic zeal."[4]

The search for strategies to implement the necessary moral, theological, and experiential infrastructure enabling Christian believers to resist becoming behavioral extensions of the empire began long before the tragedy of Ferguson. In 2009, a group of clergy and laity within a network of faith congregations was in Washington, D.C., dialoguing about the need for reforms to healthcare that would make it accessible and affordable. As we sat around a table with clergy from Flint, Michigan; Camden, New Jersey; Oakland, California; New Orleans, Louisiana; and other cities, we realized that our communities could not benefit from healthcare while they were continually drowning in the realities of death and carnage related to gun violence and incarceration. Since people cannot be saved if they are already dead, we committed to going back to our communities as architects of a national strategy to reduce violence and incarceration as a prerequisite for any meaningful social justice agenda.

Over the next eighteen months we gathered clergy in the Bay Area and across the country during the Lenten season, in family conferences, clergy cohorts, and study groups to reflect on a "theo-praxis model" of social justice formation. This led us to host major gatherings in cities nationwide within our network and within historically black denominations more broadly (including Pentecostal, Methodist, and Baptist groups). The culmination of this effort was the launching in New Orleans of the Lifelines to Healing Campaign in November 2011, in collaboration with Michelle Alexander, author of *The New Jim Crow* (2010) and U.S. Assistant Attorney General Laurie Robinson, and with over five hundred national faith leaders and twenty-five hundred lay leaders participating. The message and aim were clear: we must stop the onslaught of gun violence and incarceration. The strategy of this campaign involved training clergy and

---

3. Martin Luther King Jr., "The Role of the Behavioral Scientist in the Civil Rights Movement," speech to the American Psychological Association, September 1967, reprinted in *Journal of Social Issues*, 24, no. 1 (1968): 1–12, http://www.apa.org/monitor/features/king-challenge.aspx.
4. Martin Luther King Jr., *Strength to Love* (New York: Harper & Row, 1963), 11.

laity over the next eighteen months to flood neighborhoods surrounding our churches with night walks, ceasefire strategies, and support services for people at highest risk of shooting or being shot.

We challenged the systems and stewards of these systems to dismantle structural barriers which lock people in cycles of incarceration, poverty, and violence. In pursuing this work, we were transformed by a deep engagement in the communities where too often our churches only visited on Sundays and during midweek services when we commuted to worship. If we were going to have communities where people could "live free" from violence in all its forms and incarceration in all its manifestations, walking the neighborhoods and shedding our fear, self-righteousness, judgment, and respectability were required. As such, this strategy of direct engagement prepared us for the Ferguson uprising. So when we were invited by local clergy in Ferguson who had been working with us on this Lifelines to Healing/LIVE FREE campaign, we were prepared to show up with a curiosity about the pain of the young people and community, and the capacity to be surprised by the emerging work of God among the young people.

Being Challenged by Ferguson

There were some who believed it was the clergy who were needed to bring God to the Ferguson uprising; instead, it was in Ferguson where I was reintroduced to the Jesus who was constantly bringing disruptive fire to the systems and powers through prophetic truths of Scripture and acts of healing and deep commitments to the poor and marginalized.[5] In Ferguson I found anew the dark body, unfairly arrested, convicted by a kangaroo court, sentenced to die, and executed by the empire of his day. This Jesus, the prophet, the healer, the liberator, the organizer, the exorcist of both individuals and systems, was already there in Ferguson when we showed up—and it was the voice of this Jesus that I heard declare to whosoever would listen, "Follow me!"

The killing of Michael Brown, the militarized responses of the local law enforcement, and the complicity of the political and religious establishment to maintain a negative peace and silence around the brutality of

---

5. The early church repeatedly described and defined the life of Jesus of Nazareth in varied and unmistakable quotations from Isaiah's "suffering servant" language (passages from Isa. 53:1–8; Luke 22:37; and Acts 8:26–39 provide some representative examples) similar to the characteristics of many individuals I met in Ferguson.

the force of the state left me deeply scarred and traumatized. To know that all this happened under the leadership of administrations at the federal, state, and local level, stewarded by black Americans, progressive politicians, and professed Christians or people of faith has unmasked the woeful insufficiency of the practice of American faith and democracy when it comes to protecting dark bodies from the violent and destructive forces of empire.

All of these realities help me understand that being progressive politically is not good enough for black people. Because as Tef Poe, local leader, organizer, and hip-hop activist from St. Louis, was known to say: "I voted for Barack Obama twice and I still got tear gassed."[6] It has definitely shown me the inadequacy of our theological and ecclesiological commitments. For example, when over one hundred clergy showed up one night to be present in the protests and resistance, I remember a young man asking me, "Why are all these preachers out here tonight? They don't come out at night [or] when there are no cameras!" I said in response, "We are here because we care." The young man looked at me and said, "Fa real?"

I sense a more faithful church responsiveness to our twenty-first-century, post-Ferguson urban contexts is within our grasp if churches are willing to be transformed in several ways by these new urban realities and youth social justice movements. For example, are churches willing to shed the false dichotomy between the sacred and the secular and the church and the streets? Are churches willing to do things differently and develop new alignments in this post-Ferguson moment? Can churches recover that Spirit modeled by past church leaders that resisted empire's coercive sabotage of justice? I believe the voices of the emergent street prophets and prophetesses numbered among the poor, high school dropouts, lesbian, gay, and transgendered—generally persons not committed to respectability politics or overly invested in the status quo of religious or secular institutions—are being used by God to ask what too many churchpersons have gotten too comfortable or distracted to ask: "Will we be chaplains or will we be prophets?" Any theology of resistance to injustice must create a daily moral crisis for the faithful that forces us to answer the age-old question of every generation of freedom fighters: which side are you on?

The greed-based, impersonal, and exploitive values of our day must be transformed through continuous and strategic use of our resources of

---

6. Mustafa Dikeç, *Urban Rage: The Revolt of the Excluded* (New Haven, CT: Yale University Press, 2017), 218.

body, ballot, and bucks to create what King called the "Beloved Community," a society where mutual affirmation and respect for life-affirming values is public policy. Putting bodies to use in this instance includes showing up to engage and dismantle the exploitive consequences of empire functioning. First, as institutions of faith, we must re-imagine our congregational activities as not simply weekly worship, but also as an institutional body or collective power base with the communal agency to leverage and invent a future for poor or oppressed persons and families. Second, we must preach, pray, and act in ways that disciple our congregants to be open and willing to put their personal body in the fight for freedom through principled nonviolent direct action, mentoring, or any form of physical engagement in support of justice. While we may place our bodies on the line in various ways, what is non-negotiable in these instances is showing up in concrete ways that leverage our unique privileges of power, wealth, talent, and numbers to reaffirm that black faith matters in the future of black lives.

Making use of the ballot entails utilizing it as a tool of accountability for elected officials and political leaders in addressing the depth and complexity of suffering in black communities caused by mass criminalization and incarceration, police brutality, and state-sponsored violence. Black faith must incubate and unleash the moral outrage necessary to inspire needed and sustained engagement in electoral and political engagement, community organizing, and policy advocacy—prioritizing and resourcing these activities within our ministries. Organizations such as the Values Partnership and Let My People Vote are powerful resources which have year-round capacity to support local congregational efforts. Values Partnership works with faith-based and community-based organizations to help these organizations develop "creative engagement campaigns" and sort out "complex issues" to magnify their organizational impact.[7] Let My People Vote is a Pacific Institute for Community Organization (PICO) National Network initiative, focused on "agendas of family unity and the freedom to live with dignity in America, declaring that Black and Brown lives matter and ensuring that we live up to the promise of our democracy."[8]

Utilizing our bucks includes finding ways to harness the $1 trillion of economic wealth flowing through the black community to create an alternative economic vision that allows our financial resources to be tools

7. See http://valuespartnerships.com/.
8. See https://www.piconetwork.org/let-my-people-vote/report.

of communal economic liberation and strengthening. The church should mine the theological and moral values of our traditions to critique the dominant and excessive spirit of materialism and unfettered capitalism grinding our communities into dust. Can we sustain a rhythm of boycotts and economic interruptions that are targeted to demonstrate the power of wealth already at our disposal? Black faith institutions can channel business and parishioners to minority and women-owned businesses to keep our wealth circulating within our communities. Rahiel Tesfamariam's Not One Dime campaign and the Blackout for Human Rights campaign provide structural models of sustainable movements. #NotOneDime was launched by Rahiel Tesfamariam of Urban Cusp as a nationwide economic boycott focused on racial justice in the aftermath of the Ferguson non-indictment decision. #NotOneDime called for a suspension of all nonessential shopping from Thanksgiving through Cyber Monday and reclaiming Black Friday as a national day of action and service. Throughout #BlackDecember, continue the boycott by abstaining from all retail spending and urging support for black-owned business if you must shop. In a similar spirit of economic solidarity, Blackout for Human Rights is "a network of concerned artists, activists, filmmakers, musicians and citizens who committed their energy and resources to immediately address the staggering level of human rights violations against fellow Americans throughout the United States."[9] More strategic utilization of our resources along these lines could increase our access to jobs, entrepreneurship, and self-sufficiency, all the while alleviating economic poverty in our communities.

Concluding Thoughts

The twenty-first-century, post-Ferguson age requires churches to move into greater solidarity with communities of struggle through our presence and our emphasis on making full use of the human, financial, and political resources at our disposal—in the pursuit of justice. But that pursuit will require a theological recapturing of the biblical roots of "justice." In the Greek New Testament, the word *dikaiosynē* (or "justice") is typically rendered in English as "righteousness." It is an important biblical concept and is a word repeated more than three hundred times in the New Testament. Consistently it is used to describe both the identity of Jesus and his earthly mission and purpose. Yet I do not recall ever seeing it translated

---

9. See http://www.notonedimeboycott.com and http://www.blackoutforhumanrights.com/.

in English as *justice. However*, in the biblical languages and texts, justice and righteousness are the same word. To be faithful in a post-Ferguson era, we hold justice and righteousness must be held together as one aim. *"Blessed are those who are persecuted for righteousness' [and justice] sake, for theirs is the kingdom of heaven"* (Matt. 5:10).

Chapter 12

Listening, Undergirding, and Cross-Sector Community Building

Kimberly Gonxhe

Pittsburgh, Pennsylvania, is undergoing extensive gentrification across its urban landscape, even as many in the urban community remain unemployed, underemployed, and systemically marginalized. Local newspapers are filled with reports of community resistance to gentrification. A recent protest at a local groundbreaking ceremony for a rental housing unit featured signs and chanting, "Affordable for who? Not you" and "We won't be silent no more."[1] In the state of Pennsylvania, renting a two-bedroom apartment requires an average hourly wage of $17.57, while the state minimum wage is $7.25.[2] In poor neighborhoods facing gentrification, increases in the cost of living have transformed the social and physical landscape in ways that stack the deck against the urban poor and that impact the viability of local congregations.

Some within the community say that gentrification is the new colonialism as it forces lower-income black families out of their neighborhoods and into situations of greater vulnerability, while allowing outsiders to redefine their spaces. In his review of Peter Moskowitz's book *How to Kill a City*, Dan Arel argues, "gentrification takes a community's personal tragedy, loss and destruction, and monetizes it."[3] While the phrase

1. Kate Giammarise, "Demonstrators Protest Groundbreaking for Homewood Development," *Pittsburgh Post-Gazette*, May 4, 2017, http://www.post-gazette.com/local/city/2017/05/04/Homewood-residential-development-protests-Pittsburgh-gentrification/stories/201705040157 .

2. Tanvi Misra, "Mapping the Hourly Wage Needed to Rent a 2-Bedroom Apartment in Every U.S. State," CityLab, May 27, 2015, https://www.citylab.com/housing/2015/05/mapping-the-hourly-wage-needed-to-rent-a-2-bedroom-apartment-in-every-us-state/394142/.

3. Dan Arel, "How Gentrification Is Killing US Cities and Black Lives," Truthout, April 19, 2017, http://www.truth-out.org/opinion/item/40260-how-gentrification-is-killing-us-cities-and-black-lives.

"urban renewal" has a flourishing connotation, it is always important to ask, renewal for whom? Oftentimes development organizations will boast of declining crime rates in newly gentrified areas so as to substantiate the perceived good coming to the community. Nevertheless, these statistics are touted without noting that very little change has occurred within the community from a people-investment perspective. Moreover, most of the people engaged in criminal activities were simply relocated to different communities. While some redevelopment initiatives bring clear positive benefits, many others do more harm than good (especially as it relates to the preexisting residents of these gentrifying areas).

There are development entities and community leaders who have worked hard to foster a more equitable kind of redevelopment that ensures the least number of preexisting residents are affected and displaced. Although an outside catalyst is needed at times to jumpstart the renewal process, ultimately the community knows best how to facilitate its own change. This organic approach often takes longer, but it is necessary for long-term sustainability and for enhancing long-term resident viability and the preservation of culture.[4] Community-based and community-oriented congregations can be a part of this change as they are often already interwoven into the fabric of the local community. If not careful, however, congregations can be gentrifiers as well.

The Metro-Urban Institute (MUI) of Pittsburgh Theological Seminary places importance on walking alongside the most vulnerable in our communities, lifting up their concerns, and advocating on behalf of their stated interests. When I began my work at MUI in January 2014, we initiated engagement with the greater community through a listening tour. We went neighborhood by neighborhood listening to key stakeholders, learning from those in the trenches, documenting the community's strengths and challenges, observing neighborhood connectivity and isolation points, and embracing the collective hopes and dreams of long-term residents for their community. Since that initial outreach, we have come alongside several communities wrestling with neighborhood and congregational change, while striving to maintain authentic neighborhood and institutional identity.

In one such instance, MUI was commissioned by a Pittsburgh-based foundation to assess connections and disconnections between a broad-based neighborhood development initiative being facilitated in Pittsburgh's Northside neighborhood and the congregations within that

4. Peter Moskowitz, *How to Kill a City* (New York: Nation Books, 2017).

neighborhood (which in most cases had very little involvement with the development initiative). The sponsoring organization's core commitments were to a grassroots people-focused approach to urban renewal, and while many neighborhood residents and (to a lesser degree) faith leaders were integrally involved in the project from its inception, the community development entity wisely discerned that the project would not fully succeed without greater support from local congregations.

The remainder of this essay focuses on MUI's assessment of congregational intersections with this Northside community development initiative, outlining findings derived from thirty-five structured interviews with Northside faith leaders, and assessing the potential by these leaders for working together toward the betterment of the greater community.

Observations

During MUI's Northside listening tour during the summer of 2014, we found that Northside faith leaders as a whole were much more receptive to one-on-one dialogue, so our subsequent, commissioned Northside research utilized one-on-one or small group dialogues. Our interviewees came from twenty distinct faith groups, including Byzantine Catholic, Presbyterian Church (U.S.A.), Church of God in Christ, Seventh-day Adventist, and Sunni Islam. The majority of the congregations had mostly neighborhood-based memberships, while a noticeable segment had primarily commuter memberships. Either way, the faith leaders interviewed expressed concern for the neighborhood in which they worshipped, as well as for the broader Northside community.

Interviews were conducted during the second half of 2015, gleaning information related in each case to congregational/organizational mission, ministry context, strengths and challenges, and neighborhood involvement. There was also conversation in each instance about the comprehensive renewal strategy and potential alignments by faith leaders with existing or emerging elements of the Northside development initiative. The majority of faith leaders knew little to nothing about the initiative, so information was shared. The overwhelming majority of faith leaders expressed enthusiasm about future involvement, with most of these leaders agreeing to attend an initial group meeting and then identify a representative from their congregation or organization to represent them at ongoing strategy meetings. Some of the faith leaders, however, expressed skepticism about large-scale multi-neighborhood initiatives, about their acceptance as marginalized faith communities by mainstream churches, and about the value of such collaborations by poor and declining congregations.

It is important to point out that the primary forms of participation envisioned by faith leaders had a communications emphasis, including sharing information with the congregation related to beneficial services and volunteer opportunities, and also representing the vantage point of the congregation in the larger community meetings. Faith leaders clearly viewed communication as a prerequisite to intersecting with the community development initiative.

But the importance of communication was also expressed in another very instructive way. Many of the meetings and interviews went overtime because the pastors were so passionate about sharing their personal stories of ministry within these communities and contexts. Some sessions consisted entirely of listening with care and consideration to these personalized stories and narratives. It seemed clear that these faith leaders had few safe and affirming spaces in which to share or process their journeys and experiences as leaders operating within often challenging contexts. For many of these leaders, the constant leadership demands made it difficult to step away from a leadership frame of mind into a more reflective posture. Many also appeared distinctively lonely in their service—relishing the personal levels of interaction offered by the interview process, but also desirous of more systematic professional camaraderie and interactions in the form of a ministry network or association (nonexistent within this context).

These relational aspects though must be systematic and sustained if true cross-sector community building is to take place. Several of the long-term pastors in the community have seen numerous highly touted community development initiatives come and go, so their enthusiasm toward the next new project would be understandably minimal. Ministries coming into these neighborhoods from other locations sometimes behave the same way toward preexisting neighborhood congregations, organizations, and populations as more secular community development undertakings. Some of the pastors commented on the destructive impact on a neighborhood when external ministries establish satellite locations in urban communities without talking to the preexisting churches that have journeyed with the community over the long term. Many come in with their vacation Bible study on steroids and their Disneyland children's ministries, siphoning off members from the faithful congregations who have been there through thick and thin and know the fabric of the community.

There are, of course, congregations that have existed in these urban communities for many years but that have long transitioned from neighborhood churches to commuter churches and no longer feel themselves to be fully part of the community fabric. Often, these churches have little investment in their geographical location and are often dreaming of relocating to contexts far removed from their present location. Very little acknowledgment or embracing of neighborhood needs and identity is taking place in these instances and, therefore, very little genuine community building is occurring.

For holistic, healthy community building to transpire (especially across sectoral boundaries), input and involvement by all key community stakeholders must be facilitated. The work of listening, learning, acknowledging, and undergirding must be an integral component of such efforts.

Chapter 13

Internal Dimensions of
Church Connectedness to Community

Randall K. Bush

Consider this premise: Pastors are not called to minister to a congregation of people; they are called to minister to a congregation with a *history* that includes people. In making this distinction, a fundamental reality is being named. No church congregation is a *tabula rasa*, a blank slate just waiting for a new pastor to write their next chapter for them. Congregations all have a history that precedes each new pastor's arrival. This history is unavoidable, influential, and must be acknowledged (if not confronted) if true ministry is going to occur in that congregational setting. In addition, urban settings for ministry add another layer of complexity to the overall pastor-congregation relationship. An urban church's history is intimately tied to its region's history. Therefore, a city congregation's ministry has been, is, and will continue to be shaped by its setting.

I was called to serve East Liberty Presbyterian Church in March 2006. For the purposes of this brief essay, I propose to delineate a series of five challenges related to urban ministry that I have noted in my pastoral tenure here. The descriptions of these challenges will also include some suggested responses that can be effective tools for maintaining, and hopefully improving, any urban church's God-given gifts for ministry.

#1—People love and hate cities.

"City life" is something about which most people have strong opinions. Some may love the hustle and bustle of an active location, having access to stores, cultural events, a variety of restaurants, and other amenities. Others are quick to complain about the noise, litter, traffic congestion, difficulty in finding and affording parking, and the general stress that comes with navigating urban life. The congregation of an urban church will likely contain people who live nearby as well as those who commute in for worship. This means that within a single congregation there are both people who love cities and those who prefer to put down their roots in greener suburban (or exurban) locations.

The fact that these different groups find a common place to worship does not mean that the tension between loving cities and hating cities has been resolved. In fact, this dynamic will often impact the church's capacity to prioritize and implement community mission and outreach efforts. Before battles erupt over whether to favor neighborhood ministry over mission trips abroad, I have found it helpful to instill in the congregation a commitment to broad-based approaches to Christian mission (balancing local and global interests) coupled with the "10 percent rule." This rule says that not everyone has to participate in everything the church does. If only 10 percent wish to volunteer for a program and the other 90 percent are at least willing to be supportive of this effort (through prayer or concurring with necessary budget expenditures), then the program has a good chance of being successful.

#2—Can anything be done to fix our old building?

There is no perfect church building. Every church, whether old or new, urban or suburban, is something constructed for worship, education, and mission as primarily understood by the group who was present when the church plans were first drawn. Some churches look back, having been modeled after earlier, idealized buildings and architectural styles. Sometimes the congregation has prayerfully sought to prepare a place for the new things God is doing in their midst, so their architecture is to some degree flexible and forward-looking. Yet invariably day-to-day ministry in any church has to adapt itself to the limits associated with their specific building. Thus, the old adage is true: we shape our buildings, and then our buildings shape us.

Urban churches are typically older and larger structures struggling with some of the following problems: being the wrong size, too expensive to repair and maintain, energy-inefficient, not up to code or accessible in lots of areas, or perhaps all of the above. Solving these problems can take a tremendous amount of time, energy, and money. And in terms of church growth, how many new members are anxious to be saddled with the care and upkeep of a beloved yet aging architectural family member? One creative response is to make a strong commitment to fully use your space. To the best of your ability, open your doors to the community. Minimize the amount of dedicated, single-use space in the church to allow for flexible usages reflecting a variety of needs. With some creative scheduling, one classroom could serve for a 12-step group, an English as a second language class, and a studio for private piano lessons. Give priority to the needs of those who come into your doors needing a safe, welcoming place for their program, and you will be surprised how the focus shifts from architectural liabilities to ecclesiastical and community possibilities.

#3—Parking, parking, parking.

When I'm shaking hands after worship at the sanctuary door, I'll either get a "nice job" (when the sermon is good) or "nice tie" (when the sermon's not so good). Yet I can always count on one or two people mentioning that they had trouble finding a parking space close to the church, and given their bad knees or hips, they are not so sure they can attend as regularly as they would like unless we do something about this problem.

Parking is as much about perception as it is about literal spaces. People do need places to park their cars, but I contend that most people feel like their parking place is a good one only if they can see their car as soon as they exit the church building. For an urban church, this can be a real challenge. Educating people about the range of parking options available around their church, whether through handouts, PowerPoint presentations, or information sessions, can help alleviate some of this problem. But in the end, if they feel in their gut that it was cumbersome to find a place to park, then that will be the dominant mentality with which the church leadership has to contend.

A helpful way to reframe this issue is to expand people's definition of their church so that it includes what goes on beyond the exterior walls. Get outside whenever you can. Hold events on your sidewalks, front lawns, or out in the streets near the building. Do things like a blessing of the bikes or blessing of the animals, street fairs, information displays, or ice-cream socials to which the community is invited. This serves the double purpose of providing visible outreach in the neighborhood while reminding your congregation members that parking even a block or two away is still technically within the range of your church.

#4—The needs are overwhelming at times.

If you put up sheets of newsprint and ask people to list off the ways the church should live out its mission in the congregation, community, and world, you will quickly be inundated with suggestions limited only by the amount of paper on the walls and ink in the markers. Whatever category you choose to consider, the needs will exceed your ability to address them (e.g., time, resources, skills). In many cases, this leads to a type of mission inertia—doing what you've always done because you've got a structure in place to keep doing it. Whether that means regular food drives, housing daycare centers, organizing letter-writing campaigns, delivering meals to shut-ins, hosting Scout troops, or any number of things, our bulletin boards and Sunday announcement sheets are filled to the brim. Yet despite our best efforts, the needs seem to grow and never diminish.

If you will forgive the poor grammar, many churches do good badly. Too often efforts to help others are shaped by what we think they need, as opposed to empowering others to share in both the need-analysis and solution-creating process. When the former dynamic is in place, it can easily lead to volunteer burnout; or worse, an established program that is so inflexible and unresponsive to the actual needs it was meant to address that it ultimately serves the givers more than the receivers.

Urban settings mean that churches will be surrounded by a host of social issues affecting every aspect of their public ministry. If the neighborhood is in decline, there will be needs around housing, employment, and the public welfare to consider. If the neighborhood is healthy and growing, there will still be challenges around justice, gentrification, and protecting equal opportunities for both long-term residents and new arrivals. The church will, for better or worse, always be in the center of those competing, and at times overwhelming, dynamics of change.

No single institution can be all things to all people. Nor will any church have the resources and available skill set to address the range of ministry challenges waiting right outside its doors. That is why it is always helpful to establish sunset clauses for programs. New initiatives should build on healthy dialogue between recipients and caregivers, as well as have clear understandings around how long this trial program is going to last. It is far easier to extend something that is working well than it is to end something that has become entrenched yet dysfunctional or counterproductive.

#5—The stuff we don't want to talk about.

Let us go one step further beyond the topic raised in the preceding paragraph. Urban settings do mean that city churches are surrounded by a host of social issues. But what makes ministry challenging in these settings is that the issues are often linked to topics contemporary society has difficulty discussing, much less solving. For example, is crime in an urban area simply an issue involving laws and police resources, or is it a byproduct of inequities in the overall criminal justice system, public school system, and labor market? Is urban blight simply a cyclical problem tied to aging housing stock or is it a reflection of a deeper community malady around race, unjust economic models, underfunded public transportation resources, and extortive practices of property owners?

It is never possible to address or correct the larger inequities around us unless we are willing to listen, speak out, and prayerfully consider all the nuances associated with the problem at hand. For the church to play a positive role in this process, it needs to be a place where someone can speak the words that too often we avoid mentioning. Whether in times of worship, prayer, Bible study, or fellowship, the church needs to offer a level of safety and commitment to social justice so that people can name things like domestic abuse, cutting, depression, addiction, incarceration, abortion, heterosexism, racism, and all other scars emerging from life today. When the language of a church becomes overly sanitized or morally cautious, then ministry will not be able to be offered on the perceived margins of life. Yet that is precisely where Christ sent us to do work in his name.

For years, the handwriting on the wall for East Liberty Presbyterian Church (ELPC) seemed to point to an inevitable decline, slowed only by endowment financial resources available to help keep our doors open. But congregational and pastoral leadership over the past three decades have both made the church healthier and turned it into one of the few growing congregations in the region. This rebirth has been tied to reclaiming an active, outspoken vocabulary of full inclusion, racial diversity, and social justice.

Instead of simplistic church growth models based on formulas around contemporary worship liturgies and downplayed denominational identities, ELPC opened its doors to the greater Pittsburgh community by offering programming and resources for homeless men and single-parent households in the neighborhood, while publicly hosting events that focused on social justice, antiracism, and economic empowerment issues. In addition to intentional engagement with the African American community, ELPC took a prophetic stance early on challenging regional homophobia, including hosting two LGBT-friendly community choirs and establishing an active fellowship and outreach program on LGBT issues. In order to better serve the youth of the urban area, an initiative called Hope Academy of Music and the Arts was begun that offered music and theater instruction to underserved populations.

More recently, the church session adopted a mission statement that named radical hospitality as a primary goal, opening the church's doors and meeting rooms to a wide range of programs, 12-step groups, advocacy gatherings, and cultural events. Whether by organizing a prayer vigil during the time of the Iraqi war, sponsoring a float in the PrideFest parade, or nurturing active relationships with the local NAACP and Urban League branches, the community has come to recognize ELPC as a place where current issues and Christian faith are kept in dialogical tension. This pattern of courageous programming and community involvement has made ELPC a place that not only attracts young adults, seeking a church home as they start their career life, but also reaches out to people of faith who had disengaged from congregational life years earlier because they felt the church no longer spoke with relevance about today's issues.

There are other ideas that, for reasons of space and editorial brevity, I have not yet mentioned. Urban churches can discover new life and surprising opportunities through intentional ecumenical and interfaith collaborations, especially with Jewish, Muslim, or Buddhist communions. Urban congregations invariably contain members passionate around issues related to the environment and green practices, so lifting up those priorities as ways to care for God's creation will resonate positively with members and visitors alike. And even if church membership is generally in decline, spirituality and spiritual practices remain a strong component of life in American society. ELPC has found that offering Taizé sung prayer services, centering prayer and mindfulness meditation sessions, along with tai chi or yoga classes, helps connect our rational, liturgical minds with our contemplative, spiritual bodies. Last, urban churches can benefit from social media outreach and programs like live streaming of services, since both allow the church's impact to extend far beyond its literal walls.

Earlier in this essay, I mentioned that the discussion of challenges associated with urban ministry would include ideas and suggestions on how to respond to these issues. I am reluctant to identify anything I have mentioned as a definitive solution for I am well aware that there are no *true* solutions; at best, there are only faithful responses whose effectiveness is tied to God's grace, our willing hearts, and the mutual nurturing of humble servant-spirits. Yet there is always a way forward, especially for urban congregations. Sometimes those paths involve the buildings prior generations have blessed us with; sometimes the journey ahead sends us away from our sanctuaries and out into the streets of our changing neighborhoods. Innovative, responsive, and healthy ministries never emerge simply by finding right techniques and trendy recipes for success. Rather, as we listen, adapt, speak boldly, pray fervently, and trust sincerely, faithful gospel work for today and tomorrow becomes easier to envision, and thus more capable of implementation and expression by urban congregations.

Chapter 14

Prison Ministry with Women and Girls of African Descent

Angelique Walker-Smith

Prison ministry has been centered in long-established models and approaches regarded by many as useful and effective, but we face the very clear reality that these conventional approaches to prison ministry are not nearly sufficient.[1] Given the dramatic increase of incarcerated and formerly incarcerated women of African descent, this essay probes this concern and advances a renewed definition of prison ministry that provides a variation on ministry of visitation approaches. What is encouraged here is a ministry model that carefully considers the contextual challenges and opportunities of these women and girls while also furthering a mutual vision of social justice that empowers these women and girls.[2]

Ministries of visitation have been foundational to the conventional prison ministry model. This ministry model to those who are incarcerated typically emphasizes prayer, worship services, ministries of kindness including sharing of practical items prisoners can use, Bible study, and pastoral and priestly support particularly during difficult times of loss.[3] I regularly witnessed these acts of ministry and the challenges associated with these ministry approaches while serving

1. Prison Fellowship and Kairos Prison Ministries are contemporary examples of these conventional approaches that have been supported and encouraged by standard models of prison ministry chaplaincies in correctional facilities. https://www.prisonfellowship.org. Website for Kairos Prison Ministry, http://www.kairosprisonministry.org/our-core-values.php.
2. The distinction between women and girls is made in this essay because attention to "women" under the age of 18 who are incarcerated in prison is often understated and not reported. This is of particular concern given disproportionate numbers of women and girls of African descent.
3. Dale K. Pace, *A Christian's Guide to Effective Jail and Prison Ministries* (Old Tappan, NJ: Fleming H. Revell Company, 1976), 87–107.

115

from 1991 to 2014 as assistant volunteer chaplain at the Indiana Women's Prison (IWP). In this role I primarily ministered to women on the units of death row, administrative segregation, and disciplinary (including solitary confinement), as well as ministering in the general population.

From these experiences I have observed that conventional prison ministries tend to focus on what church visitors do to and for currently or formerly incarcerated persons as opposed to an approach that engages with and empowers the recipients of these ministries. In addition, with conventional approaches the emphasis is placed more on personal redemption than on the transformation of systems, penal processes, and societal conditions that contribute to the reasons why persons of African descent, including women and girls, have become incarcerated and frequently recidivate after their release. I focus here on the need for recognition of the societal conditions that effect this particular population and on more contextualized forms of ministry engagement that may contribute to more empowering ministry results.

The Contextual Challenges
of Incarcerated Women of African Descent

There has been a growing critical inquiry within churches and the broader society about the criminal justice policies and systems that disproportionately affect people of African descent, Latinos, and women. In the case of women, the research shows that women are the fastest growing prisoner population in the United States.[4] Since 1980, the number of women incarcerated in United States and federal prisons and local jails has increased by over 800 percent, and when all forms of correctional supervision—probation, parole, jail, and state and federal prison—are considered, more than one million women are currently under the control of the U.S. criminal justice system.[5] Women have been found to suffer higher rates of physical and sexual abuse (40 percent in federal prison and 57 percent in state prison) compared to their male counterparts

---

4. John Irwin, Vincent Schiraldi, and Jason Ziedenberg, *America's One Million Nonviolent Prisoners* (Washington, DC: Justice Policy Institute, 1999), http://www.justicepolicy.org/images/upload/99-03_rep_onemillionnonviolentprisoners_ac.pdf.

5. Lenora Lapidus, Namita Luthra, Anjuli Verma, Deborah Small, Patricia Allard, and Kirsten Levingston, *Caught in the Net: The Impact of Drug Policies on Women and Families*, American Civil Liberties Union et al., March 17, 2005, https://www.aclu.org/sites/default/files/field_document/asset_upload_file431_23513.pdf.

(7.2 percent in federal prison and 16 percent in state prison); and higher rates of mental illness (23.6 percent of women in state prison and 12.5 percent in federal prison) compared to men (15 percent and 7 percent, respectively).[6] Women are also more likely to report having been under the influence of drugs when committing their crime (40 percent of females compared to 32 percent of males), less likely to have been employed prior to their incarceration (40 percent of women in state prison compared to 60 percent of men), and more likely to have been receiving welfare assistance prior to incarceration (30 percent of women inmates versus just 8 percent of men).[7]

The popular book *The New Jim Crow: Mass Incarceration in the Age of Colorblindness*, by Michelle Alexander, provides a probing contextual analysis of why these trends are occurring with people of African descent. Alexander argues that mass incarceration stems largely from a "war on drugs" that placed a disproportionate enforcement and sentencing emphasis on patterns of drug use more prevalent in black and poor communities. The result, Alexander points out, has been an enormous increase in the numbers of incarcerated African Americans and a significant expansion of the prison industry, designed to function as a new caste system along the lines of the Jim Crow policies that previously kept blacks trapped in an inferior social position. She promotes a movement of social change targeted at reforming these tragic and misguided criminal justice policies and approaches.[8]

Christian public policy advocates such as Bread for the World believe that reforming mass incarceration policies and practices is crucial to ending hunger and poverty in America.[9] They have stated that the U.S. criminal justice system is broken and that the inequalities that the system operates have led to hunger and poverty. They argue that people in prison are more likely to have struggled with hunger and poverty before entering prison, which puts them at high risk for returning to those conditions after prison. They support this argument with the following facts:

---

6. Patricia O'Brien and Nancy Harm, "Women's Recidivism and Reintegration: Two Sides of the Same Coin," in Josephina Figueira-McDonough and Rosemary Sarri, eds., *Women at the Margins: Neglect, Punishment, and Resistance* (New York: Haworth, 2002), 295–318.

7. Ibid.

8. Michelle Alexander, *The New Jim Crow: Mass Incarceration in the Age of Colorblindness* (New York: New Press, 2010).

9. Bread for the World, "Hunger and Mass Incarceration," http://www.bread.org/sites/default/files/downloads/gar-issues-mass-incarceration.pdf.

- More than 1 in 10 prisoners were homeless before incarceration;
- Nearly 1 in 51 suffer with mental illness;
- Persons living in shelters were almost five times more likely to have a post-release shelter stay;
- People living in poverty who experience trauma or have a mental illness are less likely to get treatment and some turn to illegal drugs as a way to cope. The government's war on drugs increased the number of people in prison with long sentences;
- Previously incarcerated people generally experience higher unemployment and below-average wages due to criminal histories, poor work history, low educational attainment, and higher prevalence of health problems;
- Formerly incarcerated people and their families are more likely to be poor and food insecure;
- More than two-thirds of people who were incarcerated were legally employed before incarceration. More than half were the primary source of financial support for their children;
- A prison record cuts wages for workers by 11 percent, cuts annual employment by nine weeks, and reduces yearly earnings by 40 percent; and
- Children of incarcerated parents are more likely to fall into poverty when a parent is incarcerated due to loss of a second income. This is especially true when the parents have lower levels of education.[10]

Bipartisan public policymakers have proposed federal policies like the Sentencing Reform and Corrections Act of 2017 (S. 1917). The Sentencing Reform and Corrections Act (SRCA) is a bipartisan bill that would reform some U.S. sentencing laws and better prepare incarcerated persons to reenter the workforce and the community.[11] While the legislation will not address all of the concerns identified above, the organization believes this is an important step in the direction of systemic change. Bread for the World (along with other advocates within faith communities, various public policy organizations, and ex-prisoners) is promoting the passage of this bill.[12]

---

10. Ibid.
11. Bread for the World, "Sentencing Reform and Corrections Act of 2017 (S. 1917)," http:// http://www.bread.org/sites/default/files/bill-analysis-sentencing-reform-201.
12. "New SRCA Faith Support Sign-On—May 2016.pdf," May 5, 2016, https://drive.google .com/file/d/0B7oDBkKtwsiYMk10ekZfZEJlMFU/view.

Transforming the Context: Solidarity and Structural Empowerment

The critical contextual inquiry by academics, faith movements, and public policymakers offers important content for identifying the systemic issues contextually framing the relationship between African Americans and American criminal justice. These critiques also should inform and help direct prison ministry approaches by leading to a fuller embrace of a holistic balance of prison ministry presence through visitation and other related acts of ministry, and a prophetic justice emphasis that promotes ministry *with* and not simply *to* incarcerated women. Social empowerment of these women must be a priority in this justice model, addressing ways African American women have been unjustly burdened and harmed by racism, poverty, and gender bias. Therefore, a renewed prison ministry paradigm with these women should not only lead to systems change that speaks to these contextual biases but also a ministry practice of personal and structural empowerment.

In the 2015 Hunger Report of Bread for the World, titled *When Women Flourish . . . We Can End Hunger*, positive personal and systems change that empowers women means, among other things: (a) developing a plan to end hunger in the United States as part of the post-2015 global development goals; (b) eliminating the wage gap by sex and race and enforcing antidiscrimination laws; (c) supporting women's ability to work by raising the federal minimum wage to a livable standard, protecting collective bargaining rights, mandating paid sick leave and family leave, and providing high-quality, affordable child care with sufficient public and private funding; (d) eliminating mandatory minimum sentencing and support reintegration of returning citizens; (e) reducing poor maternal and child health outcomes by making affordable health care available to all; (f) promoting practices and norms that share care responsibilities more equitably between men and women; and (g) increasing women's representation in public office and other decision-making bodies critical to building a more just and equitable society.[13]

These recommendations insist on reforms of public policies and on a pastoral ministerial practice that engages the social context of disproportionate hunger, poverty, and gender and race bias.[14] These contextual

---

13. Bread for the World, *2015 Hunger Report: When Women Flourish . . . We Can End Hunger*, Washington, D.C., 2015: http://www.bread.org/sites/default/files/hunger-report-2015-sm.pdf; see also, Bread for the World, "The Bible and Mass Incarceration," Washington, D.C., 2015, http://www.bread.org/sites/default/files/downloads/gar-how-to-bible-mass-incar.pdf.
14. Bread for the World, *2015 Hunger Report*.

realities compel churches to engage in a prison ministry that not only serves, worships, and prays with these women but finds ways to empower them to lift up their own stories and voices so as to inform and direct their investment in seeking justice. The sharing of their stories and lifting of their advocacy voices should center upon the naming of their own experiences of struggle and agency, which can foster personal empowerment of these women when their stories are listened to and received without judgment.[15] When approached from a spirit of humility, churches are better able to assume a posture of receiving and thereby following the lead of incarcerated and formerly incarcerated women and girls with respect to their personal vision of healthy, readjusted lives during imprisonment and upon reentry to society.

In 1994, I wrote a training manual titled *I Was in Prison and You Came to Visit Me* that captured the stories of imprisoned women by working with them to write their stories and to convey to the churches what they should do.[16] It was shared widely in trainings with churches. The stories reflected the challenging contexts of systems and policies that have reinforced approaches that marginalize communities based on race and gender. Naming these challenges and delineating these stories matters, as does linking and integrating these stories with a social ministry agenda of public policy and other systemic changes (including economic development) capable of improving conditions for these women.

If prison ministries, then, are to achieve greater impact, then they will need to better connect issues such as hunger and poverty, then integrate those policy dimensions with ministry dimensions related to visitation and related means of empowerment utilizing listening and other processes of mutual discovery.

Moving Forward

In sum, churches are invited to be part of a prison ministry process that nurtures the spiritual and social narrative of women of African descent in ways that facilitate their dreams and imagination and move beyond the limitations of their social location.

An exciting example of where this paradigm shift is occurring is

---

15. Angelique Walker-Smith, "The Legacy, Leadership, and Hope of Pan-African Women of Faith in Building Sustainable Just Communities as a Missional Focus," *International Review of Mission* 105, no. 2 (2016): 226–42.

16. Angelique Walker-Smith, *I Was in Prison and You Came to Visit Me*, Prison Ministry with Women Manual (Indianapolis: The Church Federation of Greater Indianapolis, 1994).

with the National Council for Incarcerated and Formerly Incarcerated Women and Girls.[17] This council, recently created under the leadership of incarcerated and formerly incarcerated women and girls of African descent, galvanizes their collective knowledge and experience of the criminal justice system in efforts to reform that system. These women and girls know the realities of incarceration, the many hurdles this demographic faces after returning home, and the changes necessary to shift the system to one based on human dignity and social justice.

By bringing together the faith community, policy makers, academics, researchers, and the public in dialogue with council members, they strive to ensure that when policies, laws, practices, organizing, and services with women and girls of African descent who are or were incarcerated are decided upon, their voices and ideas are included. Their mantra is "Nothing about us, without us!" This is a big goal but they believe it is attainable. Through connecting with each other and freely sharing information, insights, and strengths, they believe they can create the opportunities to have their voices heard and collectively build new and just policies grounded in human rights. Coming alongside women who are incarcerated or who are returning citizens in efforts like this is needed to strengthen the church's witness and ministry with women and girls whose lives have been affected by the criminal justice system.

17. The National Council for Incarcerated and Formerly Incarcerated Women and Girls: http://thecouncil.us/.

Chapter 15

Christian Community Responses to African Immigrants in the United States

Laurel E. Scott

Despite the fact that America is a nation of immigrants, people migrating to the United States in the past decade have been experiencing a particularly difficult time because of prevailing attitudes about immigration. These attitudes are the result of years of increasingly restrictive immigration policies combined with a declining economy and the variety of cultures in the mix. Immigrants who trace their heritage back to Africa, in whole or in part, find things especially difficult because of deepening complications when matters of race and class are added to the main issues of nationality and economics within a white-majority culture. Nevertheless, these immigrants come to the United States seeking improvements in their social, material, and emotional circumstances—a cause that has driven migrants of every stripe to leave otherwise satisfactory lives in search of new horizons.[1]

When in strange and potentially estranging circumstances, human beings gravitate toward whatever might be familiar, whatever might provide a sense of grounding and security. In this case, African-descended immigrants often look in the familiar direction of church life for assistance in their time of need. For example, Jacob K. Olupona found that faith-based immigrant organizations, in addition to serving as sacred places for worship and the social construction of ethnic identity, also provided a renewed sense of values for immigrant communities and their host communities; and Olupona confirms that religion is increasingly viewed as

---

1. Pew Research Center, "African Immigrant Population in U.S. Steadily Climbs," February 14, 2017, http://www.pewresearch.org/fact-tank/2017/02/14/african-immigrant-population-in -u-s-steadily-climbs/.

integral to social and cultural processes by which new immigrants collectively define a sense of belonging.[2] So as these immigrants find themselves appealing to the church for assistance, the challenge to the church is how to respond to these expectations of hospitality and generosity.

I focus here on three congregations in the Northeast United States with large numbers of Ghanaian immigrants, examining how those congregations responded to demands placed on them by new members of African descent. Of particular interest are the diverse responses employed by these congregations and the extent to which they serve as indicators of the likelihood for successful engagement with immigrant members. A primary finding is that there are phases congregations pass through in arriving at successful integrative multicultural ministries with immigrants, and these are outlined below.

African-Descended Communities in the United States

Among the fastest growing groups of immigrants in the United States today are those whose country of birth is on the continent of Africa. The American Immigration Council reports that the foreign-born African population in the United States doubled between 2000 and 2010 and further describes the group as follows: nearly half are naturalized citizens, seven in ten speak only English or speak English very well, two-fifths have a bachelor's degree, and one-third work in professional jobs. African immigrant communities are settled mainly in the states of California, New York, Texas, Maryland, and Virginia, with the largest numbers coming from Nigeria, Ethiopia, Ghana, Kenya, and Egypt. Seventy-four percent of Africans in the United States are black.[3]

The Caribbean is a much smaller region geographically, but with an African heritage, given that much of the forced agricultural labor force in the Caribbean in the late 1600s and 1700s came from Africa's west coast. Like the African continent, this region accounted for 4 percent of the foreign-born population in the United States in 2010, with the largest numbers of Caribbean immigrants coming from Cuba, Jamaica, the Dominican Republic, Haiti, and Trinidad and Tobago, for a numerical total of 3.5 million persons. But while the percentage

---

2. Jacob K. Olupona, "Communities of Believers," in *African Immigrant Religions in America*, ed. Jacob K. Olupona and Regina Gemignani (New York: New York University Press, 2007), 29, 23.

3. The American Immigration Council, "African Immigrants in America: A Demographic Overview," https://www.americanimmigrationcouncil.org/sites/default/files/research/african_immigrants_in_america_a_demographic_overview.pdf.

of African immigrants in the United States has increased, the percent-age of Caribbean immigrants in the United States has declined since the 1970s. Caribbean immigrants tend to be concentrated in Florida and New York; approximately 50 percent of the Caribbean-born population in the United States identifies as black, with the same percentage being highly educated; most are highly proficient in English; and Caribbean immigrants were more likely than any other immigrant group to have graduated from secondary school.[4] Caribbean and African immigrants in the United States are found mainly in the service, construction, adminis-trative support, and transportation industries.[5]

Many of these African and Caribbean immigrants leave responsible and respectable positions in their countries of birth to pursue the Ameri-can dream of "a better life."[6] Nevertheless, immigrants to the United States today face an increasingly inhospitable atmosphere, despite high levels of achievement characteristic of many African-descended immi-grants. Immigrants are accused of taking jobs away from native-born Americans, of taking away opportunities for education, or of bringing cus-toms viewed as strange and sometimes incompatible with well-established practices within the U.S. Immigrants, who are distinct particularly because of race or language find even greater levels of rejection. More-over, most immigrants face difficulties associated with adjusting to a new culture; new customs; new ways of doing business; new systems of edu-cation, health care, and transportation; linguistic differences; as well as sudden shifts from what they experienced in their home country with respect to social and economic status (whether the shift is upward or downward).[7] So how do African-descended immigrants tackle challenges

---

4. Kristen McCabe, "Migration Policy Institute; Caribbean Immigrants in the United States," April 7, 2011, https://www.migrationpolicy.org/article/caribbean-immigrants-united-states-0.

5. Stephen Macedo, "The Moral Dilemma of U.S. Immigration Policy: Open Borders Versus Social Justice?" in *Debating Immigration*, ed. Carol M. Swain (New York: Cambridge University Press, 2007), 63–81. In this book chapter, he argues that native-born poor people in the United States are adversely affected by the low-wage jobs performed by immigrant workers.

6. Laurel Scott, "To Welcome the Stranger: Hospitality with Ghanaian Immigrants in the United Methodist Church," PhD dissertation, Boston University School of Theology, Boston, MA, 2014, 32. Ninety percent of respondents in a study of Haitian and Ghanaian women con-ducted in 2007–2011 by the Anna Howard Shaw Women's Center at Boston University School of Theology gave this as their reason for coming to America. This finding was later confirmed in the study of the three congregations, which is the main focus of this paper, with a majority of respondents giving this as the main reason for immigrating to the United States.

7. This is discussed in Elvinet S. Wilson, "What It Means to Become a United States American: Afro-Caribbean Immigrants' Constructions of American Citizenship and Experience of Cultural Tradition," *Journal of Ethnographic and Qualitative Research* 3 (2009): 199.

associated with living in the sometimes strange and foreboding contexts of their newly adopted countries?

Immigrants Look for Help

Human beings are inclined, when in new and different places, to look for the familiar, something with which they resonate—a friendly face, a familiar ritual, a language or dialect with which they are comfortable. Many immigrant groups have formed "friendly societies," organizations which under the United States IRS code are provided the legal status to operate for the welfare of their members—sports organizations, educational organizations, social welfare organizations, and immigrant churches. These provide a haven for all immigrants, whether documented or not, places of refuge in the sea of difficulties and challenges that new places present.

One of the places to which immigrants have looked for help in navigating the new culture is to the established church. The concept of hospitality to strangers is one of the core concepts of the church, and it is to this core concept that immigrants make their appeal and claim their welcome as part of the worldwide church family. For strangers in a strange land, the church as a worshiping community is the one place where they know they can go to experience the familiar and comforting, where they will be accepted, where they will find the love of God expressed.

Churches in the United States have at times made important strides toward fulfilling these expectations. A 1996 resolution from the United Methodist Church declared that it is not a crime to be an undocumented worker, and urged its congregations to "seek ways to welcome, assist and empower the refugee, immigrant, visitors, and undocumented persons in their neighborhoods and to denounce the persecution of the sojourner in the United States as prejudicial and racist."[8] Thus when the factories and fields where immigrants work and the social clubs where they relax are raided, and when immigration enforcement agents surround church

---

8. Resolution 119, 1996, The United Methodist Church General Conference. In March 2017, the Church's General Commission on Religion and Race reaffirmed this stance, issuing a "Statement on Compassion and Justice for Immigrants and Refugees" in response to President Trump's executive order of February 2017. The bishop of the New York area, which boasts the greatest diversity in race and ethnicity in the United States, encouraged the church in that region to go to extraordinary lengths to welcome immigrants and refugees in a letter written in response to the executive order.

buildings, oppressed immigrants often have looked to houses of worship to find respite."[9]

One of the ways church responsiveness has been evident is through the New Sanctuary Movement. The original Sanctuary Movement began in the 1980s along the U.S. border with Mexico.[10] The New Sanctuary Movement seeks to provide refuge and guidance to the immigrant who seeks it, regardless of their nation of origin. United Methodist congregations have had varied experiences in offering sanctuary, and with mixed results. For example, in the case of Elvira Arellano who remained for several months in 2006 in Chicago's Adalberto United Methodist Church, Arellano (against the advice of church lawyers) attended a rally for immigration reform in San Francisco and was subsequently arrested and deported to Mexico.[11] While in the confines of the church she was safe, but once outside she was fair game for the authorities. A better outcome occurred in Boston, Massachusetts, where several churches preparing in 2006 to establish a network of sanctuaries for an African immigrant local high school teacher had their plans happily preempted by a U.S. congressional bill that was passed as a result of grassroots pressures, including from the Boston high school where the immigrant had worked and several local nonprofit organizations. Although the teacher had overstayed his visa, the bill allowed him to remain in the United States and begin a path toward legalization.[12]

A practical reason churches are responding to African immigrants who settle in their communities is that they can no longer ignore a population that is increasing all around them. A 2012 study I conducted of three congregations in the northeastern United States with large numbers of Ghanaian immigrants revealed several factors accounting for congregational and community changes in these instances.[13] First, changes in the demographic and social landscape of the community directly have contributed to changes in the life and shape of the congregations. Community

9. The churches in the community came to the assistance of many children who were left without parents and to the aid of parents who were confined in detention centers out of state ("Up to 350 in Custody after New Bedford Immigration Raid," *Boston Globe*, March 6, 2007).

10. James Carroll describes the political situation in Latin America that led to the rise of the Sanctuary Movement. James Carroll, *House of War: The Pentagon and the Disastrous Rise of American Power* (New York: Mariner Books, 2006), 397.

11. "Church Is Sanctuary as Deportation Nears," *Washington Post*, August 17, 2006.

12. The author, a participant-observer, pastored one of these churches in Boston (2000–2007), which was one of the proposed networks of sanctuary locations.

13. Scott, "To Welcome the Stranger."

landscapes changed due to declines of some industries and the relocation of others, out-migrations of workers historically connected with these industries (mainly whites), and influxes of persons of color arriving to work in the remaining or emerging jobs in health care, domestic, and other service industries. In one of the towns where research was done, the largest industrial employer—an aeronautical and space engineering firm—drastically reduced its workforce in the 1990s, sending dozens of families into other regions of the country to find employment. When fully 50 percent of working-age families departed for other parts of the country, this town was left with retirement-age residents. The effect on the churches was membership attrition over the space of twenty years due to job relocation and deaths of members. As Ghanaian immigrants began attending these churches for worship, the host congregations were forced to adapt in many ways, including in their approach to worship and ministry in order to survive.

Another town where the research was carried out shifted, beginning in the 1990s, from a predominantly white town to a place having one of the highest concentrations of persons of Ghanaian descent in the United States.[14] Ghanaians familiar with the Methodist Church at home began seeking out Methodist churches in the areas in which they settled, and while they expected to find some differences in the ways of worship, many did not anticipate the cultural and racial differences and the reserve with which they were initially received. Nevertheless, for the sake of responding to the social and spiritual needs of the Ghanaian immigrant congregation and the survival needs of the host American congregation, they faced together the prospect of joining together for their mutual benefit.

In this instance, members of the faith community started discussing possible solutions to meet their current needs. Facing a deficit in their congregational operating budget, the congregation needed to both reduce expenses and maintain critical services, especially in light of the increased use of the building. After discussion, prayer, and reflection, the Ghanaian membership volunteered to provide janitorial services. They helped solve the budgetary problem by eliminating the paid janitor and replacing him with volunteers. Simultaneously, they became more invested in the vitality of the congregation.

With respect to practical responses, the simplest and most easily accomplished actions are those where American host congregations provide space, equipment, and resources for immigrant worshipers. In one

14. City Data, http://www.city-data.com/.

example in the study, the host congregation, which was largely African American and Caribbean, shared space with the Ghanaian congregation. This cooperative ministry came about as a result of a request made by the immigrant congregation and by the supervising minister who oversaw congregations in that particular geographic area. Although the two congregations came together at a basic level, there were no shared ministries; they shared only a building, equipment, and other physical resources. The two congregations came together a few times during the year—for organized women's celebrations and Good Friday services, for example, but their cooperation went only as far as sharing physical space and equipment. This is the most basic means of institutional cooperation and interaction.

Another congregation in the study went a step further. This congregation held a traditional English-speaking service on Sunday mornings, with many Ghanaians sometimes joining this service. After this worship service, the immigrant members shared in a fellowship hour with the English-speaking congregation and later held a service in their own language (Akan) in the basement chapel of the church. Ghanaians in this congregational instance sang in the host congregation's chancel choir and participated in leadership roles in the traditional worship, but it was clear the traditional worship took precedence over the immigrant community's "after worship, worship." Still this accommodation by the host congregation was intended to be helpful to the Ghanaian congregation, welcoming as they did Ghanaians into the traditional service while also providing the opportunity for immigrant members to have a separate service within their own linguistic and cultural frameworks.

Ghanaian immigrants within the third congregation participating in the study were also inclusively part of the host congregation's traditional service, but without the benefit of an additional, separate worship experience situated in Ghanaian culture. The traditional service did, however, incorporate a Ghanaian choir in which white members of the congregation also sang, and Ghanaian clothing was often worn to worship services both by the Ghanaian and white members. Other Ghanaian worship and ministry features also were adopted in an attempt to be integrative and inclusive, including opening the church for daily prayer at times when Ghanaian members who did not have traditional daytime work schedules could come to the church building and pray, as was their custom at home in Ghana.

Beyond issues related to shared or parallel worship, host churches have made their facilities available to the Ghanaian community to serve as a community center for Ghanaian immigrant members and their friends.

In these instances, Ghanaians have gathered to celebrate important life events, such as weddings, baptisms, and funerals. For example, where a family member has died in Ghana, if circumstances do not permit family members in the United States to travel to Ghana (in some instances due to being undocumented and unwilling to risk being unable to return to the United States) a significant celebration of life is held within the immigrant community in the United States—quite often within these host American churches. Conversely, where Ghanaians do have the immigration status allowing them to travel, money is collected to assist with travel and funeral expenses. These are examples of the ways in which opportunities are provided (with the assistance of American host churches at least in the instances of those studied here) for the Ghanaian community to maintain the familial and ethnic acquaintances and support networks that enable them to pass on their customs to new generations born in America, thus enhancing the potential for biculturalism for future generations.[15]

The second primary way churches have attempted to engage in practical responses to black immigrant populations in the United States has been through social relief, development, and advocacy efforts. In one of the study congregations, the growth of the Ghanaian portion of the membership led the congregation to begin looking at social needs within a targeted Ghanaian village. A group from the congregation organized a visit to the village, assessed the needs, raised funds, and started construction of a restroom intended for use by the local school and eventually serving as a much needed public restroom for the entire village. Members of the American host congregation members also brought with them the $30,000 required for the construction, along with school supplies for the children.[16]

Moreover, all three host congregations in this study provided practical assistance to immigrant populations within their contexts in the form of food pantries, sorely needed in situations where immigrant populations were facing difficult financial times often brought about by a loss of or inability to secure employment. Since newly arrived immigrants are

15. Individuals who are bicultural have the ability to identify with and exist within two different cultures. For descendants of immigrants, access to the culture of their elders is enabled through exposure to customs and language. Teresa LaFromboise, Hardin L. K. Coleman, and Jennifer Gerton, "The Psychological Impact of Bi-Culturalism: Evidence and Theory," *Psychological Bulletin* (American Psychological Association) 114, no. 3 (1993): 395–412.

16. For the Ghanaian portion of the population, these are "networks of self support." For the host congregation, these are indirect "missional activities" (Olupona, "Communities of Believers," 42–43).

ineligible for government assistance until they have lived in the United States for more than five years, and undocumented immigrants are ineligible, this is particularly helpful for those who find themselves unemployed or underemployed.

An important expression of church-based advocacy on behalf of immigrant populations is a United Methodist Church program called Justice for Our Neighbor (JFON) where attorneys provide free legal clinics and advocacy services for immigrants seeking to adjust their immigration status. For undocumented immigrants facing Immigration and Custom Enforcement hearings, JFON has provided advocates who assist these immigrants in interpreting and navigating the immigration policy process and, in some cases, advocating on their behalf. One of the study congregations helped establish a JFON clinic in a nearby community.

Churches also provide advocates for immigrants needing to navigate U.S. educational systems and procedures, including helping parents understand the reasoning behind the various school conferences, the laws that govern school attendance, and how to comply with requirements in public school systems. Many immigrant children suffer the indignity of being inadequately assessed, being labeled "special needs," and then placed in educational classes that limit the full exploration of their intellectual potential. Host congregations provide advocates to explain and navigate these situations, providing language and procedural interpretation services for immigrant families.

Concluding Thoughts

Congregations in the study demonstrated various signs of progress along this journey toward a community genuinely inclusive of new immigrants. The concept of hospitality to strangers is one of the core concepts of the church, and for strangers in a strange land (black, and largely Christian, populations from Africa and the Caribbean in this instance) the church represents a place where they can experience the familiar, where they enter into extensions of communities left behind in their places of origin, and where they gain support, acceptance, and solidarities within the context of new communities. It is the place where they can "sing the Lord's song" even in a strange land—assuming host church communities within that new land are up to the challenge.

Chapter 16

Theological Professionals, the Community, and Overcoming the Disconnection

Anthony Rivera

Graduate theological schools, like other institutions of higher learning, locate in time and space in ways making them integral to their localized and broader historical contexts. They do not exist in a vacuum. Former Princeton University president Harold T. Shapiro claimed, "All higher education institutions, both public and private, both nonprofit and for-profit, and from state colleges to research universities to community colleges to a wide variety of technical and professional schools, serve a public purpose."[1] What is the responsibility and connectivity of twenty-first-century institutions of higher education, and of graduate theological schools in particular, to our increasingly urbanizing and globalizing communities?

As someone who is a seminary graduate and who now works as an admissions and recruitment officer for an urban seminary, this is a question I find myself living with on a continuous basis. The fact is, graduate theological schools today, even when they are located in the urban contexts of core cities, are frequently unknown by their surrounding communities and seem functionally disconnected from them. This essay explores factors contributing to this disconnection between theological

1. Harold T. Shapiro, *A Larger Sense of Purpose: Higher Education and Society*, the 2003 Clark Kerr Lectures (Princeton, NJ: Princeton University Press, 2005), 1. See also Judith Rodin, *The University and Urban Revival: Out of the Ivory Tower and into the Streets* (Philadelphia: University of Pennsylvania Press, 2007), 3: "More than half of the nation's colleges and universities are located in cities. They represent significant contributors to the character of their cities and to the definition of the urban environment. By virtue of their mission, intellectual capital, and investments in physical facilities, urban universities, and their medical centers are uniquely positioned to play a leading role in their communities in powerful ways."

schools and urban communities, looking both at historical and contemporary dimensions of the developmental trajectories of Western theological education. Suggestions are then made about ways for potentially overcoming these disconnections going forward.

Historical Reflections on Western Theological Education

At least as far back as monastic and cathedral schools during the early Middle Ages, the education of clergy was central to conceptions of higher education.[2] The University of Paris, modeled after the cathedral schools, became not only the celebrated teaching center of all Christendom by the end of the thirteenth century but also served as the model for Oxford and Cambridge.[3]

The "liberal arts" curriculum of the medieval university consisted in the disciplines of grammar (i.e., Latin), rhetoric, logic, physics, ethics, philosophy (i.e., Aristotle), and theology. At the end of four years, students received the bachelor of arts degree—the equivalent of an apprentice certificate.[4] The theological curriculum, taking its cue from the medieval scholastics and known as "dogmatics," covered four areas: church history, biblical studies, theology, and practical theology. When the University of Halle, founded in 1694, "became the center of the Theological Enlightenment, theology became purely academic."[5]

When universities begin appearing in colonial America in the seventeenth century, they followed along the lines of Protestant scholasticism in Europe, with Harvard College leading the way in 1636. As historian Glenn Miller points out, the scholastic paradigms enforced in these instances tended to form ministers who were "not to be only theologians and preachers; they were to be 'learned gentlemen.'" Miller continues, "Although seminary leaders issued frequent rhetorical appeals for more ministers, they showed scant interest in the average minister or in pastoral practice. . . . The

2. Glenn T. Miller, *Piety and Intellect: The Aims and Purposes of Ante-Bellum Theological Education* (Atlanta: Scholars Press, 1990), 4; and *Global Dictionary of Theology* (Downers Grove, IL: IVP Academic, 2008), s.v. "theological education."

3. Roger L. Griger, *The History of American Higher Education: Learning and Culture from the Founding to World War II* (Princeton: Princeton University Press, 2015), xiv. Justo L. González, *The History of Theological Education* (Nashville: Abingdon Press, 2015), 51, comments, ". . . it is clear that much of the theology that was studied, discussed, and produced in the universities had no great relevance for ministerial practice."

4. Griger, *The History of American Higher Education*, xiv.

5. Ibid. See also W. Zumkeller, "The University of Halle through the Centuries," *Molecular Pathology* 54, no. 1 (February 2001): 36–37.

scholarly aspects of theology fascinated the founders of theological schools. . . . The purpose of the seminary's residence requirement was to train students to be 'gentlemen theologians.'"[6]

Theological schools soon became more like professional schools, patterned much like that of medicine and law. In the United States, this arose as a response to a demand by mainline churches for an educated clergy. For some, however, this fact gave rise to a concern that graduate theological education would lessen clergy effectiveness by encouraging a distancing from core Christian faith tenets given the increased influence of graduates from German universities drawing heavily on scientism and its enlightenment approaches.[7] As early as the eighteenth century, secularization was already settling into theological studies at schools such as Harvard and Yale.[8]

By the nineteenth century and into the twentieth, African American universities and theological schools were emerging, aimed at preparing clergy and lay-people to meet the demands of the church and the African American community.[9] African Methodist Episcopal (AME) bishop Daniel Alexander Payne, a graduate of Lutheran Theological Seminary in Gettysburg, Pennsylvania, was a pioneer of black theological education. As one of the founders of Wilberforce University in 1856, and its president (and the first black university president in the country) after the AME became sole owner of the university in 1863, Payne later founded Payne Theological Seminary in 1891 (which was an offspring of the university's theology department). Like its white counterparts, African American universities offered courses in the classics, mathematics, science, and European languages, while many African American theological schools followed the same curricula design as white schools.

---

6. Miller, *Piety and Intellect*, 26–27. Bruce Shelley comments, "The image of the pastor-theologian is the ideal for most theological faculties," in Bruce Shelley, "The Seminaries' Identity Crisis," *Christianity Today*, May 17, 1993, 42.

7. Linda Cannell, *Theological Education Matters: Leadership Education for the Church* (Newburgh, IN: EDCOT Press, 2006), 79.

8. Roger Finke and Rodney Stark, *The Churching of America, 1776–2005: Winners and Losers in Our Religious Economy* (Piscataway, NJ: Rutgers University Press, 2006), 47.

9. By way of mention: Shaw University (1865—Baptist), Morehouse College (1867—Baptist), Morgan (1867—Methodist), Fisk University (1866—American Missionary Association [AMA]), Talladega (1875—AMA), Knoxville College (1875—Presbyterian); these schools were funded by white churches. Morris Brown (1885—American Methodist Episcopal [AME]) and Livingstone College (1879—AME Zion); these were funded by black churches. See Albert J. Raboteau, *Canaan Land: A Religious History of African Americans* (New York: Oxford University Press, 1999, 2001), 65.

The late nineteenth and early twentieth centuries saw growth of the industrial economy, contributing to increasing urbanization within the United States. Urbanization, however, was accompanied by increased exploitation, neglect, disorganization, and segregation.[10] This segregation was along the lines of race, income, ethnicity, national origin, and ecclesial affiliation. These forms of segregation, especially race, turned neighborhoods into territorial battlegrounds between blacks and whites in the first two decades of the early 1900s.[11]

As educated clergy gravitated to urban pulpits, a large number of Protestant churches were ineffective in addressing societal inequities, in that "many reflected the political and social concerns of their most influential members."[12] Though a minority of faculty at theological schools (notably, persons such as Walter Rauschenbusch at Rochester Theological Seminary) spoke against the ills of society at the time, most theological schools generally did not move beyond a prevailing pedagogical approach that ignored current social conditions.[13]

10. Referenced by Henry Louis Taylor Jr. and Walter Hill, eds., *Historical Roots of the Urban Crisis: Blacks in the Industrial City, 1900–1950* (New York: Garland Publishing, 2000), 1–2, 99.

11. Henry Louis Taylor Jr. and Song-Ho Ha, "A Unity of Opposites: The Black College-Educated Elite, Black Workers, and the Community Development Process," in Taylor and Hill, *Historical Roots of the Urban Crisis: Blacks in the Industrial City, 1900–1950*, 32. Taylor and Ha comment, "Separating blacks and whites in residential space was one of the main objectives of segregation. Although the system was imperfect, it generated much tension between blacks and whites. Then in the 1920s, '30s, and '40s, as the residential environment was gradually turned into a commodity, neighborhoods became very volatile places."

12. Glenn T. Miller, *Piety and Profession: American Protestant Theological Education, 1870–1970* (Grand Rapids: Eerdmans, 2007), 310. Miller adds: "Many Anglo-American city churches were chapels of comfort for those who had moved from the countryside to the city, and they were spending much of their time and effort making their newly urban membership feel at home in its new circumstance." See also Cannell, 209, who comments, "In some instances churches became private organizations serving the devotional needs of congregational members who influenced society primarily through volunteer associations related to but independent of the churches. This development contributed to the debate concerning the nature of ministry, as clergy tended to isolate their preaching and ministerial tasks from social responsibility."

13. Walter Rauschenbusch, *A Theology for the Social Gospel* (Louisville, KY: Westminster John Knox Press, 1997). Robert C. Fennell writes, "The Social Gospel was principally a Protestant impetus that combined religious conviction with social, political, and economic analysis and programs designed to alleviate poverty and other social ills." Robert C. Fennell, "The Social Gospel and the Social Sciences," in Jeff Nowers and Nestor Medina, eds., *Theology and the Crisis of Engagement: Essays on the Relationship between Theology and the Social Sciences* (Eugene: Pickwick Publications, 2013), 42. See also John W. Coakley, *New Brunswick Theological Seminary: An Illustrated History, 1784–2014* (Grand Rapids: Eerdmans, 2014), 49–51.

The Challenge

The preceding narrative provides a historical glimpse of a systemic dilemma afflicting most institutions of theological education and society: namely, the pervasive ideology of professionalism that fosters the disconnection between the theological education and the social contexts in which it operates. Even in the twenty-first century, activist theologian Ched Myers notes, theological seminaries do not "equip everyday disciples to overcome their sense of disempowerment and denial in order to engage in the evangelical works of mercy and service, advocacy and resistance, community building and social reconstruction."[14] The concept of professionalism was originally associated with orientations expressing a "dedication to values transcendent of self-interest and monetary reward," but the concept eventually took on connotations of assessing "measurement of worth by pay and advanced individual skills."[15] These, in turn, were associated with upward career mobility, prestige, notoriety, and assumptions of competence.[16]

A second factor contributing to disconnections between theological education and society is the failure of theological institutions to consider their immediate location. Theological institutions cannot sit in urban contexts characterized by heavily concentrated inequalities, discrimination, violence, crime, and corruption without engaging these issues as part of their theological pedagogies and scholarship. This will require, among other things, theological institutions doing more to incorporate the voices of scholars who are themselves connected (intellectually and experientially) to these contextual realities.

Theological education cannot be confined to the perspectives or social locations of any one social or ecclesial group. Theology must emerge from many social locations, including different races and ethnicities, if it is to be taken seriously. If theology is to "liberate" humanity, voices from Latin America, the Caribbean, Africa, Indonesia, and Asia must be fully incorporated into the standard curriculum, including work from theological scholars such as J. Severino Croatto (Argentina), Otto Maduro (Venezuela), Kwesi Dickson (Ghana), Kosuke Koyama (Japan), James Cone

---

14. Ched Myers, "Between the Seminary, the Sanctuary, and the Streets: Reflections on Alternative Theological Education," *Ministerial Formation* 94 (July 2001): 49–52.
15. Magali Sarfatti Larson, *The Rise of Professionalism: A Sociological Analysis* (Berkeley, Los Angeles: University of California Press, 1977), xvi–xvii.
16. Ibid., 127–29.

(United States), and Gustavo Gutiérrez (Peru). This includes voices and ministry of women.[17]

Unless theological education becomes more contextualized in these ways, it will be viewed as having less and less relevance by persons within the contexts in which it operates. These contexts are changing dramatically, especially urban demographics. For example, the U.S. Census Bureau reported a 43 percent increase in the Hispanic/Latino population in the United States between the years 2000 and 2010, making it the largest U.S. minority population at 16 percent.[18] Yet too few Hispanic/Latino scholars are on U.S. seminary reading lists or are members of seminary faculties, and too few Hispanic/Latino students occupy U.S. seminary classrooms.

Moreover, too many graduate theological institutions continue to relegate themselves to the ivory tower of disseminating new philosophical and hermeneutical theories and attempting to be on the cutting edge of theological inquiry and knowledge, only to perpetuate the ongoing disconnection between themselves, the community, and the world they profess to serve. Exceptions in graduate theological institutions do exist, but they are rare.[19] The seminary where I am based has made notable efforts through its Metro-Urban Institute, which incorporates an extensive advisory board consisting of local community members, pastors, other educators; consults with urban churches, public officials, and local agencies and community-based organizations; and engages in research and pedagogies that attempt to connect theological scholarship to social realities. Another notable example is Eastern University's Esperanza College, which is a leader in connecting institutions of higher education with the community. The school offers two-year degree programs designed to prepare students to "engage the world with the gospel . . . particularly for underserved and oppressed groups [and] youth and immigrant communities."[20]

---

17. A. J. Gordon, "The Ministry of Women," *Africanus Journal*, 8, no. 1 (April 2016): 50–61, http://www.gordonconwell.edu/resources/documents/africanusjournalvol8no1ev3.pdf.
18. U.S. Census Bureau, https://www.census.gov/newsroom/releases/archives/2010_census/cb11-cn125.html.
19. To name a few, Wesley Theological Seminary (Washington, DC), Evangelical Theological Seminary (Myerstown, PA), Princeton Theological Seminary (Princeton, NJ), and Wake Forest University School of Divinity (Winston-Salem, NC). This list of institutions is not exhaustive and simply represents efforts made by theological institutions to connect with the community.
20. Esperanza College, Christian Ministry Program Overview, https://esperanza.eastern.edu/academics/associate-degrees/christian-ministry.

In order to serve the twenty-first-century globally urban environment of which they are a part, institutions of theological education must recognize the integral nature of their oneness with the communities where they serve and are localized. Disconnected curricula, myopic institutional protocols, and elitist pedagogical approaches designed to produce specialists in irrelevant disciplines cannot address the needs of urban churches or their surrounding communities going forward. By contrast, emphasis on the interrelatedness of its institutional connection with the community can produce theologically educated leaders who are prepared to be in partnership with the wider community and, with its constituents, discern a communally shared vision that helps strengthens the quality of life for all going forward. That is the vision of theological education I can gladly lift up to students considering enrolling in seminary.

Chapter 17

Theological Pedagogies and Urban Change-Making in an African City

Stephan de Beer

The Context: A (South) African City

This essay is written from within a very specific context. It is written, first, against the backdrop of the Gauteng City-Region in South Africa, with its 13.6 million inhabitants, and projections of growth estimated at 20 million people by 2025.[1] The Gauteng City-Region is made up of three large metropolitan areas and two district municipalities, all independently governed but economically and otherwise deeply interdependent.[2] Although geographically the smallest province in the country, occupying only 2 percent of the land, Gauteng represents 25 percent of the country's population, and is responsible for one-third of South Africa's GDP.[3]

The Gauteng City-Region is seeking to reconstruct itself beyond its apartheid legacy, with glaring socio-spatial-economic fragmentation still segregating people and neighborhoods. Very little dedicated theological reflection and theological critique have accompanied the process of this city-region's unfolding. This article describes an attempt to do theology in the city in a trans-disciplinary manner, being present, making

---

1. Gauteng is one of nine provinces in South Africa, known as the economic powerhouse of South Africa and even of Africa. Some also advocate for it to be understood, imagined, and managed not only as a province but as an interdependent city-region comprising different metropolitan areas and municipalities.

2. The Gauteng City-Region includes Johannesburg, the city of Tshwane, and Ekurhuleni, as well as the district municipalities of West Rand and Sedibeng.

3. Gauteng City-Region Observatory (GCRO), The Gauteng City-Region, 2017, www.gcro .ac.za.

sense, critiquing, and envisioning possible urban futures in the Gauteng City-Region.[4]

Second, the essay is written against the backdrop of substantial twenty-first-century African urbanization, as the highest rate of urban population growth is now to be found in Sub-Saharan Africa.[5] Accompanying this urbanization are many evolving challenges for African cities, including the interdependence between urban and rural, an elusive sense of home in the light of urban migration patterns, the predominance of informal patterns of lifestyle organization, increased economic and environmental precariousness, limited resources, significant religious growth and diversity, and conflicting conceptions of urban governance and urban citizenship.

Each of these matters has important implications for urban studies but also for theology. Just as cities are dynamic, under construction, and never complete, so our theologies should be. This chapter stresses the importance of *doing* theology as the task of constructing local theological responses to urban challenges, as well as the task of ongoing critical reflection on faith practices in the light of various sources informing our urban understanding and responses.

Doing Theology in an African City

Doing theology should not be an individualistic undertaking by scholars alone, but rather it should be done in community, with others, in response to actual urban dynamics and challenges. This represents an epistemological shift, understanding the generating of knowledge as a dynamic process growing out of a creative, critical, cyclical dance of action and reflection, and as a deep interaction between academic, non-academic, and experiential knowledge. This, then, acknowledges the possible contribution of diverse knowledges to the development and praxis of theology.

Theological education is still predominantly located in theological schools or seminaries, and not in local neighborhoods or ecclesial or faith communities. The contextual engagements of higher education in

4. See Stephan De Beer, "Whose Knowledges Shape Our City? Advancing a Community-Based Urban Praxis," *De Jure* 47, no. 2 (2014): 218–30.

5. United Nations Department of Economic and Social Affairs, Population Division, "World Population Prospects: The 2014 Revision" (United Nations, 2015). https://esa.un.org/unpd/wpp/publications/files/key_findings_wpp_2015.pdf.

the form of service learning or community engagement exist primarily as add-ons to the "real" curriculum, instead of belonging to the core of the pedagogical approach. Our theological interlocutors and sources of knowledge are mostly other theologians, often from the global North. The deep knowledges located in urban communities and places of vulnerability or struggle—residing with urban residents, practitioners, and activists—are mostly overlooked when shaping our theological discourses.

From the perspective of the contextual-liberationist tradition in which I position myself, urban theological engagement asserts a particular position from the margins, over against a so-called position of neutrality. It engages the city in ways that seek socio-spatial-spiritual transformation, emphasizing the interconnectedness between spatial, social, and personal or communal well-being.

In responding to the Gauteng City-Region and the City of Tshwane (Pretoria), the Centre for Contextual Ministry at the University of Pretoria, which I direct, has long embraced the use of a praxis-cycle as our pedagogical approach.[6] The praxis-cycle emerged in base ecclesial communities in Latin America where a pastoral facilitator often living in urban slums reflected with small communities of people about their situations. They would relate their faith to their realities, analyzing the causes of their struggles, reflecting on biblical texts in relation to their felt experiences, and discerning actions to be taken to address their challenges. It became a method that placed theology back in the hands of ordinary people, and particularly the poor.

The praxis-approach choreographs a continuous dance between immersion, analysis, action, and reflection. The action dimensions emerging from these community reflections are aimed at making change, and could include transformed liturgies connected to daily life struggles, specific projects aimed at reducing poverty, initiatives aimed at creating social awareness about people's circumstances, or actions aimed at longer-term systemic change. What makes the praxis-approach theological is that this communal discernment process centers upon the "lived faith" or communal spirituality operative among the people.[7] These urban spiritualties are what Johannes "Klippies" Kritzinger speaks of as "concrete spirituality": languages, rituals, and postures that emerge from concrete places, connecting concretely to real-life urban struggles.[8]

---

6. We are using and adapting the praxis-cycle as developed by Joseph Holland and Peter Henriot, *Social Analysis: Linking Faith and Justice* (Maryknoll, NY: Orbis Books, 1983).

7. Gustavo Gutiérrez, *A Theology of Liberation* (Maryknoll, NY: Orbis Books, 1988), xxxiv.

8. Johannes N. J. Kritzinger, "Concrete Spirituality," *HTS Teologiese Studies/Theological*

These immersive approaches to *doing theology in the city* take place as a cycle of four moments: entering the city, reading the city, imagining the city, and co-constructing the city. "Urban immersions" (*entering the city*) are woven into many of our courses. The emphasis is not on participants offering anything to the places of immersion but rather on students experiencing urban places with all their senses (in "not-knowing" ways), and for them to discern the gifts these places might possess. Students reflect on how these places challenge or disrupt them, whether personally, theologically, or in their understanding of ministry. These often mobile classrooms attend to ways in which the apartheid framework is still pervasive in South African cities, as well as to signs of hope, resistance, or reconstruction in response to specific urban fractures. In *reading the city*, we ensure exposure to multiple critical assessments of urban space and landscapes, including urban neighborhoods, urban churches, urban cultures, and urban systems and power. We invite socio-historical readings of the New Testament, gendered readings of the Old Testament, and insights from city planners, political scientists, or sociologists. We create spaces in which to listen carefully to the voices of urban ministry workers, activists, and social movements and to hear the laments and dreams of ordinary citizens and those marginalized by the workings of the city. We provide tools and resources for community analysis. Our urban assessments focus on the urban both as socio-political-economic and spatial construct, but these assessments are also interested in an understanding of ecclesial, religious, or faith expressions in response to the city.

The moment of *theological reflection*—or *imagining the city*—is a moment of critical-creative fusion of diverse experiences and readings, being deliberate about making theological sense of the city's complexities. Dominant narratives are deconstructed, phantom narratives identified, and strong alternative narratives considered.[9] In this moment of imaginative theological reflection, participants are encouraged and assisted to foster an alternative imagination of what the city and urban neighborhoods could be(come), discerning preferred realities for both city and church.[10]

The fourth moment—*planning for action* or *co-constructing the city*—places a strong emphasis on the agency of participants in the process

---

Studies 70, no. 3, 2014, http://dx.doi.org/10.4102/hts.v70i3.2782.

9. On usage of the term "phantom narratives," see Johann-Albrecht Meylahn, "Ecclesiology as Doing Theology in and with Local Communities but Not of the Empire," *Studia Historiae Ecclesiasticae*, vol. 37, supplement (2011): 287–313.

10. Cf. Walter Brueggemann, *Prophetic Imagination* (Minneapolis: Fortress Press, 2001).

of constructing not only responsive local urban theologies but also co-constructing urban communities. The purpose of reading or imagining the city is not simply to deconstruct current realities or imagine utopian alternatives, but to become the embodiment of such imagination, co-constructing the preferred reality into being.

An inherently strong element of *self-criticality* is built into our peda-gogical processes, in every moment of the praxis-cycle. Using the met-aphor of Parker Palmer—"to know as we are known"—we design our spaces and processes in ways that allow for all of us to be confronted with ourselves, our biases and complicities, not only to reimagine or co-construct new urban neighborhoods or ecclesial responses but also to reimagine and re-story ourselves.[11]

Conscientization, Change-Making, and Prophetic Urban Leaders and Communities

Being rooted in a spirituality of transformation, the praxis cycle has the potential to be a liberating theological method for facilitating personal, ecclesial, and larger societal change-making. Paralleling analysis by Paulo Freire, there is an inherent emphasis here on theology as conscientiza-tion, with every moment of the cycle being able to contribute to a critical and prophetic urban consciousness.[12]

The Cameroonian theologian Jean-Marc Éla said of his ministry with poor mountain people, "I did not feel called to become the manager of a form of decaying Christianity . . . so I decided to keep my distance from a model of church designed elsewhere by people who do not know the conditions of the mountain people."[13]

Similarly, the emphasis of our pedagogical approach is not first to cul-tivate leaders who will serve as custodians of suburban, or anti-urban, churches but to prepare a generation of reflective practitioners and com-munities willing to immerse themselves in urban places, able to reimag-ine ecclesial responses, and committed to making urban change. Our emphasis is to provide people with tools to discern and develop their own local urban theologies that are not "designed elsewhere by people who do not know" their conditions.

---

11. Parker J. Palmer, *To Know as We Are Known: A Spirituality of Education* (San Francisco: HarperOne, 1993).
12. Paulo Freire, *Pedagogy of the Oppressed* (New York: Conti, 2000).
13. Jean Marc Éla, *My Faith as an African* (Maryknoll, NY: Orbis Books, 1988), 5.

If we are to be faithful to our vocation, I have proposed five areas for theological and political consciousness-raising and change-making in the direction of God's urban *shalom*: (1) fostering a consciousness from below, (2) discerning a new economics, (3) practicing a different kind of politics, (4) exploring radical socio-spatial transformation, and (5) engaging in collaborative knowledge generation.[14]

The Centre for Contextual Ministry, based in the faculty of theology at the University of Pretoria, imagines the theological faculty as a gateway into cities that are humane and just. At the same time the centre is inviting the voices of the city into the faculty, convinced that the city could contribute to our ongoing transformation. With these objectives in mind, I highlight here three activities embodying the center's urban agenda.

1. The Urban Studio

The Urban Studio is both a concept and a place. It is intentional about the city as classroom for engagement and reflection, bridging the gap between theory and practice, inviting different knowledges and experiences into conversation with each other. Currently the Urban Studio is primarily based in two locations—the inner city of Pretoria and Mamelodi East, an area combining established urban townships with sprawling informal settlements.

The Urban Studio aligns itself with Edgar Pieterse's vision of decolonized knowledge production in urban Africa, in conversation with emerging urban knowledge in the global South as well as his argument for the coproduction of knowledge at different levels.[15] This takes the form of a city-level studio in our case, in which practitioners, citizens, and city officials could "work with academic researchers to jointly decipher the most urgent questions that require sustained attention."[16] Various modules in our center and in the faculty of theology are hosted in one or

---

14. See Stephan De Beer, "'The Good City' or 'Post-Colonial Catch-Basins of Violent Empire'? A Contextual Theological Appraisal of South Africa's Integrated Urban Development Framework," *HTS Teologiese Studies / Theological Studies*, 72, no. 4 (2016): a3543, http://dx.doi.org/10.4102/hts.v72i4.3543.

15. Edgar Pieterse, "Epistemological Practices of Southern Urbanism," paper presented at the ACC Academic Seminar, February 21, 2014, 1, http://www.africancentreforcities.net/wp-content/uploads/2014/02/Epistemic-practices-of-southern-urbanism-Feb-2014.pdf.

16. Ibid., 20.

more of the Urban Studio spaces, including engaged research activities, the feast@UP, and the Biennial Consultation on Urban Ministry.[17]

2. Leadership in Urban Transformation

This is a one-year program, specializing in equipping leaders who will engage in the important work of transformational urban ministry. Currently we host two cohorts of students per year—in Gauteng Province and in Cape Town. The program carries credits toward postgraduate degrees in practical theology with an emphasis on urban ministry or urban theology.

Almost all participants in this program come deeply immersed in challenging urban contexts, as urban pastors, community practitioners, or activists. The whole program—offered in the form of five intensives of four days each—is designed around the praxis cycle, and participants are encouraged to use the cycle as theological method as they engage their own communities or themes of inquiry during the year.

Classroom-bound pedagogies assume intellectual paradigm shifts in a vacuum, disconnected from contextual immersion, personal relationships, wisdom from "below," and knowledge from the "other." In this program we are deliberate about practicing and fostering an epistemological and methodological shift—emphasizing urban theological pedagogy as conscientization for change-making.

3. Faith in the City

Faith in the city was conceptualized as a dedicated research project, exploring the (dis)engagement of theology and the church in relation to healing urban fractures. Sub-themes have grown out of this research focus.

One sub-theme, pathways out of homelessness, involves more than forty researchers from different disciplines and universities, as well as

---

17. Engaged research activities refer to research projects with a direct impact on local communities, such as recommending a strategy to address homelessness or urban spatial interventions by churches. Feast@UP is an annual collaboration with the Feast of the Clowns, an inner-city festival hosted by the Tshwane Leadership Foundation. The aim is to foster consciousness for social justice among students and academics through workshops, service learning, arts, and creative protest, both in the inner city and on campus. The Biennial Consultation has been hosted since 1996 by the Institute for Urban Ministry, gathering 250 to 300 urban practitioners, activists, students, and scholars, for a time of information, imagination, and inspiration.

practitioners, city officials, and formerly homeless people, developing a policy and strategy on street homelessness for the city of Tshwane, through a participatory process of knowledge generation. The outcomes of the research are being implemented by the city, academic institutions, and civil society and faith-based organizations. Tshwane, as a result of this praxis-based research, was selected as one of twelve pilot cities globally to implement innovative solutions that will showcase sustainable alternatives to street homelessness.

A second sub-theme, spatial justice and reconciliation, considers ways in which spatial injustice and fragmentation in the (post-)apartheid city hinder sustainable reconciliation, with specific attention to the city of Tshwane. Part of our research is to formulate concrete recommendations for churches and faith-based organizations in terms of how their properties, land, or buildings could contribute to spatial justice, restitution, and reconciliation.

The center also hosts or participates in more limited-scope research projects, exploring churches' responses to urban vulnerability and change; investigating transnational migration, precarious housing, and faith-based responses; and researching youth on the urban margins (specifically in the inner city of Tshwane).

Concluding Thoughts

The danger exists for a praxis-approach to become just another domesticated theological method: replacing preexisting safe and detached theological orthodoxies with a newer orthopraxy, bias for the poor, and insistence on discerning prophetic actions. It is equally possible for black, liberation, feminist, or other such theologies, and the important insights they offer, to be co-opted into mainstream theological curricula, in ways that domesticate their potentially liberating implications. The methodologies inherent in doing such theologies need to be allowed to help deconstruct institutional hierarchies and colonial constructs inherent to our inherited theological curricula.

A praxis-approach to doing urban theology, if practiced consistently, holds the potential to foster a new kind of personal, theological, ecclesial, and urban consciousness. To the extent that happens, prophetic leaders and communities may emerge, committed to making urban change in the direction of God's *shalom.*

Can schools of theology embrace such a pedagogical praxis? They can if they take our cities seriously—and in (South) Africa, this must become increasingly the case as well.

III

Urban Social Policy

Chapter 18

Church Pursuits of Economic Justice, Public Health, and Racial Equity

John C. Welch

As I traveled across the country meeting with and training clergy, I discovered that many religious leaders have a discomfort mixing politics with their call to ministry. Most have argued for the need to separate church from state without understanding the intent of the First Amendment to the U.S. Constitution, which was intended to protect the church from the state, not to inhibit the freedom of religious expression. In addition, these leaders fail to realize the fallacy in thinking religion is apolitical. Religion not only involves exploring our relationship with the divine but also our relationship with one another. Religion is shaped by the ways we exercise influence and power as well as share resources in our personal and professional relationships. Indeed, religion is a political maneuver.

Clergy often fail to realize their call to pastoral ministry is indistinguishable from public witness. This is not fortunetelling, it is speaking truth to power like Ezekiel (2:1–5), Isaiah (3:13–15), Haggai (1:1–7), and the other Old Testament prophets who called nations to justice and repentance. Acknowledging the powers that have built structures of oppression in this country since its inception is critical to effective urban ministry. Members of our congregations are either victims of unjust systems or perpetuators of the injustice. They are either shut out of opportunities, or they fabricate the proverbial doors and locks.

In true transparency, I was once an uninformed pastor. I believed my sermons were connecting with my congregation, and from all indications, they were. Sunday mornings and weekly Bible studies, however, were the only days when those connections were taking place. The cycle I operated in was merely preparing for each week's sermon and Bible study. I was able to successfully use my seminary training to form a relevant hermeneutic that drew linkages between biblical stories, inspirational texts, and contemporary challenges of our communities. That I made few efforts, though, to confront structures and root causes of community challenges left my ministry hollow.

It wasn't until I attended a Race and Regionalism conference in Minneapolis, organized by the Gamaliel Foundation, that I learned how policies determined spatial configurations and that these policies have created our own American caste system. Determined by race and class, these spatial configurations shaped access to jobs, education, housing, health care, and other resources, which produced communities of concentrated poverty and concentrated affluence. I began to understand that from the first segregated public housing projects of the New Deal era to the G.I. Bill of 1944 and the 1949 Housing Act that encouraged the exodus of middle-class whites to newly created suburbs, government policies favored whites and disadvantaged African Americans.[1] The lightbulb went on in my head and my eyes were opened.

My preaching not only changed, but I also became an activist. I became a national leader in faith-based community organizing. In this role, I began training other clergy and encouraging them to look and think more deeply about their call to join pastoral ministry with a prophetic ministry beyond the walls of the church. I desired to awaken my fellow clergy to the paradoxical conditions faced in our communities despite the advances of the civil rights movement, or maybe because of it. I began calling attention to what may seem obvious to many: our inner-city residents and congregations are economically challenged, and this challenge has implications that diminish the population's health. My concern for the individual in the pew also extended to the entire city and what population health experts call the distribution of health across the population.[2] These intersections between social inequality and public health and church engagement with these matters are explored here.

Knowledge Is Power

Over the years, I have been struck by the correlation between socioeconomic status (SES) and health. One of the more comprehensive Centers for Disease Control reports, "Health Disparities and Inequalities

1. Richard Rothstein, *The Color of Law: A Forgotten History of How Government Segregated America* (New York: Liveright Publishing Corporation, 2017).

2. David Kindig. "Improving Population Health: Ideas and Action," April 2014, https://uwphi .pophealth.wisc.edu/publications/other/blog-collection-final-2014-04-05.pdf.

Report," examines available national data on health disparities across a variety of measurement categories, such as morbidity, mortality, health care access, social determinants, and behavioral risk factors. The factors of interest to me include more than health care access, but also factors such as socioeconomic status, education, physical environment, employment, and social support networks. These social determinants of health are conditions in which "people are born, grow, live and age." This report warned that if programs for the most vulnerable in this country are not supported, in light of the economic recession of 2009, health disparities might worsen.[3]

A key to these health outcomes is *stress*, induced by recessionary consequences such as unemployment and the secondary effects of loss of health insurance and pension fund accumulation. This leads to mental health deficiencies and behavioral and physiological changes.[4] Loss of income also results in involuntary dislocations through evictions or foreclosures. According to Harvard scholar David R. Williams, racism and the associated stigma of inferiority and institutional discrimination are added stressors that adversely affect health for African Americans and other communities of color.[5] These negative outcomes are largely the result of a faulty economic infrastructure that disproportionately allocates fewer resources to those at the bottom.

For example, much of the economic and health disparities evident in the twenty-first century are the result of policies and other factors that suppress educational opportunities for African Americans. Despite the championing and celebrations of the *Brown v. Board of Education* case in 1954, scholars attest that the decision did not go far enough. Tara J. Yosso and colleagues argue that this Supreme Court ruling failed to require a timetable for school desegregation and also assumed that school integration would also mean equality in education.[6] According

---

3. Centers for Disease Control, "CDC Health Disparities and Inequalities Report—United States," January 14, 2011, https://www.cdc.gov/mmwr/pdf/other/su6001.pdf.

4. Sarah A. Burgard, Jennifer A. Ailshire, and Lucie Kalousova, "The Great Recession and Health: People, Populations, and Disparities," *The Annals of the American Academy of Political and Social Science* 650, no. 1 (2013): 194–213, http://journals.sagepub.com/doi/pdf/10.1177/0002716213500212.

5. David R. Williams, "Race, Socioeconomic Status, and Health: The Added Effects of Racism and Discrimination," *Annals of the New York Academy of Sciences* (1999): 173–88, https://doi.org/10.1111/j.1749-6632.1999.tb08114.x.

6. Tara J. Yosso, Laurence Parker, Daniel G. Solórzano, and Marvin Lynne, "From Jim Crow to Affirmative Action and Back Again: A Critical Race Discussion of Racialized Rationales and Access to Higher Education," *Review of Research in Education* 28, no. 1 (2004): 1–25, https://doi.org/10.3102/0091732X028001001.

to a report produced by the Civil Rights Project of Harvard University in 2002, relaxing the judicial requirements of school districts led to increasing antidesegregation efforts, requiring schools that want to voluntarily desegregate to prove it is a "compelling government interest." Further, the report states, "We find decreasing black and Latino exposure to white students is occurring in almost every large district as well as declining white exposure to blacks and Latinos in almost one-third of large districts."[7] This resegregation of schools ultimately left urban school districts lacking access to the resources of their counterparts in more affluent schools. African American students are unfortunately disproportionately represented in these low-resourced, low-expectation, low-performing, and highly punitive schools.[8] The cascade begins: students who perform poorly in school typically engage in activities resulting in suspensions. This leads to increased school disengagement, and students eventually drop out with only preparation for low-wage jobs. Ultimately, this contributes to the crisis of concentrated poverty and a series of other urban challenges.

Faith-Based Community Organizing

What should the faith community do in response to the challenges that affect population health? Some suggest we should pray. While this is irrefutable and prayer is powerful, sometimes we need to pray with our feet to sufficiently address the root causes. Another recommendation is faith-based or congregational-based community organizing, which has been around since the creation of social justice movements. Examples of these networks developing leaders in congregations across the nation in direct action organizing include Gamaliel Network of Chicago, PICO National Network of Oakland, Industrial Areas Foundation (IAF) of Chicago, and Direct Action and Research Training Center (DART) of Miami.

One of the important tools of this methodology is agitation, a tool that if used properly can shift the center of power. Agitation is not appreciated by some. W. E. B. Du Bois, a champion of political agitation, recognized others devalued this strategy and believed that "agitation is

7. Erica Frankenberg and Chungmei Lee. "Race in American Public Schools: Rapidly Resegregating School Districts" (UCLA: The Civil Rights Project, 2002), http://escholarship .org/uc/item/1tz5k622.

8. Talisha Lee, Dewey Cornell, Anne Gregory, and Xitoa Fan, "High Suspension Schools and Dropout Rates for Black and White Students," *Education and Treatment of Children* 34, no. 2 (2011): 167–92.

destructive or at best negative."[9] Conversely, supporters of direct action methodologies echo the perspective of Martin Luther King Jr. that waiting for justice is no option because delayed justice is denied justice. Similar to the direct action protests of the civil rights movement, the purpose of actions in congregational-based community organizing is to "open the door to negotiations."[10] As author/minister, Dennis Jacobsen suggests in his book *Doing Justice: Congregations and Community Organizing* that the purpose of congregational community organizing is to recognize the world as it is and move to the world as it should be. He goes on to say that the world as it is "is driven by abusive power, consuming greed, relentless violence, and narcissistic pride," while the world as it should be is "rooted in truth, love and community" and it involves people acting "according to their values and faith."[11]

Finding Our Power

I found my power to stand against injustice and oppression through the Gamaliel Foundation and the example of leaders such as Joseph Ellwanger. According to Ellwanger, a retired Lutheran pastor, "Part of the mission of the Church, and especially in urban congregations, is to raise up leaders, to empower people who think they have no power, to discover their power, and to use their power for the building up of the Body of Christ, and for the common good of all."[12] As a white pastor of an African American congregation, he knew racism up close. Ellwanger tells the story of accepting the invitation of a white pastoral intern, James Fackler, to join the youth of the University Lutheran Church in Tuscaloosa for a Sunday service. He took two of his youth, fifteen-year-old girls. The service was an open and enriching exchange for the black and white youth. The following Wednesday, the Birmingham newspaper reported that the KKK had accosted Fackler, severely beating him and leaving him to walk back to Tuscaloosa. Ellwanger received a phone call issuing a threat that he and the two girls would be next.[13]

9. W. E. B. DuBois, "Agitation," *The Crisis* 1 (1910).
10. Martin Luther King Jr., "Letter from Birmingham Jail," http://kingencyclopedia.stanford.edu/kingweb/popular_requests/frequentdocs/birmingham.pdf.
11. Dennis A. Jacobsen, *Doing Justice: Congregations and Community Organizing*. (Minneapolis, MN: Fortress Press, 2017), 1.
12. Joseph W. Ellwanger, *Strength for the Struggle* (Milwaukee, WI: Henschel HAUS Publishing, 2014), 11.
13. Ibid., iv.

Motivated by his experiences in the South, Ellwanger became an organizing pastor in Milwaukee, Wisconsin, where he helped establish the organization Milwaukee Inner-City Congregations Allied for Hope (MICAH). One of MICAH's more significant accomplishments was the securing of a $500 million loan fund from seventeen banks for inner-city housing loans, forcing law enforcement to close 138 drug houses in a year and successfully getting the county to allocate an additional $5.8 million for the treatment of addicts with no insurance.[14] This is putting faith into action.

Putting My Faith into Action

In my native city of Pittsburgh, one in four households make less than $20,000 per year, 11 percentage points higher than the state of Pennsylvania.[15] Yet the city was selected as the most livable city in America on more than one occasion, most recently in 2014 by the *Economist* and *Forbes* magazine.[16] African Americans make up 26 percent of the city's population, according to 2010 census data, with a disproportionate number of them earning less than the area median income. Reports revealed that Pittsburgh ranked first in the country with working-age African American men living in poverty and also first in the country with children under five years of age living in poverty.[17] Pittsburgh has almost double the national percentage of African Americans working full-time jobs making less than $20,000 a year.[18] According to a recent report, lead levels in Pittsburgh's water were higher than that reported

14. Dave Condren, Mike Vogel, and Susan Schulman. "Church-Based Group Helps Clean Up City's Mean Streets," *Buffalo News*, May 10, 1997, http://buffalonews.com/1997/05/10/church-based-group-helps-clean-up-citys-mean-streets/.

15. City-Data.com, Pittsburgh, "Pennsylvania (PA) Income Map, Earnings Map, and Wages Data," 2016, http://www.city-data.com/income/income-Pittsburgh-Pennsylvania.html.

16. See: "The Economist Names Pittsburgh the Most Livable City (on the Mainland) Again," *Next Pittsburgh*, March 17, 2017, http://www.nextpittsburgh.com/business-tech-news/economist-names-pittsburgh-livable-city/; and "Forbes Once Again Names Pittsburgh 'Most Livable City,'" *Pittsburgh Business Times*, May 3, 2010, https://www.bizjournals.com/pittsburgh/stories/2010/05/03/daily4.html.

17. United States Census Bureau, "Quick Facts: Pittsburgh City, Pennsylvania," *United States Census Bureau*, U.S. Department of Commerce, 2016, https://www.census.gov/quickfacts/fact/table/pittsburghcitypennsylvania#viewtop.

18. Harold Miller. "Regional Insights: High Black Poverty a Shame," *Pittsburgh Post-Gazette*, July 4, 2010, http://www.post-gazette.com/Biz-opinion/2010/07/04/Regional-Insights-High-black-poverty-a-shame/stories/201007040132.

in Flint, Michigan.[19] Pittsburgh also faces an affordable housing crisis with an estimated shortage of 17,000 units, all while low-income families continue to be dislocated to make room for high-end developments.[20] Dynamics such as these are part of the social determinants that contribute to poor health outcomes in Pittsburgh. These issues, among others, are what call the faith community to put its faith into action and organize for the common good.

For six years, I served as president of Pittsburgh Interfaith Impact Network (PIIN). This placed me on the front lines leading marches and protests for employment rights and other issues that affect the health of the city and region. On February 27, 2014, a sixteen-degree day, nine other PIIN clergy, including my wife, stood in solidarity with University of Pittsburgh Medical Center (UPMC) service workers subjected to intimidation, wrongful termination, and suppression of their right to organize a union.[21] We were arrested. We also successfully shifted the narrative away from union greed and power and toward the moral imperative to protect workers' rights and human dignity. As a result of this advocacy, the National Labor Relations Board cited UPMC.[22] At the time, this nonprofit health care system and the largest employer in Western Pennsylvania had the highest-paid CEO of any nonprofit health care provider in the country. It amassed $4 billion in reserves and paid several executives' salaries that tipped $1 million while neglecting to pay their service workers family-sustaining wages. Instead, they thought it best to set up their own food pantry for their low-wage workers.[23] With starting salaries for their workers at $11 per hour, the average annual

19. Jessica Glenza, "Pittsburgh Water: Expensive, Rust-Colored, Corrosive, and High in Lead," *The Guardian*, September 12, 2016, https://www.theguardian.com/environment/2016/sep/12/pittsburgh-water-expensive-rust-colored-corrosive.

20. See "Funding Stream Sought for Proposed Affordable Housing Fund in Pittsburgh," http://triblive.com/news/allegheny/10747440-74/housing-affordable-fund; and "Penn Plaza Developer Files Countersuit against Pittsburgh," http://www.post-gazette.com/local/city/2017/04/04/Whole-Foods-Pittsburgh-Penn-Plaza-apartments-East-Liberty-redevelopment/stories/201704040072.

21. Alyssa Marsico, "10 Clergy Members Arrested during UPMC Protest," *Pittsburgh Post-Gazette*, February 27, 2014, http://pittsburgh.cbslocal.com/2014/02/27/10-clergy-members-arrested-during-upmc-protest/.

22. Ann Belser, "Labor Board Issues Complaint against UPMC," *Pittsburgh Post-Gazette*, January 29, 2015, http://www.post-gazette.com/business/healthcare-business/2015/01/29/National-labor-board-NLRB-issues-complaint-against-UPMC/stories/201501290292.

23. Luis Fabregas, "UPMC Presby, Shadyside Food Pantry Becomes Dividing Line," *Tribune Review*, December 13, 2012, http://triblive.com/news/allegheny/3124464-74/upmc-mercy-employees.

salary was a little more than $26,000.[24] When one takes into consideration housing and transportation costs, food, and health care premiums, there is very little discretionary income remaining.

Two months later about 1,200 protestors, including clergy, parishioners, health care workers, and union leaders and members from the Service Employees International Union and United Food and Commercial Workers, again protested for better wages for UPMC service workers. This shut down the streets in downtown Pittsburgh at midday. While the work of the coalition of unions and congregations did not lead to immediate concessions from UPMC, it did get the attention of another local hospital in the city, Allegheny General Hospital. As a result, the service and technical workers at Allegheny General agreed to form a union.[25] After two years of protesting and attempted negotiations, UPMC agreed to raise their starting salaries to $15 per hour.[26]

Politics in Ministry

Faith-based and congregational community organizing can be effective but only when the clergy leading these congregations realize there is politics in ministry and ministry in politics. Clergy and other community leaders should consider promoting civic engagement as a requirement of the call. While endorsing candidates has always been prohibited in order to protect the tax exemption status of the house of worship, educating the congregation on issues and candidates and encouraging voter turnout is important. There will be times when as religious leaders we will have to lead from in front of the pulpit and outside the church walls. There will be times when religious leaders will have to make unpopular decisions to speak truth to power. Clergy must be willing to operationalize their faith and organize for significant political power in order to dismantle

---

24. Robert Zullo and Moriah Balingit, "UPMC Protests to Resume Tuesday," *Pittsburgh Post-Gazette*, March 3, 2014, http://www.post-gazette.com/local/region/2014/03/03/Pittsburgh-police-begin-closing-streets-for-Downtown-protest/stories/201403030124.

25. Rebecca Nuttall, "Allegheny General Hospital Workers Vote in Favor of a Union," *Pittsburgh City Paper*, June 4, 2015, https://www.pghcitypaper.com/Blogh/archives/2015/06/04/allegheny-general-hospital-employees-vote-in-favor-of-union.

26. Kris Mamula, "UPMC to Boost Starting Wage to $15 an Hour over the Next Five Years," *Pittsburgh Post-Gazette*, March 29, 2016, http://www.post-gazette.com/business/healthcare-business/2016/03/29/UPMC-pledges-to-boost-starting-wage-to-15-an-hour-by-2021/stories/201603290126.

the stress-inducing structures that have inhibited human flourishing and produced poor population health on a city, state, and federal level.

I have experienced first-hand how speaking truth to power goes beyond Sunday preaching and weekday Bible studies to civic engagement, community activism, and perhaps even electoral politics.[27] If we are going to change our communities, it will require clergy and congregations to act boldly. Whether the congregation is urban or suburban, black, white, Latino, or multiethnic, true progress will only take place if such boldness also includes targeting the covert, overt, and latent effects of racism. As Martin Luther King Jr. stated in 1968, "Among the moral imperatives of our time, we are challenged to work all over the world with unshakable determination to wipe out the vestiges of racism."[28]

27. I ran for mayor of Pittsburgh in 2017. I had no prior experience in electoral politics but felt God calling me to bring "disruptive politics" to this primary season.
28. Martin Luther King Jr., *Where Do We Go from Here: Chaos or Community?*, vol. 2 (Boston: Beacon Press, 2010), 183.

Chapter 19

The Accra Confession and Theological Reflections on Urban Economic Justice

Setri Nyomi

Much has been written about the trend of urbanization in the world today. In a good part of the global South many young people are abandoning the villages and small towns and heading toward cities in search of jobs, a better quality of life, and other perks. This trend has affected the ministry of the church in profound ways. Even many graduates of theological seminaries seem first and foremost to seek a call in urban or metropolitan areas. Although the challenges associated with inner-city ministries sometimes make it a less attractive option for some ministers, the fact remains there is need to pay great attention to urban mission.

Some of the challenges and community struggles encountered in intensified ways in urban contexts include: (1) population diversity, and the racism, tribalism, classism, and economic polarization that often accompany this diversity; (2) violence; (3) population mobility due to in-migration and out-migration; (4) pervasive consumerism and the religious and social ideologies supporting it; and (5) environmental degradation due to pressures on ecosystems and reliance on technologies and energy sources that create a significant carbon footprint. The list is not exhaustive; nevertheless these represent some of the significant challenges urban pastors and churches are called upon to address.

Globalization has transformed the world into a global village. Many who live in urban areas, whether in neoliberal capitalist settings or in state-planned economies, are often at the receiving end of the injustice inherent in these and other systems. From Pittsburgh to Johannesburg, Chicago to Tokyo, New York to London, Los Angeles to Accra, no matter where one turns for news and analysis of what is happening in any city around the world, the dominant news outlets report bad news, unsettling news. There is great need for good news of transformation that will shift the tide of death-dealing realities into life-giving opportunities. Churches must be active partners in seeking to address urban challenges, and there are important theological resources that speak effectively to some of these issues—namely, formal confession documents such as the Accra Confession—on which churches can draw to address today's social ills and participate in the creation of more just societies.

Shifting the Urban Mission Mindset

A theologian who has contributed to our understanding of the paradigmatic shifts in the Christian mission mindset is South African missiologist David J. Bosch. In his book *Transforming Mission: Paradigm Shifts in Theology of Mission*,[1] Bosch delineated six shifts in the theology of mission that emerged throughout the history of Christianity. He calls the last shift the emerging ecumenical missionary paradigm, which is characterized by its rootedness in a view of mission as (1) the actions of God and (2) the reign of God. By placing the authority of missions with God, we refocus the work of urban mission as God bringing the kingdom to the world "wherever Jesus overcomes the power of evil."[2] He expands the scope of mission to include such contemporary missiological issues as justice and contextualization.

According to Bosch, "Mission is, quite simply, the participation of Christians in the liberating mission of Jesus, wagering on a future that verifiable experience seems to belie. It is the good news of God's love, incarnated in the witness of a community, for the sake of the world."[3] An effective metropolitan mission that makes it possible for people to experience good news should take this definition of mission into account. The liberating mission of Jesus into which we have been invited to participate calls us to experience the good news of God's love and God's new reality characterized by God's righteousness and justice. The Greek term *dikaiousoune*, which is rendered as righteousness, or justice, has to do with right relationships. This view places the building of right relationships and the quest for justice at the heart of ministry in urban areas today. It

---

1. David Bosch, *Transforming Mission: Paradigm Shifts in Theology of Mission* (Maryknoll, NY: Orbis Books, 1991), 349.
2. Ibid., 32.
3. Ibid., 519.

is an urgent task to which a transformed church which is not chained to business as usual must pay attention.

Living the Good News: Embodying *Shalom* and *Ubuntu* Principles

Fostering communities of right relationships becomes good news when the communities experience *shalom* and *ubuntu*. Generally, in urban areas more than in rural areas, the tendency is to be lost in individual concerns—focusing on one's self, one's family, one's career, how to navigate the stress that often accompanies urban living, and how to find meaningful worship space. Corresponding questions for urban ministry should therefore include how to maintain worshiping communities in which all feel at home within the larger community. This is characterized by a sense of meaning and well-being for all, justice and right relationships, and community belonging.

How can we foster worshiping communities in which the rich meanings of the Hebrew concept of *shalom* and the African concept of *ubuntu* are combined? These are two words that the English language lacks the proper words to translate. The concept of shalom expresses a sense of deep peace characterized by justice and well-being of all.[4] The concept of *ubuntu* conveys a meaning that can be characterized by three simple principles:

- "I am because we are;"
- "what I am is only because of the gifts of others in the community;" and
- "meaning in my life is deepened the more I use my gifts to combine with others to build a healthy community."[5]

Those called to be members of God's household should be committed to fostering the sense of shalom and *ubuntu*. Christian persons or institutions committed to this worldview would therefore link their own peace and well-being to the peace and well-being of others. Community peace and right relations go together. Ministries that neglect this linkage may not be engaging fully in the theological obligations of ministry, in that standing for justice is part of our urgent calling.

---

4. Bernhard Haring, *Shalom: Peace: The Sacrament of Reconciliation* (New York: Farrar, Straus and Giroux, 1968).

5. Dirk Louw, "Ubuntu: An African Assessment of the Religious Order," The Twentieth World Congress of Philosophy, in Boston, Massachusetts, August 10–15, 1998, https://www.bu.edu/wcp/Papers/Afri/AfriLouw.htm.

The role of the church is to live the good news, to proclaim it, and to engage in practical actions that bring life-giving transformation to our communities. This includes impacting the unjust, death-dealing forces of this world that compromise the lives of urban dwellers and their communities, including matters bearing upon economics, environment, social prejudices, and social injustices. Any proclamation coming from the church that does not positively impact the lives of urban communities may be inadequate or even inadvertently complicit in compromising the lives of such communities.

Theological Tools for Justice

Using theological resources as a base for effective moral and social critiques of society and as a catalysis for positive, life-enhancing change in communities has a long history. German Reformed theologian Jürgen Moltmann traces this back to the cross of Calvary and affirms this as a form of critical theological reflection at the heart of being Reformed Christians. He writes, "To realize the theology of the cross at the present day is to take seriously the claims of Reformation theology to criticize and reform, and to develop it beyond a criticism of the church into a criticism of society."[6]

Centuries before Moltmann, French Protestant reformer John Calvin revealed a great passion for justice in communities and the need for the church's commitment. Operating in the city of Geneva, which doubled in population during the time of his ministry, Calvin's writings reveal opposition to all forms of social injustice:

> All those arts whereby we acquire the possessions and money at the expense of our neighbours are to be considered as thefts. Although those who behave in this way often win their case before the judge, yet God upholds them to be none other than thieves. For he sees the intricate deceptions with which crafty people set out to snare those of simpler mind; he sees the rigour of the exactions which the rich impose on the poor to crush them.[7]

6. Jürgen Moltmann, *The Crucified God: The Cross as the Foundation and Criticism of Christian Theology*, trans. R. A. Wilson and John Bowden (London: SCM Press Ltd., 1974), 4. The original German is on page 9 of Jürgen Moltmann, *Der gekreuzigte Gott* (Chr. Kaiser Verlag München), 1972.

7. Andre Bieler, *Calvin's Economic and Social Thought*, trans. James Greig, ed. Edward Dommen (World Alliance of Reformed Churches and the World Council of Churches, 2007), 301. See also John Calvin's *Institutes of the Christian Religion* (II, viii, 45), translated from the original Latin, and collated with the author's last edition in French with John Allen (William Fry Printer, 1816).

Commenting upon this passage, Andre Bieler, a twentieth-century Swiss theologian, suggests Calvin saw in the disparity between the rich and the poor a scandal, which is "unworthy of a church reformed by the Word of God."[8]

In the Reformed Christian tradition, confessions and catechisms have become key instruments for addressing moral and social challenges of past eras. Thus, the Heidelberg Catechism of 1563, the Westminster Confession of 1646, and other such confessions have served as resources for the church's understanding of Christian calling and relevant actions in their eras.[9] In the twentieth century, two key confessions were developed to address the major injustices to large numbers of people in Germany and South Africa. In 1934, the Barmen Declaration was a tool developed to articulate a clear confessional stance with which the church could battle the menace of Nazism in Germany and territories influenced by Germany. The confession addressed this peril and served as a beacon for justice in the face of an absurd, death-dealing political system that corrupted human relationships in communities.[10] In 1986, the Uniting Reformed Church of Southern Africa developed the Belhar Confession to counter the evil apartheid system as a contradiction to the reconciling good news of Jesus Christ.[11] Here again, there was a need for churches to have a tool to engage in effective life-giving ministry for communities. This confession certainly provided the "medicines" needed to sustain communities and draw churches to effectively minister in their contexts. It offered a vision for making God's household everywhere (including urban areas) a more just dwelling place for all. Nevertheless, it is the Accra Confession, developed in 2004, on which I want to focus here.

---

8. Bieler, *Calvin's Economic and Social Thought*, 135.

9. The Heidelberg Catechism was developed with the backdrop of emerging religious and educational reform in the palatinate. Its aim was to unify and solidify the religious reform while meeting the curriculum needs of students and future leaders. See http://www.heidelberg-catechism.com/en/. The Westminster Confession of Faith is a reformed statement of faith influenced by both Calvinism and Puritanism. Beyond the Church of England and the Church of Scotland, it has been influential around the world. See http://www.reformed.org/documents/index.html?mainframe=http://www.reformed.org/documents/westminster_conf_of_faith.html.

10. The Barmen Declaration responded to Hitler's national church as a statement of unified Christian resistance to false nationalist teachings destroying the peace and unity of the church in Germany. See http://www.sacred-texts.com/chr/barmen.htm.

11. The Belhar Confession stands as a challenge to the South African apartheid system as noted here: https://www.crcna.org/welcome/beliefs/contemporary-testimony/confession-belhar.

The Accra Confession and My Context

Accra, the capital of Ghana, is a sprawling metropolis with a population of more than four million people, the eleventh largest metropolitan area in Africa.[12] Some estimate that in Accra one can find a church within a thousand feet of wherever one is standing. While many are bringing the good news of the love of God, few holistically address the spiritual needs of members or help with specific challenges of urban living. As a minister in Accra, I have encountered many who are struggling with many of the five challenges listed above, and yet churches do not seem to be attentive to these needs. Large metropolises such as Accra can be places where people feel most isolated when dealing with the challenges characteristic of urban spaces. Churches desiring to address urban challenges more systematically may ask what theological tools are available as resources for analyzing such situations. Having served the World Communion of Reformed Churches as General Secretary for almost fifteen years, I offer one of its products, the Accra Confession, as one example of a theological critique that inspires life-giving action.[13]

In 2004, the then World Alliance of Reformed Churches held its 24th General Assembly in Accra, Ghana, under the theme "That all may have life in fullness" (adapted from John 10:10).[14] This theme inspired delegates to question the situations that compromise life for millions of people in the world, including many in urban areas. One of the key instruments that came out of that General Council is the Accra Confession. Following in the footsteps of previous Reformed Confessions, the Accra Confession emerged as a prophetic statement on Christian life that placed before the church a vision and a challenge for moving toward just and right relationships in communities so that all might live life in its fullness. Some of the tenets of the Accra Confession that provide meaningful tools of analysis include the following:

- We believe in God, Creator and Sustainer of all life, who calls us as partners in the creation and redemption of the world. We live under the promise that Jesus Christ came so that all might have life in fullness

---

12. Ghana is a country in western Africa with a rich history and many assets and continues to face many challenges. See https://www.newsghana.com.gh/ghana/.
13. The Accra Confession calls the church to stand in solidarity against economic and ecological injustices as an expression of faith in Jesus Christ. See http://wcrc.ch/accra.
14. As a result of the merging of the World Alliance of Reformed Churches and the Reformed Ecumenical Council, the World Communion of Reformed Churches was formed in 2010.

(John 10.10). Guided and upheld by the Holy Spirit we open ourselves to the reality of our world.

- We believe that God is sovereign over all creation. "The earth is the Lord's and the fullness thereof" (Psalm 24.1).
- Therefore, we reject the current world economic order imposed by global neoliberal capitalism and any other economic system, including absolute planned economies, which defy God's covenant by excluding the poor, the vulnerable and the whole of creation from the fullness of life. We reject any claim of economic, political and military empire which subverts God's sovereignty over life and acts contrary to God's just rule.
- We reject the culture of rampant consumerism and the competitive greed and selfishness of the neoliberal global market system or any other system which claims there is no alternative.
- We believe that any economy of the household of life given to us by God's covenant to sustain life is accountable to God. We believe the economy exists to serve the dignity and wellbeing of people in community, within the bounds of the sustainability of creation. We believe that human beings are called to choose God over Mammon and that confessing our faith is an act of obedience.
- Therefore, we reject the unregulated accumulation of wealth and limitless growth that has already cost the lives of millions and destroyed much of God's creation.[15]

The parts of the *Accra Confession* on economics may be difficult for some city dwellers to hear because for many it may indeed be the allure of accumulation of wealth or what is seen as financial growth that led them to the city. Therefore, this may not necessarily be experienced as positive news by all. Nevertheless, a prophetic urban ministry approach necessarily includes exposing societal commitments to unjust systems and contrasting those systems to God's intentions for our life together. Those relational intentions are outlined in the following paragraphs from the Accra Confession:

- We believe that God is a God of justice. In a world of corruption, exploitation and greed, God is in a special way the God of the destitute, the poor, the exploited, the wronged and the abused (Ps 146.7–9). God

---

15. *Accra 2004: Proceedings of the 24th General Council of the World Alliance of Reformed Churches*, World Alliance of Reformed Churches, Geneva 2005. Articles 17, 18, and 19, page 156; Articles 20 and 21, page 157; Articles 22, 23, 24, and 25, page 158.

calls for just relationships with all creation.

• Therefore, we reject any ideology or economic regime that puts profits before people, does not care for all creation and privatizes those gifts of God meant for all. We reject any teaching which justifies those who support, or fail to resist, such an ideology in the name of the gospel.[16]

This section of the confession holds up a high standard of justice for all, suggesting those who have embraced corrupt societal values premised upon injustice would need to realign themselves with God's intentions of more just communities. In the face of growing urban injustices (in an era of empire brought about by "the coming together of economic, cultural, political and military power . . . led by powerful nations to protect and defend their own interests"), God's reign provides a counterforce.[17]

Concluding Thoughts

In the face of evil, and the intensified systemic and structural forms it can take within our high-density urban existences, churches are called not only to pray and proclaim, but also to act; not only to expose evil in society, but also to stand up for justice, even if this leads to the anger of powerful forces.

When churches take actions that challenge powerful forces benefiting from systems that cause human suffering, God's presence in the world (especially among those facing social hardships) is manifested for all to see. As we become living critics of structures and systems that contradict life, reforming, criticizing, and changing whatever contradicts the fullness of life, we bear witness to the fullness of life for which Jesus Christ came. The good news in this case includes lifting up and pursuing ways people can live qualitatively meaningful lives that bring them hope in the middle of social challenges. Such hope should not merely be about some future life beyond life in this world. It includes impacting. Any proclamation coming from the church that does not counter the unjust, death-dealing forces of this world shaping our life together, including its concentrated urban forms, may be complicit in compromising the lives of such communities. Churches need to do everything

16. *Accra 2004*, Articles 24 and 25, page 158.
17. World Communion of Reformed Churches, *Accra Confession: Ten Years Later*, Accra Confession: Global Consultation Report. See http://wcrc.ch/wp-content/uploads/2015/05/Accra-GlobalConsultationReport.pdf.

possible to refrain from knowingly or unknowingly participating in perpetuating the bad news embodied within too many of our systems and structures. This requires not simply offering charity but doing the critical analysis and actions that make for transformation from the roots. This requires accompanying those who are struggling, and committing to a journey alongside them that leads to justice.

Chapter 20

School Voucher Programs
and Black Clergy Responses in Two Cities

R. Drew Smith

Educational inequalities within America are readily apparent, and so is the lack of consensus about how to respond to these inequalities. When the problem is seen as having mainly to do with factors internal to underperforming schools and the familial and cultural milieu of their students, the primary strategic focus is generally on getting more out of teachers and administrators within these schools and, short of that, getting students out of underperforming schools and into schools that can put taxes allocated for those students' education to better use.[1] With respect to the latter, significant disagreement exists over whether tax dollars allocated to public school systems should be reassigned to families as vouchers that can be used in purchasing private school alternatives for their children.

Often, students have used these school vouchers to attend faith-based schools. As of 2016, Catholic schools were the largest recipients of these voucher-supported students, receiving 1.9 million such students nationally.[2] With respect to private K–12 schools in the United States, faith-based schools constitute the largest segment (22,000 schools serving 4.1 million students in 2006). These faith-based schools outnumber nonreligious schools by more than three to one—and Catholic schools outnumber

---

1. President George W. Bush's major educational initiative, "No Child Left Behind," placed significant emphasis on rewarding and punishing teachers based upon student performance. Ironically, President Barack Obama's educational initiative announced in March 2010 was criticized for maintaining some of the same emphasis.

2. Lesli A. Maxwell, "Why Trump's Plan for a Massive School Voucher Program Might Not Work," *Education Week*, November 28, 2016, http://blogs.edweek.org/edweek/charterschoice /2016/11/trump_voucher_primer_and_reality_check.html.

religious schools of other traditions by the same margin.[3] Included in the segment of Protestant faith-based schools are a growing number of historically black independent schools in the United States (reportedly 400 as of 2000, serving 52,000 students, and with many of these schools operated by black churches).[4] Given the robust number and variety of faith-based K–12 schools, and the quite discernible streams of support for school voucher programs, the competition and challenges these programs represent for urban public schooling may prove considerable.

The debate over school funding bears not only upon matters related to educational effectiveness, it also embodies a larger wrestling over how tax dollars are appropriately spent and how broad-based public purposes are effectively advanced. Urban churches and clergy are unavoidably in the middle of this battleground—with their responses serving as key indicators of their theological and social commitments to urban community well-being, including to how many urban youth those commitments extend. This essay briefly explores black clergy engagement from both sides of the school voucher struggle, focusing especially upon local battles in Washington, D.C., and Milwaukee.[5]

School Vouchers as an Urban Policy Flashpoint

Support for the idea of school vouchers in the United States began at least as early as the 1950s when southern governments proposed tuition grants as a means of circumventing mandated school desegregation. These southern strategies proved largely unsuccessful, but by the 1960s, the school voucher concept caught the attention of parochial school advocates who recognized the potential vouchers possessed as a buttress for parochial schools (mainly Catholic ones).

Apart from a few limited examples, there was not much progress in implementing voucher programs prior to the 1990s.[6] Voucher programs

3. White House Domestic Policy Council, *Preserving a Critical National Asset: America's Disadvantaged Students and the Crisis in Faith-Based Urban Schools* (Washington, DC: U.S. Department of Education, September 2008), 5.

4. Gail Foster, "Historically Black Independent Schools," in *City Schools: Lessons from New York*, ed. Diane Ravitch and Joseph Viteritti (Baltimore: Johns Hopkins University Press, 2002), 299.

5. Portions of this essay come from a much fuller, previously published discussion by the author of the topic. See R. Drew Smith, "Black Clergy, Educational Fairness, and Pursuit of the Common Good," in R. Drew Smith, ed., *From Every Mountainside: Black Churches and the Broad Terrain of Civil Rights* (Albany: State University of New York Press, 2014), 167–88.

6. There were small, short-lived pilot programs in California and in New York during the 1970s.

of notable size and scope were implemented in Milwaukee in 1990, in Cleveland in 1995, and on a statewide basis in Florida in 1999. By 2007, twelve states and the District of Columbia provided publicly funded tuition scholarships to approximately 150,000 primary and secondary school students across the United States, and the number of states with voucher programs has now grown to twelve.[7] Indiana's "Choice Scholarship Program," which was established in 2011, is among the largest and fastest growing school voucher programs in the nation, with more than 34,000 participating students and more than 300 participating schools during the 2016–2017 academic year.[8] Additionally, Arizona passed legislation in 2017 that promises to make it one of the nation's most expansive voucher programs.[9]

Despite the support vouchers have gained at state and local levels, federal backing for voucher programs has been blocked by forces opposed to vouchers—with the exception of the District of Columbia's program (a five-year program providing tuition grants for 1,700 students as of spring 2009). Even the "No Child Left Behind" legislation, widely viewed as a rejoinder to public schools, gained congressional approval in 2001 only after all voucher proposals had been removed from the bill. Nevertheless, President Donald Trump is a strong supporter of vouchers, as evidenced by his campaign promise to invest $20 billion in federal funding in support of voucher programs, and by his appointment of voucher advocate Betsy DeVos as his secretary of education.

Support for voucher programs within African American communities has been mixed. Polling data, for example, from the Joint Center for Political and Economic Studies showed 57 percent of African American respondents in 1997 and in 2002 favored voucher programs. In a 1998 Gallup poll, 62 percent of African Americans supported vouchers. These data would seem to indicate solid black support for vouchers among African Americans. But, as some scholars have argued, the reality may be far more complicated than the data suggest. For example,

7. Dan Lips and Evan Feinberg, "Utah's Revolutionary New School Voucher Program," Heritage Foundation, WebMemo #1362, February 16, 2007, http://www.heritage.org/Research/Education/wm1362.cfm#_ftn2.

8. "Indiana—Choice Scholarship Program," https://www.edchoice.org/school-choice/programs/indiana-choice-scholarship-program/.

9. Yvonne Wingett Sanchez and Rob O'Dell, "Arizona Is Expanding Its School Voucher Program. What Does It Mean for Parents?" *Arizona Republic*, April 20, 2017, http://www.azcentral.com/story/news/politics/arizona-education/2017/04/20/arizona-expanding-its-school-voucher-empowerment-scholarship-account-program-now-what/100352304/.

BlackCommentator.com points out that surveys attempting to measure support for vouchers have operated largely in a hypothetical realm, given the paucity of existing voucher programs on which respondents can base their opinions. Instead, the argument continues, black support for vouchers is more accurately measured by how blacks have voted on voucher issues when put to a referendum—and consistently blacks have voted against voucher programs in these instances.[10]

Among black survey respondents, it has been shown that support for vouchers has been strongest among younger, lower-income black respondents, and opposition to vouchers strongest among black elites, including clergy and elected officials. For example, a 2000 Joint Center poll showed 76 percent of African American respondents ages 26–35 favored vouchers. When asked in a 1992 California survey whether they would use a proposed $2,600 voucher to send their children to private school, 69 percent of African Americans with school-age children and 62 percent of respondents with household incomes of $25,000 or less said they would.[11] Similarly, analysis of a 2000 and a 2004 National Annenberg Election Survey showed that support for vouchers was strongest at lower income levels among black respondents (which was just the opposite of white respondents, whose support was strongest at higher income levels).[12] Although black elite opposition to vouchers may constitute a minority viewpoint within the black population in general, black elite opposition to vouchers is fairly systematic, especially among black elected officials—69 percent of whom were opposed to vouchers in a 2001 Joint Center poll.

Black Clergy and Voucher Programs

Black clergy appear to be a bit more evenly divided on vouchers, according to data from Morehouse College's 1999–2000 Black Churches and Politics (BCAP) Survey. When asked whether educational tax dollars could be put to better use in the form of vouchers, 44 percent of the largely

---

10. BlackCommentator.com, "Poll Shows Black Political Consensus Strong," issue 17, November 21, 2002, 7.

11. Janet Beales, "Survey of Education Vouchers and Their Budgetary Impact on California," Reason Foundation Working Paper, no. 144, August 1992, http://reason.org/files/09e700faf2 3a677e337560724f675840.pdf.

12. Andrew Gelman, "Who Wants School Vouchers? Rich Whites and Poor Nonwhites" Columbia University Department of Statistics online, June 15, 2009, http://www.stat.columbia .edu/~cook/movabletype/archives/2009/06/who_wants_schoo.html.

clergy respondents agreed, while 54 percent disagreed. That black clergy are a bit more supportive of vouchers than other black elites may derive both from their agreement with the principle of expanding educational alternatives for black students and with their interest in increasing black enrollment in faith-based schools, including a growing number operated by black churches. Nevertheless, black clergy opposition to voucher programs was discernible early in the national debate on vouchers, especially in two cities where there were pioneering efforts to advance the voucher cause: Milwaukee and Washington, D.C.

Milwaukee's voucher program was initiated in 1990 as one of the first in the United States. The program originally provided vouchers to 341 low-income students from public schools but grew incrementally, receiving legislative approval in 2006 to extend vouchers to approximately 22,500 of Milwaukee's public and private school students. Black clergy featured prominently on both the pro-voucher and anti-voucher sides of the debate.

A local leader who played a principal role in voucher advocacy and in generating support for vouchers among local black clergy was Bishop Sedgwick Daniels, who pastors the 8,000-member Holy Redeemer Institutional Church of God in Christ in Milwaukee. Daniels, a former Democrat, developed strong ties to the Republican Party during George W. Bush's tenure, receiving both a $1.5 million federal grant as part of Bush's initiative to fund faith-based social services and a visit to his congregation from Bush himself.[13] Daniels also became closely identified with an influential Milwaukee foundation, the Bradley Foundation, which provided major funding in support of the Milwaukee voucher campaign—not to mention that it also awarded $1 million in grant money to Sedgwick's congregation for community programming.[14] Nevertheless, Daniels argues that it was not monetary incentives but, rather, his commitment to a politics emphasizing faith and values that led him to support policies such as vouchers and to endorse Bush in 2004.[15]

Another black minister prominently involved in school choice advocacy in Milwaukee has been Archie Ivy, pastor of Milwaukee's New Hope Missionary Baptist Church, a former school principal and an alternate

13. Peter Wallsten et al., "Bush Rewarded by Black Pastor's Faith," *Los Angeles Times*, January 18, 2005.

14. BlackCommentator.com, "Voucher Tricksters: The Hard Right Enters through the Schoolhouse Door," issue 7, July 11, 2002, http://www.blackcommentator.com/7_voucher_tricksters .html.

15. Wallsten, "Bush Rewarded by Black Pastor's Faith."

delegate to the 2000 Democratic National Convention. Ivy has contributed to school choice causes by serving as a board member of Milwaukee's Alliance for Choices in Education, a board member of the Milwaukee branch of Black Alliance for Educational Options (BAEO), and as cochair of a Milwaukee group called Clergy for Educational Options. Unlike Daniels, there are no conspicuous benefits that have accrued to Ivy's congregation as a result of his connection to school choice causes, but the school choice organizations he is involved with are themselves connected to major funding streams such as the Bradley Foundation and the Walton Family Foundation.

The Milwaukee version of Clergy for Educational Options is a less extensive version of South Carolina's Clergy for Educational Options (CEO). The South Carolina organization was founded in 2004 by a small number of South Carolina ministers, at least two of whom were black—Maurice Revell, who pastors Agape International Ministries, and Richard Davis, a former military chaplain, schoolteacher, and CEO's current executive minister. According to its mission statement, CEO is concerned with "equity and quality in education," but its overarching objective, as alluded to in its organizational name, is to promote educational alternatives and choice for students. As Davis points out, South Carolina has one of the highest dropout rates in the nation, so CEO has responded by encouraging churches "to start schools . . . [and] do things to make sure these children are not left on the side of the road."[16] According to Davis, three hundred South Carolina congregations are members of CEO and account for a good deal of the organization's funding. But it has also been reported that the pro-voucher Walton Family Foundation has been an important CEO funder as well.[17]

Milwaukee has given rise to considerable pro-voucher momentum locally and nationally (especially through the far-reaching influences of its Bradley Foundation), but it has been a context where both local and national opposition to vouchers has been galvanized as well. During the mid-1990s, Milwaukee was often the site or the focus of anti-voucher advocacy by national leaders. In his early years in Congress, Jesse Jackson Jr. directed a great deal of his criticisms of vouchers toward the Milwaukee program, even traveling to Milwaukee for anti-voucher rallies.

16. Thomas Hanson, "Black Groups Advocate Parental Choice in Education," http://thomashanson.com/voucherblack.htm.
17. Gervais S. Bridges, "More on Clergy for Educational Options," *Barbecue and Politics* blogosphere, July 26, 2007, http://scbarbecue.blogspot.com/2007_07_01_archive.html.

At a 1998 citywide rally held at an African American church, Jackson shared speaking duties with two prominent leaders of People for the American Way (PFAW), an organization that has mobilized national opposition to vouchers and which brought in approximately $2 million a year in charitable funding during the early 2000s (mostly in five-figure sums).[18] PFAW's national president spoke, as did Timothy McDonald, who chairs PFAW's African American Ministers Leadership Council (AAMLC). McDonald, an Atlanta pastor and former president of Atlanta's Concerned Black Clergy, has been an outspoken critic of vouchers, as displayed in the following quote: "Dangling the conservatives' voucher agenda in front of the nation's most disenfranchised Americans under the guise of helping them is both immoral and hypocritical. Inner-city parents whose schools are not performing well are desperate for solutions and the Religious Right is exploiting that frustration."[19] McDonald has fought voucher initiatives in his home context of Atlanta and has traveled the country speaking against vouchers. McDonald also testified before Congress on vouchers in 1997 and in 2002, the year of a Supreme Court ruling affirming the constitutionality of a voucher program in Cleveland, Ohio (where 95 percent of voucher students used their vouchers to attend religious schools).[20]

The same day the ruling was handed down, Congressman Richard Armey (R-TX) introduced a bill in Congress to make vouchers available to public students in Washington, D.C. In 2004, a bill was successfully passed after being put to a surprise vote while a number of congressional opponents (including many Congressional Black Caucus members) were out of Washington on other business and therefore absent from the vote.[21] So despite being opposed at the time by 85 percent of D.C.'s black residents, a voucher program was launched that served approximately 1,900 of the District's students—making it the first federally funded voucher program in the United States. The program required but did not

18. Gregory B. Bodewell, "Grassroots, Inc.: A Sociopolitical History of the Cleveland Voucher Battle, 1992–2002," dissertation, Case Western University, 2006, 342, https://etd.ohiolink.edu/pg_10?0::NO:10:P10_ACCESSION_NUM:case1133366159.
19. "False Choices: Vouchers, Public Schools, and Our Children's Future," *Rethinking Schools Online*, spring 1999, http://www.rethinkingschools.org/special_reports/voucher_report/v_quotes.shtml.
20. Terry Frieden, "Supreme Court Affirms School Voucher Program," *CNN*, June 27, 2002, http://www.cnn.com/2002/LAW/06/27/scotus.school.vouchers/.
21. BlackCommentator.com, "D.C. Voucher Passage Is Huge Defeat," September 11, 2003, http://www.blackcommentator.com/55/55_cover_vouchers.html.

receive congressional reauthorization in 2008, largely due to high levels of opposition to the program, opposition that gained additional traction with the release of a 2007 federal study indicating that D.C. voucher students performed no better than the general population of D.C. public school students.

Black clergy in D.C. have not been supportive of vouchers straight down the line, however. Black clergy were primary opponents of a 1998 D.C. voucher initiative by a Walton-funded group called American Education Reform Foundation (AERF). Many of these clergy opponents had endorsed AERF a year earlier, but stated later that they were misled into thinking they were endorsing educational scholarships and not a voucher proposal.[22] One of the few black clergy voicing clear and consistent opposition to D.C.'s voucher program has been Graylan Hagler, pastor of Plymouth Congregational Church in Washington and president of Ministers for Racial, Social, and Economic Justice. Hagler's perspective on vouchers is: "The [civil rights] battle has always been around public schools, not around private academies." After desegregation, says Hagler, there was "an immediate drain of white participation from public education, going into parochial and private schools. And ever since, they have attempted to redirect public dollars out of public education and into private schools."[23] Hagler was a highly visible protester at rallies outside the Supreme Court during its deliberations over the Cleveland case. Hagler indicates that support for vouchers and charter schools among black clergy in D.C. has come mainly from a small number of clergy whose congregations operate private schools. "We didn't have a groundswell of support for vouchers and charters," says Hagler, "because there weren't many clergy operating private schools. Folks understood that the common denominator was the ability to get educated in a public environment."[24]

Concluding Thoughts

There are clearly competing instincts about how best to respond to the problem of under-resourced and poorly performing educational options for urban poor and minority youth. On one side, black clergy have been

22. People for the American Way Foundation, "Privatization of Public Education: A Joint Venture of Charity and Power," April 20, 1999, http://files.pfaw.org/pfaw_files/file_74.pdf.
23. Barbara Minor, "Distorting the Civil Rights Legacy," *Rethinking Schools Online*, spring 2004, http://www.rethinkingschools.org/special_reports/voucher_report/v_kpsp183.shtml.
24. Rev. Graylan Hagler interview with author, Washington, D.C., October 21, 2010.

guided by a concern with marshaling resources (via vouchers) toward private (and especially faith-based) alternatives to urban public school systems and, on the other side, a commitment to facilitating improved educational prospects for the large number of students who will remain reliant on public schools as the only realistic option for their education. Given that the achievement of either of these two objectives is reliant upon the same tax revenue streams, it is hard to see how the two objectives could be considered complimentary. Either a smaller segment of urban students receive potentially enhanced educational prospects by reducing available revenue for students remaining in public school systems, or else the revenue should be retained within the public school systems as well as a commitment to improving that system for the benefit of all of its students.

The few versus the many—that is a problem of increasing urgency in a nation and a world where inequalities and disparities between the haves and have-nots have become ever-more glaring. Against that backdrop, the school voucher issue serves as an important window into the bigness and broadness of American church leaders' vision for urban community possibilities.

Chapter 21

Creating an Oasis Food Ecosystem in a Post– "Faith-Based Initiatives" Environment[*]

Stephanie C. Boddie

Across the United States more than 300,000 houses of worship, particularly black congregations, open their doors beyond the traditional worship service, religious education, and pastoral care of their church members. Many of these congregations respond to the call to serve by offering food-related ministries. According to Duke University scholars Mark Chaves and Alison Eagles, of the 1,331 congregations that participated in the National Congregations Study 52 percent provide some type of food-related program.[1] The involvement in food assistance, however, is much more varied than traditional soup kitchens and food pantries. Congregations reported donating funds to a local food bank, serving meals at a homeless shelter, or participating in fundraisers for food projects. These programs do not come close to meeting the demands of the 42.2 million people living in food-insecure homes[2] or the 25 million people who live in communities that are the product of food "redlining" or categorized by the United States Department of Agriculture (USDA) as food deserts.[3]

[*]This author serves as the co-leader for the Oasis Foods Demonstration project. She acknowledges Dr. John M. Wallace, the project leader, and the Bible Center's Oasis Foods team members for their commitment to developing this demonstration project over the last five years, particularly Dr. Cynthia Wallace, Casey Clauser, Kerri Clauser, Steve Davis, Arielle Donelan, Brooke Durham, Breanna Goff, Stephanie Lewis, Jomari Peterson, John Scarbough, Donna Taylor, Debralyn Woodberry-Shaw, and Romie Yates.

1. Mark Chaves and Alison J. Eagles, "Congregations and Social Services: An Update from the Third Wave of the National Congregations Study," *Religions* 7, no. 55 (2016): 1–9.

2. United States Department of Agriculture Economic Research Service, "Food Security in the U.S.," USDA, 2016.

3. Michele VerPloeg, Vince Breneman, Tracy Farrigan et al., *Access to Affordable and Nutritious*

Chaves and Eagles found that 83 percent of the congregations provide social services; however, only 9 percent do so with external funding or form a separate nonprofit. Only 14 percent of these congregations have at least one staff member devoting a quarter or more of their time to social services. The average social service spending reported by these congregations is $1,500. Even with modest estimations, $3.3 billion of the $115 billion given to all religious organizations benefited nonmembers in 2014. Overall congregations invested an estimated 15 to 30 percent of their budget in ministries beyond their walls, thus considered a collectivistic orientation, according to Burton Weisbord.[4] Congregations are best equipped to use their social capital to mobilize volunteers and collaborate with other congregations or social agencies. Food ministry is one service that matches the congregations' desire to serve and their most available means to do it, small cadres of volunteers helping one person at a time. Consistent with other research on congregation social service, these congregations were less likely to offer services that require longer commitments, greater resources, and more intensive engagement with those in need.[5]

In *Sweet Charity? Emergency Food at the End of Entitlement,* Janet Poppendieck, a Hunter College sociology professor, calls this type of emergency food response to poverty and hunger, "the kinder but less just" solution.[6] She documents the exponential growth of emergency food programs and the fascination with rescuing waste since the 1980s. She raises these questions: Has charity so intoxicated us that we fail to see the opportunities to examine and critique policies that leave people hungry and malnourished? Are we distracting people from the root causes of these problems with food pantries, soup kitchens, and "gleaning" centers? Poppendieck recognizes the ritualistic experience, the emotional draw, and the relational value of the services provided. However, she warns us not to trade the good for the better, charity for justice.

In this essay, I assert the need for comprehensive and cooperative

---

Food: Measuring and Understanding Food Deserts and Their Consequences: Report to Congress, USDA, Administration Publication No. AP-036, June 2009.

4. Burton A. Weisbord, *The Nonprofit Economy* (Cambridge, MA: Harvard University Press, 1988).

5. Ram Cnaan, Stephanie C. Boddie, Charlene C. McGrew, and Jennifer Kang, *The Other Philadelphia Story: How Local Congregations Support Quality of Life in Urban America* (Philadelphia: University of Pennsylvania Press, 2006).

6. Janet Poppendieck, *Sweet Charity? Emergency Food and the End of Entitlement* (New York: Penguin Books, 1998).

urban ministries to address complex food challenges within the changing policy context. I recognize the opportunities and limitations of congregations seeking to go beyond helping the individual to establishing a more just society. I use concepts from the story of Nehemiah and the rebuilding of the wall of Jerusalem to frame the development of new ministries. Nehemiah integrates his faith practice, community development, and policy practice. Nehemiah respected God's influence in his life, the help of others, the assets of the community, the "discernment process," and policies of his context. The case study of Bible Center Church's Oasis Foods Project demonstrates how the congregation moves beyond charity to partnering with other organizations to rebuild its local community and transform the local food landscape.

The Policy and Practice Backdrop

By 1996, the door had swung open to policies encouraging faith-based social service and more charity. The passage of the Personal Responsibility and Work Opportunity Reconciliation Act and its Charitable Choice laws under the Clinton administration followed by the Bush administration's Faith-Based Initiative launched under the George W. Bush administration ushered in a new policy context.[7] These policies reunited religion and social policy within the context of welfare state retrenchment and government restructuring, significant socioeconomic changes, and the increasing importance of personal responsibility. This continued under the Obama administration with a new emphasis on the collaborative and advisory role of faith groups. The remaining legacy of these policies is "leveling of the playing field" to support faith-based social services receiving government funding without diminishing their religious character. The infrastructure of these faith-based policies remains—the 13 federal faith-based offices affiliated with the White House Office of Faith-Based and Neighborhood Partnerships.[8]

In the wake of many changes in the political and religious landscape, black churches hold on to a steady percentage of members as Christians are

---

7. Ram A. Cnaan and Stephanie C. Boddie, "Charitable Choice and Faith-Based Welfare: A Call for Social Work," *Social Work* 47, no. 3 (2002): 224–35. David Wright, *Taking Stock: The Bush Faith-Based Initiative and What Lies Ahead* (The Roundtable on Religion and Social Welfare, The Nelson Rockefeller Institute of Government, State University of New York, 2009).

8. Adelle Banks, "Still No Sign of Leader for White House Faith Partnership Office," *Religion News Service*, March 31, 2017, http://religionnews.com/2017/03/31/still-no-sign-of-leader-for-white-house-faith-partnership-office/.

losing their share of the U.S. population, Pew Research Center reports.[9] Black churches also tend to go against the tide in the ways they provide social and community services.[10] Out of the crucible of slavery, segregation, and discrimination and into new eras that have reshaped race and class in social policies, black churches continue to birth food-related ministries to nourish and nurture both members and the wider community.

While black congregations primarily employ benevolence strategies for their food-related ministries, examples of community development and advocacy pre-date this current policy context. Most notably, Pastor Charles Albert Tindley and Tindley Temple United Methodist Church of Philadelphia established a soup kitchen during the years of the Great Migration.[11] The soup kitchen launched in 1929 as one of a set of services to help southern blacks escaping Jim Crow laws and reestablishing themselves with church-sponsored housing, job training, and job placements. The soup kitchen continues to serve 100 community members each week.

In 1962, Pastor Leon Sullivan and Zion Baptist Church of Philadelphia designed the "10-36 plan," the start of his "community investment cooperation movement" to revitalize the North Philadelphia community.[12] He asked church members to save $10.00 a month for thirty-six months. Over 4,000 people came forth, and Sullivan demonstrated that black people can cooperate, coordinate their assets, and create collective wealth. In 1968, this African American faith community developed the first shopping center with a grocery store. The Progress Plaza still operates and is developed, owned, and operated by African Americans.

Daughter of a sharecropper and woman of great faith, Fannie Lou Hamer established the Freedom Farm Cooperative (FFC) in 1967.[13] Owned and worked cooperatively by 1,500 families, this 680-acre farm included a livestock share program, Head Start program, commercial kitchen, and affordable housing and other programs. Based in Sunflower

9. Pew Research Center, *The Religious Landscape Study*, May 12, 2015, http://www.pewforum .org/2015/05/12/americas-changing-religious-landscape/.

10. Stephanie C. Boddie, "Social Services of African American Congregations in the Welfare Era," *African American Research Perspectives* 10, no. 1 (2004): 36–43, http://www.rcgd.isr.umich .edu/prba/perspectives/springsummer2004/Boddie.pdf.

11. Ralph H. Jones. *Charles Albert Tindley: Prince of Preachers* (Nashville: Abingdon Press, 1982).

12. V. P. Franklin, "The Lion of Zion: Leon H. Sullivan and the Pursuit of Social and Economic Justice," *The Journal of African American History* 96, no. 1 (Winter 2011): 39–43.

13. Monica M. White. "'A Pig and a Garden': Fannie Lou Hamer and the Freedom Farm Cooperative," *Food and Foodways* 25, no. 1 (2017): 20–39.

County in the Mississippi Delta, her initiative sought to achieve greater citizenship for blacks by giving them the resources and tools to control their diet and destiny. She also protested the Johnson administration's shift from commodity food distribution to the food stamp program.

Though these faith leaders experienced a sense of exile in their own country, these leaders demonstrated the kind of faith, vision, tenacity, and community organizing that allowed them to "build houses and live in them; plant gardens and eat what they produce . . . seek the welfare of the city . . ." (Jer. 29:5–7). They imagined something new.

Bible Center Church's Oasis Foods Project

Bible Center Church was founded in 1956 and has continued to be actively involved in the social and physical transformation of its Pittsburgh community.[14] For the past sixty years, this church has been an anchoring institution in Homewood, an east-end neighborhood encompassing one square mile. The founding pastor, Ralph Groce, was known for his visionary leadership, pioneering spirit, and backyard gardening. In the second chapter of this church his grandson, John M. Wallace, is casting a bolder vision in his roles as senior pastor, social work professor at University of Pittsburgh, and board chair of two local community-based organizations. Under his leadership, this 130-member church has purchased and rehabilitated more than two dozen vacant parcels of land and six abandoned properties.[15] These properties have been adaptively reused for a range of activities including a KABOOM! community playground, a ministry house for college students, sites to teach youth construction trades, classrooms for afterschool programs, the administrative office, and rentals for community events.

The Oasis Foods Project advances the ministry life of the church while cooperating with other community leaders to address Homewood's complex food challenges. Based on research from Wallace's Comm-Univer-City Project and the PHRESH RAND Study, the church had access to valuable data about Homewood and its food insecurity and accessibility status. Most notable, Homewood residents' eligibility rates for Temporary Assistance for Needy Families cash assistance and food stamps are

14. See "Bible Center Church History and Annual Report" at http://biblecenterpgh.org. Also see https://www.facebook.com/bcpgh/.
15. The adaptive reuse strategy helps faith and community leaders to reclaim properties that might otherwise deteriorate and require demolition. Homewood has a 28 percent rate of vacant and abandoned residential buildings.

more than double those of the rest of the city. More than 80 percent of the public school students are eligible for free or reduced-price meals. Forty percent of the residents were food insecure.[16]

Influence of the pastor: In 2006, Dr. Wallace returned to his hometown with a desire to rebuild Homewood. He recalled the glory days of his old neighborhood with the sights, sounds, and smells of vibrant businesses. While Pittsburgh is considered the "Most Livable" and best city for "foodies," Homewood was known more for its crime, donuts, and pit beef. The community is changing. By creating an oasis—a place of peace, safety, and happiness in the midst of trouble and difficulty—Wallace envisioned making Homewood a little bit more like heaven (Matt. 6:10). "Old men and old women shall again sit in the streets [of Homewood], each with staff in hand because of their great age. And the streets of the city shall be full of boys and girls playing in the streets" (Zech. 8:4–5). The most notable signs that this vision is being realized include the transformation of an old crack house into the church's administrative building, the development of Oasis Farm and Fishery (DC HEART project solar-powered bio-shelter with an aquaponics system),[17] and the launch of Everyday Café, a new hub for innovation and inspiration located near the Homewood busway.[18]

The involvement of others: Bible Center is a 130-member, tithing church with a diverse membership of active older adults, energetic college students, and socially minded, well-educated adults and young families. In addition to the senior pastor, the church staff includes an executive pastor, farm manager, chef, social worker, educational director, minister of

16. Samantha Teixeira and John M. Wallace, "Data-Driven Organizing: Community University Partnership to Address Vacant and Abandoned Property," *Journal of Community Practice* 21, no. 3 (2013): 248–62. Also see 2010 U.S. Census data. See https://www.rand.org/health/projects/phresh.html. Based on the 2010 U.S. Census, Homewood has 6,442 residents, of whom 30 percent are children under 18 years old, 94 percent African American, 32 percent live below the poverty level, and 39 percent are in the workforce. According to the RAND study, nearly half of the 429 respondents reported diet- and nutrition-related health problems, including hypertension, arthritis, high cholesterol, diabetes, and heart disease. The average respondent in the study traveled 3.5 miles to grocery shop, and about 40 percent had limited access to a car.
17. Daniel Moore, "An Ambitious Energy Project in Homewood Powers Up," *Pittsburgh Post-Gazette*, March 17, 2017, http://powersource.post-gazette.com/powersource/consumers-powersource/2017/03/17/Clean-energy-Pittsburgh-Fleury-Way-Homewood-solar-farm-bioshelter-microgrid-John-Camillus-Pitt/stories/201703160039. See http://www.dcpower.pitt.edu/about/pittsburgh-project.
18. Bob Bauder. "Homewood Café Hopes to Create Bridge between Neighborhoods." Trib-Live, November 28, 2016, http://triblive.com/local/allegheny/11527944-74/homewood-cafe-pittsburgh.

music, administrative support staff, as well as property managers. The church annually sets aside time to teach on Strength Finders or S.H.A.P.E. to identify the gifts and skills that members can invest in the church and community ministries.[19] As educators and entrepreneurs, Wallace and his wife, Cynthia Wallace, attracted others with similar mindsets. Like them, many of these members were also connected in various industries that would bring additional networks like local chefs, urban agriculture practitioners, and food policy experts.[20] The church has collaborated with at least eighteen institutions from multiple sectors: higher education, urban agriculture, philanthropy, business development, community organizing, and health care. Bible Center expanded its networks even more through the exposure of the UpPrize Social Innovation Challenge.[21] This transdisciplinary network sparked new ideas for innovative food programs.

The assets of the community: The people in the community and the local organizations are significant assets. A short list includes the thirty congregations and related emergency food programs, other urban agricultural organizations with youth programs and farm stands, as well as health and educational resources.[22] The WARM Center, the Oasis Farm and Fishery with its outdoor classroom, and the Everyday Café are spaces the church now opens to the community as assets and food sites. Bible Center's summer meal program was one of the few to operate during dinner time. Volunteers served food and also provided lessons on table etiquette along with fun activities to allow children an opportunity to interact with supportive adults. The Oasis Foods project currently focuses on its Field to Fork youth program. This novel program provides local youth

---

19. See tests like these: http://www.sdfa.org/pdf/shape-test.pdf; http://www.ministryinsights .com/leaders/leading-from-your-strengths-profile/; http://www.gallup.com/press/176561/living -strengths.aspx.

20. Robert Wuthnow, "Religious Involvement and Status-Bridging Social Capital," *Journal for the Scientific Study of Religion* 41, no. 4 (2004): 669–84.

21. Amanda Waltz. "Meet the UpPrize Healthy Food Access Finalists," Next Pittsburgh, March 20, 2017, https://www.nextpittsburgh.com/business-tech-news/meet-the-upprize-healthy -food-access-finalists/.

22. The food ecosystem in Homewood is slowly evolving. There are thirty congregations and the Salvation Army with related emergency food programs, the food bank programs and Farm Stand, Homewood Children's Village, and their weekend Powerpack food program; other urban agricultural projects, including Phipps Conservatory's Home Grown program, Sankofa Community Farm and urban agricultural youth programs, two public schools with gardens, the Black Urban Gardeners Farm and Farmers' Market, Operation Better Block and the Junior Green Corps, the Community Empowerment Association community garden; as well as related health and educational resources such as Alma Illery Medical Center, the Allegheny Community College, and the YMCA and YWCA.

opportunities for education, entrepreneurship, employment, and environmental leadership. The Everyday Café's chef along with the development team continue to try new menus and programs to attract a broad base clientele. These first two projects lay the foundation for future collaborations and other projects (e.g., food incubator, restaurant, commercial kitchen) as the local food ecosystem begins to take shape.

The discernment process: Prayer, discerning, brainstorming, networking, planning, more prayer, more planning, more networking, preparing for opposition, and celebration: this was the recipe for advancing in this work. There were teams that prayed, teams that planned, and teams that continued brainstorming and networking. There was also the anticipation of opposition and hence the need to remain focused on rebuilding the wall and loving the people.

The policies: Dr. Wallace and Bible Center members were well aware of the friendly policy context created by the Charitable Choice legislation and the Faith-Based Initiatives that eased churches into the social welfare mix. Hence, the work to establish the Café and micro-farm has all been accomplished under the auspices of the church. After consulting with legal and nonprofit experts, the church decided against creating separate businesses for these new entities. Meetings with USDA representatives also made the pastors aware of other opportunities to apply for the Community Foods Projects (CFP) program. The CFP was part of the 2014 reauthorization of the Agricultural Act of 2014 (Farm Bill). Along with polices, there is always politics to navigate in these community building projects.

Concluding Thoughts

The Bible Center Church's Oasis Foods Project is an example of a congregation moving beyond charity to entrepreneurial approaches to address food accessibility and community food security.[23] This congregation recognizes that food challenges are entangled with other social, economic, and environmental factors that limit well-being and the flourishing of any community. These faith leaders are benefitting from knowledge of government and local agency policies as well as their community conditions.

23. Wei-ting Chen, Megan L. Clayton, and Anne Palmer, *Community Food Security in the United States: A Survey of the Scientific Literature*, vol. 2 (Baltimore: Johns Hopkins Center for a Livable Future, Spring 2015). According to these authors, community food security seeks to "ensure the availability, stability, and access to food at a community level," 7. This definition also includes promoting food production and the well-being of the community.

These leaders have armed themselves with the information to determine how, where, and with whom to begin building their community's wall.

The kindness of charitable service will always have a place. However, congregations should not stop there. Justice is needed. The lesson from Bible Center teaches us to allow congregations to be stretched in new ways of thinking, doing, and being. Once congregations have moved beyond charity toward innovation they should also consider going upstream to change the structures that allow people to fall into cycles of hunger, poverty, low educational attainment, and unemployment. Duke Divinity School scholar Gregory Jones calls this nurturing "third way" innovation strategies.[24] Such "Spirit-guided" disruptive strategies build upon Christian values such as hope, creativity, imagination, hospitality, forgiveness, and love.[25]

By pursuing this "third way," congregations can be attentive to both the aspirations and challenges of their neighbors and come alongside them to rebuild the community. Together the congregation and the community can establish connections, a collective mission, and capacity while holding each other and policymakers accountable for the flourishing of the city.

24. L. Gregory Jones, *Christian Social Innovation: Renewing Wesleyan Witness* (Nashville: Abingdon Press, 2016).
25. Ibid., 61.

Chapter 22

One Congregation's Ministry to Immigrants

Jean Stockdale

In 1999, right after I began attending the Reformed Church of Highland Park (New Jersey), the pastor retired, and soon thereafter I found myself (a newcomer) serving on the pastoral search committee of this thirty-five-member congregation. One and a half years later, we selected as our copastors a young married couple just graduating together from Princeton Theological Seminary, who came with a commitment to reaching the needs of the community.

The small congregation, which had already made its facility available for Alcoholics Anonymous meetings for years, opened its doors to Narcotics Anonymous and Overeaters Anonymous sessions, yoga classes, Jewish services on Saturdays, and Buddhist meetings on Thursdays. The new copastors also encouraged a summer day camp for neighborhood children on the church's front lawn, cultivated the leadership of church members, and enlivened our worship services, Sunday school, vacation Bible school, and weekday Bible studies. Our congregation grew.

But be forewarned: when you fling open the doors of a church, not only will the happy aspects of life gain entrance (more baptisms, larger Christmas pageants, and church softball games) but so too will the problems of desperate people. In line with the congregation's commitment to meeting community needs, we set up an afterschool drop-in center for middle school students in the church basement. Within a year it was assisting about fifty children and their families. Most kids came for the games and snacks, but our tutoring assistance was also popular with those whose parents spoke limited English. Some of these kids confided living in situations where two or three families were crowded into a single-family home. The parents in these families did not have work authorization

185

and thus could not apply for a decent job but instead worked two or three "under-the-table" jobs involving long hours and low pay to put food on the kids' plates. Our church was brushing up against hidden realities that beset many immigrant families. I had little idea of the larger struggles ahead of us, because I had not yet grasped the systemic nature of this oppression or my responsibility to help dismantle it. I would soon learn more (as would our entire congregation) about these urgent aspects of our ministry.

Congregational Solidarities with Immigrant Populations

Our congregation founded a nonprofit community development agency called Who Is My Neighbor? Inc. that would allow our afterschool program to raise external funding through corporate and municipal grants and donations, increasing our capacities for providing neighborly services to the global community forming around us. The nonprofit's mission expressed itself in a fair trade store, a concert series by folk bands from various countries, and in a language bank providing interpreters to accompany low-English parents to school conferences and doctor appointments (before there was a Google translation app to help with that).

While I directed the afterschool drop-in center and ran the summer day camp through Who Is My Neighbor, the pastors and elders were exploring additional local needs that had come to the church's attention. The major way we learned about community problems was by listening during Sunday morning worship service to the prayers of the people, the part of our service where the minister encourages persons in attendance to lift up concerns for which they are seeking prayer. In response to the question For whom should we pray?, people voiced answers such as, "pray for my grandson, he's home from the service and can't find a job"; or "pray for my daughter's classmate, she's in a foster home and the state is going to cut off her benefits because she has become adult. She will have no place to live and she has no job skills yet." We prayed on behalf of these concerns, and we put our hearts, heads, and hands to these prayers by establishing a second nonprofit organization—Reformed Church of Highland Park Affordable Housing Corp. This organization's purpose is to facilitate construction of permanent housing for veterans, youth aging out of foster care, and other special sectors of the homeless population, including formerly incarcerated citizens. Soon afterward came prayer requests and inquiries about helping immigrants caught in the trap of labor trafficking.

Our church did not work on all these matters in a linear fashion but in a jumble of events and developments, surges of exhilarating success, simultaneous crises, and the complexities of our own personal lives. Encountering the hidden problems of low-income immigrant families in our midst through serving their preadolescents at our drop-in center was one way God was preparing us to understand the insidious connections between U.S. immigration policies, mass incarceration, and human trafficking. An event that happened in our midst hastened our learning.

On a night in 2006, in a town up the road from our church, Immigration Customs and Enforcement (ICE), which is a branch of the U.S. Department of Homeland Security, raided an apartment complex and forcibly removed thirty-two fathers and husbands from their families. These hardworking, taxpaying, law-abiding people had no criminal records. They had entered the United States on tourist visas and business visas in the early 1990s, fleeing vicious persecution in their native country where they were an ethnic and religious minority. Their entry visas had long ago expired, and a law passed in 1996, the one-year time bar, stipulated that people with asylum claims must file them within one year of entering the United States. Although many had since become parents of U.S.-born children, these out-of-status parents of U.S.-citizen children had no avenue to initiate the citizenship process for themselves. That situation created mixed-status families.

The predawn raid resulted in the deportation of thirty-two breadwinners and the devastation of their families. Not knowing where else to turn, some of the women and children fled to our church and lived there over the next two weeks while coping with the trauma that ICE had rained down upon their lives. This situation catapulted our congregation to the front lines of immigration reform, earning us "criticism" as a "sanctuary church." How profoundly these two words were redefined in their relationship to each other. Meanwhile, our congregation was caring for these people among us whose cooking aromas smelled different from our own.

One man who had not answered the knock on his door that night was becoming a leader in our church, caring for the children who had lost their fathers, traveling with our pastors to meetings with government officials, throwing himself wholeheartedly into volunteer tasks of maintaining our building and grounds, and all the while continuing his full-time work at a warehouse. But because he had followed a U.S. law and registered with the post-9/11 National Security Entry Exit Registration System (NSEERS) program that went into effect in 2002, he was low-hanging fruit for ICE to pick up. They knew his name and address, birthdate, year of entry, and many other facts about him that he voluntarily provided in good faith when NSEERS declared that all noncitizen men between the ages of sixteen and sixty-five from any of twenty-five majority-Muslim countries must register or be considered terrorist fugitives. He was one of the 82,000 people who registered. ICE treacherously deported over 13,000 NSEERS registrants before the program was suspended in 2011 and dismantled in 2016 without netting a single terrorist and meanwhile trampling the human rights and civil liberties of those whom this law profiled on the basis of racial, ethnic, and religious backgrounds.

In 2009, our brother felt it was just a matter of time before he fell prey to an ICE dragnet, and he was right. ICE agents surrounded him as he was getting out of his car returning home from a night shift, and while his wife watched in horror from the kitchen window. They took him to Elizabeth Detention Center, a for-profit prison in Elizabeth, New Jersey, run by one of ICE's major contractors, Core Civic (formerly Corrections Corp of America). The multibillion-dollar company makes its money from a little-noticed quota that was quietly slipped into a congressional appropriations bill and became law, requiring ICE to detain at least 34,000 people every night of the year, costing taxpayers $2 billion annually. No other law enforcement agency in the United States has a quota. This quota results in the detention of more than 415,000 people per year, many of whom are basically abducted by ICE from homes, workplaces, cars, or public transportation, then held indefinitely in ICE's network of over two hundred prison facilities. Hence, immigrant detention has become a main pillar of the prison-industrial complex.

Our brother was detained for three months. Our tax dollars paid $130 per day to keep him captive. Our attempts to visit him daily were frequently thwarted by the facility's "policies." We would make the hour-long drive from church to the detention center, stand in an overcrowded waiting room for hours, and then be told the detainees are on lockdown or are being counted and that visitors must go home. Detention centers have low-paid staff, high turnover, and no concept of customer service.[1] Visitors were often told we do not meet dress code, do not have sufficient ID, or cannot bring paper into the room as we are not allowed to write down anything detainees say. Sometimes we got far enough to sit in a row of booths in a cinderblock room where we could see our brother through

---

1. Dagmar Myslinska, "Living Conditions in Immigration Centers, Nolo.Com, http://www.nolo.com/legal-encyclopedia/living-conditions-immigration-detention-centers.html.

a Plexiglas wall and talk into a phone to speak with him. The din of all the other conversations, however, made it very hard to hear.

Although the "rules" of the place heaped indignities upon visitors, they were minimal compared to the humiliations suffered by detainees, who had to wear prison jumpsuits, sleep in under-heated barracks, and could never go outside to hear a bird or breathe fresh air. Their insufficient food could be supplemented by purchasing overpriced junk food if any friend or relative had put money in their commissary account. Detainees were locked up without being charged, tried, or sentenced for a crime, in a profit-driven system that has hijacked U.S. immigration law and rewritten it for its own purposes, greatly expanding the scope of punishable activity. ICE and its contractors know no transparency or accountability.[2]

Twice our brother was put in solitary confinement, a space called "the Shoe" in reference to its size as well as its acronym—SHU—for Special Housing Unit. He had organized a Bible study attended by twelve other detainees. As any kind of organizing was seen as a threat, he was transferred to a pod where no one spoke his language. He soon had four guys reading the Bible together. Guards apparently felt intimidated, and again transferred our brother to the Shoe. Later he was moved to a remote detention center 2,689 miles away, making it impossible for family members and attorneys to visit.[3]

By now our church was aware of the desperation of inmates at the Elizabeth Detention Center and of the family members we met in the waiting room. We kept on visiting, weekly. Our detention visitation ministry has continued several years, offering sympathy to people suffering needless separation from their families. In addition to noncitizens who have been in the United States for a long period of time, detention centers hold newly arriving asylum seekers who must establish a credible fear of return to their country. People without documents are detained until they can establish their identity and prove that they present no flight risk. Some detainees have no one they know within the United States. These individuals often languish in detention without friends or resources.

Over the years our church has requested the release of hundreds of detainees. Usually ICE has declined these requests for "community supervision as an alternative to detention" but on occasion has released

2. Lutheran Immigration and Refugee Service, "Immigration Detention," http://lirs.org/immigrationdetention/.

3. Immigration, "ICE's New Prisoner Transfer Policy: Something Old, Something New," May 15, 2012, http://crimmigration.com/2012/05/15/ices-new-prisoner-transfer-policy-something-old-something-new/.

people into our care. One such man released to us was a victim of labor trafficking. We would not have known about him except that he was brought to our attention by another detainee we were visiting who told us about his bunkmate, a man who spoke little English and seemed to be suffering from a horrendous injustice. We came to understand he had been recruited from abroad by an American company, which had paid its steep fees to cover the immigration paperwork required for U.S. employment and a green card (permanent resident status). He arrived in the United States, reported to the job site, and found himself forced to work in dangerous conditions in an isolated area and to live in crowded housing with other workers from his country. These workers had been tricked into paying dearly for a nonexistent green card job opportunity. The company also heavily deducted from their paychecks for the room and board they had promised would be free. They were often threatened with deportation if they did not work faster. He escaped and fell into further problems.

Congress enacted the Trafficking Victims Protection Act in 2000, making illegal "the recruitment, harboring, transportation, provision, or obtaining of a person for labor or services, through the use of force, fraud, or coercion for the purposes of subjection to involuntary servitude, peonage, debt bondage, or slavery (22 USC § 7102)."[4] Although U.S. citizens can be victims of labor trafficking, most victims are noncitizens; the coercion used against them as a weapon to exploit their labor is often the threat of deportation. It tends to be an effective threat. Returning to one's country saddled with debt incurred by accepting the job offer may seem like a worse prospect than continuing in the hostile work environment. Workers entering the United States on this type of visa are not allowed to work for any employer other than the one that sponsored their visa. As such, these persons are especially vulnerable to exploitation. When their short-term visas expire, they are out of status—meaning that they are in the country "illegally"—and cannot renew their work authorization. Most unauthorized workers currently have no legal route or application process by which they qualify to gain lawful status and the right to work.

So what can an unauthorized worker do? His or her employer may cheat a little or a lot through various forms of wage theft, including failure to pay an agreed-upon wage, or a fair wage, or the legal minimum wage, or overtime, or for every hour worked. Abuses also include delaying

---

4. National Human Trafficking Hotline, "Federal Anti-Trafficking Laws," https://humantraffickinghotline.org/what-human-trafficking/federal-law.

payment, not giving promised benefits, misclassifying an employee as an independent contractor, or illegally deducting fines or supplies from the worker's earnings. Sometimes employers take advantage of workers' lack of English skills or limited knowledge of immigration laws or their legal rights, while also asserting that the worker will be safer from deportation if he or she keeps a low profile and stays in the job.

Noncitizen workers you may see every day may be working for $5 per hour on a twelve-hour shift in a six- or seven-day work week. They could be on staff in a hotel, restaurant, beauty salon, gas station, grocery, convenience store, or in construction, landscaping, fishing, farming, factory, or office work. They can be working side by side with Americans who are being paid fairly and know nothing about "special arrangements" moderating the earnings of their foreign-born coworker. Unauthorized workers can be anywhere on the continuum from occasionally cheated to severely exploited and entrapped to the point of being trafficked.

We assisted this man and many of his former coworkers in obtaining a humanitarian visa that the United States offers to victims of trafficking. The process can take many months. The application can be denied if any of several stringent criteria is not met in the person's situation. Meanwhile, applicants are not authorized to work, so it is hard for them to support themselves. In the summer and fall of 2011, eight victims of trafficking schemes lived on the charity of our congregation, waiting for federal adjudicators to decide whether to grant each of them a T Visa.[5] Our congregation alone could not provide all the necessary supports, so we reached out to all corners of our community in meeting their needs for food, shelter, medical care, legal services, and language assistance. We called on cultural groups, university departments, other houses of worship, and human rights organizations—and in the process, we moved into deeper solidarity with socially vulnerable immigrants. In addition to assisting individuals, our congregation has advocated for changes in laws and policies so as to reduce mass incarceration, worker exploitation, and labor trafficking.

---

5. The T Nonimmigrant Status (T visa) is a federal immigration visa designated for victims of human trafficking. These visas provide for the protection of victims of human trafficking and allow these victims to remain in the United States to assist with the investigation and prosecution of human trafficking violations. Additional information on the T Visa can be found at "Victims of Human Trafficking: T Nonimmigrant Status," U.S. Citizenship and Immigration Services. See https://www.uscis.gov/humanitarian/victims-human-trafficking-other-crimes/victims -human-trafficking-t-nonimmigrant-status.

Concluding Thoughts

Being present and in dialogue with vulnerable immigrant populations and willing to extend a helping hand has allowed our congregation to stand in the gap between abusive U.S. immigration policies and fairer policies that could be established. By inserting ourselves into these situations, we have experienced the surprising ways God can work in the breaking of chains and the recovery of persons who have been abused by an unjust system.

The exploitation and abuse of foreign-national workers in the United States are so prevalent that if you scratch the surface you will see it for yourself. Express care and concern for the immigrants you come across in your daily life. Ask them about their well-being, about their family, and about where their family lives and when they saw them last. Press government officials for changes to immigration law and policies so that immigrant labor is not being stolen and so that the few million people in the United States who are without work authorization might receive it—in the interest of the economy, the social fabric, and immigrant families.

Our current labor and immigration laws virtually invite employers to take unfair advantage of noncitizen workers. Let us seek solutions with others who care about this: unions, human rights organizations, and faith groups—and let us ask God to bless our efforts. There is a Scripture that says, "Ask, and it will be given you; search, and you will find; knock, and the door will be opened for you" (Matt. 7:7). Let us keep asking and seeking in pursuit of God's reign on earth and walk through every open door.

Chapter 23

Gun Violence and African American Churches

Katie Day

On June 17, 2015, a young self-proclaimed white supremacist shot and killed nine members of the Emanuel African Methodist Episcopal Church, including their pastor, Rev. Clementa Pinckney. The young killer had sat with them for an hour during their regular Bible study and opened fire when they bowed their heads in prayer. Although he was a stranger to the church members, they had followed the widespread custom of African American Christians of welcoming persons into their midst. The country and the world were shocked not only by another mass shooting in the United States but also by the heartless violation of sacred space and of loving hospitality. Two days later, the piety of the black Christians affected by this tragedy again caught media attention as several grieving family members of murdered victims attending the shooter's bond hearing tearfully declared they forgave him. The tragedy in Charleston left many black churches with a heightened sense of their vulnerability, as violence had come into the sanctuary.

There was an expectation that after this massacre, African Americans would join the wave of consumers buying guns for protection—especially members of the faith communities that were among the softest of targets. But African American Christians have continued to demonstrate unique patterns in the meanings they attach to gun ownership, gun violence, and gun laws. I explore in this chapter some of the quantitative data on these patterns, and also present findings from ethnographic research I have been conducting in black churches. The chapter outlines a nuanced combination of moral and theological reasoning, focused pragmatism, and echoes of a violent history that inform African American attitudes related to guns.

The relationship between faith and firearms has been an understudied area. Many studies on gun attitudes and practices were conducted in the 1980s, before Congress limited and then cut off funding for gun studies by the Centers for Disease Control and Prevention in 1996.[1] Further, the focus on religion as a variable in the construction of meanings around gun ownership, violence, and regulation has received even less attention. New quantitative studies by David Yamane, Carson Mencken, and Paul Froese at Baylor supplement earlier work by Public Religion Research Institute (PRRI) on race, religion, and guns.[2] Other studies, by Pew and soon-to-be-published research by Harvard and Northeastern scholars offer current data on gun ownership and attitudes across many variables, including race but not religion.[3] Research related to the critical issue of "God and guns" is shallow, but it appears to be growing.

Background

According to a Harvard/Northeastern study, handgun ownership grew by 71 percent between 1994 and 2015, even as gun violence decreased. Pew data show personal protection is now the primary reason given for handgun acquisition (48 percent) and is reflected in the increase in female gun owners who feel more at risk.[4] While the percentage of personal gun ownership overall is decreasing slightly (down from 25 percent to now 22 percent), there is a phenomenon of stockpiling, with 3 percent of

1. Michael Hiltzik, "The NRA Has Blocked Gun Violence Research for 20 Years. Let's End Its Stranglehold on Science," June 14, 2016, ahttp://www.latimes.com/business/hiltzik/la-fi-hiltzik-gun-research-funding-20160614-snap-story.html.

2. David Yamane, "Awash in a Sea of Faith and Firearms: Rediscovering the Connection between Religion and Gun Ownership in America," *Journal for the Scientific Study of Religion* 55, no. 3 (September 2016); F. Carson Mencken and Paul Froese, 2014, "In the Valley (the Grip?) of the Gun: Measuring America's Gun Culture," unpublished paper presented at the annual meeting of the Society for the Scientific Study of Religion, Indianapolis, IN; and Daniel Cox and Robert Jones, "A Slim Majority of Americans Support Passing Stricter Gun Laws," August 15, 2012, http://www.prri.org/research/august-2012-prri-rns-survey/.

3. Pew Research Center, "Gun Rights vs. Gun Control," August 26, 2016, http://www.people-press.org/2016/08/26/gun-rights-vs-gun-control/#race; and Lois Beckett, "Gun Inequality: U.S. Study Charts Rise of Hardcore Super Owners," September 19, 2016, https://www.theguardian.com/us-news/2016/sep/19/us-gun-ownership-survey.

4. Pew Research Center reports 32 percent of men and 12 percent of women own guns (up from 9 percent in 1994). Pew Research Center, "Why Own a Gun? Protection Is Now Top Reason," March 14, 2013, http://www.people-press.org/2013/03/12/why-own-a-gun-protection-is-now-top-reason/.

American adults having 50 percent of all guns in circulation—averaging 17 guns each.[5]

Different patterns of gun ownership emerge by race. Pew data from 2013 show 31 percent of whites as opposed to 15 percent of African Americans personally own guns.[6] Similarly, 2015 Harvard/Northeastern data put the percentage of white individual handgun ownership at 25 percent but only 14 percent for African Americans.[7] Other data identify gun ownership by household, but the trends of lower rates in African American households remain consistent. Only recently has research begun to consider religion as a variable, so sources are sparse. Consider these 2012 findings from PRRI displayed in figure 1.[8] The patterns of race are consistent with the individual data; non-whites have less than half the proportion of gun-owning households of whites (51 percent vs. 23 percent). When breaking out by religion, Protestants show higher rates of gun ownership, and Evangelicals have the highest level of any religious group shown here—58 percent compared to 42 percent of all sampled. The Catholic rate is well below national standards, at 32 percent. Dan Cox of PRRI reported, however, when separating out ethnic groups, white Catholics look much like the national sample (at 43 percent), but Latino Catholic households are much less likely to own guns (24 percent).[9] These

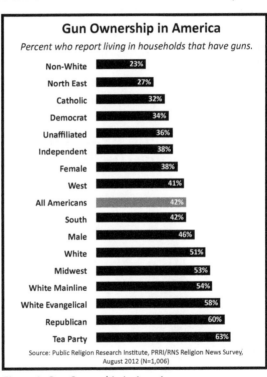

Figure 1: Gun Ownership in America

5. Ibid.

6. Pew Research Center, "Gun Ownership Trends and Demographics," March 12, 2013, http://www.people-press.org/2013/03/12/section-3-gun-ownership-trends-and-demographics/.

7. Beckett, "Gun Inequality."

8. Cox and Jones, "A Slim Majority of Americans Support Passing Stricter Gun Laws."

9. Additional data provided to author by PRRI from their 2012 data set, November 5, 2015.

data suggest that ethnic minority status is not highly correlated with gun ownership within a religious tradition.

Other research on attitudes toward gun laws shows, again, different patterns by racial groups. Trends in Pew Research show increasing support for "gun rights" over "gun control."[10] Their data found that whites more strongly support gun rights (55 percent) over gun control (42 percent). For African Americans, the opposite is true: 3 out of 4 support stronger gun control and only 1 of 4 support expanding gun rights.

Other research from Baylor University found that as white men felt increasing anxiety about their personal economic situation, their attachment to guns increased, but for non-white men the opposite was true: the more "economic despair" they reported, the less they looked to guns for a sense of safety and empowerment.[11] This same study found the more religious a person reported being, the less attachment he felt toward guns. But again, there was a racial difference. For white men, their religious faith weakened their "gun empowerment," but only slightly. Religion had a much greater impact on attachment to guns for black respondents.

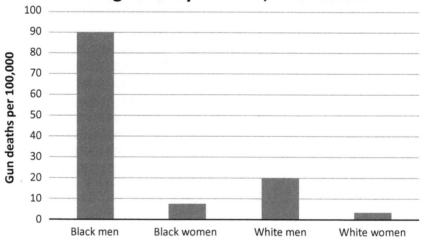

U.S. gun deaths by race and gender among 20–29 year-olds, 2011–2013

Note: These figures have all been calculated using a 2011–2013 average to smooth single-year fluctuations.
Source: CDC Injury Prevention & Control database.

BROOKINGS

Figure 2: U.S. Gun Deaths

10. Pew Research Center, "Gun Rights vs. Gun Control."
11. Mencken and Froese, "In the Valley (the Grip?) of the Gun."

In summary, African Americans as a whole have different attitudes toward guns than do whites. This raises two questions: First, since the top motivation for gun ownership is personal protection, why are African Americans who have been and remain more at risk than white Americans not rushing to arm themselves? Second, given that African Americans are much more likely to be victims of gun violence than whites (see figure 2), how are religious belief and practice mediating a response to gun violence among this constituency? How are African American Protestants (mostly Evangelical in their theology) constructing meanings of security and protection as well as gun ownership and regulation?

Churches, Guns, and Staying Safe

I have been conducting lengthy interviews with African American clergy and church members about gun violence (including leaders of programs addressing gun violence and people of faith stymied by this complex issue). Virtually every black churchperson I interviewed in my research reported their lives had "been touched" by gun violence—that is, they had lost family members, friends, and neighbors. For these persons this issue was not abstract or just another news story. All the clergy had done funerals, "too many funerals," for victims of gun violence.[12] When asked about why there is lower gun ownership in the African American community, there were two general interpretations. Those who did not question the lower levels of gun ownership attributed it to financial inaccessibility or being "disassociated from the NRA." But their first response was consistently, "Black Christians believe God will protect them" and, therefore, they do not need guns.

Most informants, however, questioned the reliability of the numbers, feeling that African American gun ownership was greatly underreported. Explanations for underreporting were revealing. Some felt many owned guns illegally and did not want to reveal that to a pollster. Often respondents referenced the complex history of African Americans and guns in this country, a historical memory that impacted their cautiousness. When referring to "our slave narrative," they recalled the fear of slave rebellions as deeply entrenched in the racial reasoning of states such as South Carolina (where whites were in the minority). In many states, white patrols could legally raid homes looking for weapons, and it was illegal

---

12. Although one clergywoman reported that they were "really memorial services because they can't afford funerals."

for slaves or free blacks to own guns. Of course, the very structure of white hegemony was maintained by guns. Still, some blacks armed themselves and, claiming citizen rights based on the equal protection clause guaranteed by the Fourteenth Amendment passed during Reconstruction, formed their own militias for protection during the nineteenth and twentieth centuries. The repercussions could be deadly, however, leading historians Robert Cottrol and Raymond Diamond to conclude: "When blacks used firearms to protect their rights, they were often partially successful but were ultimately doomed."[13] This history was no doubt a backdrop to a black respondent's explanation of African American reticence about revealing to a phone survey they owned guns: "A black guy with a gun strikes fear in the white imagination," an image that invites a violent response. Still, black respondents knew their parents' and grandparents' generation had quietly kept guns in their closets for protection, and those guns were sometimes passed down.

Despite the reasons for underreporting, a minority of the clergy interviewed revealed they were handgun owners, but none regularly carried them. They kept the guns locked up. The theological frame used in interpreting gun ownership always stressed the prior source of security in God. One African Methodist Episcopal (A.M.E.) pastor (who owned a handgun) was typical in expressing what was heard from many: "They [guns] might protect you but they won't save you. Ultimately, God is in control." A Christian's "walk of faith," stressed several preachers, is incompatible with a reliance on firearms.

No one felt the tragedy in Charleston could have been stopped had one of the members been armed. They spoke of mental illness, racist hatred, the advantage of preparation, and the element of surprise. No intervention could have stopped the attack yet this did not seem to create a theological question of theodicy for them; no one in my research so far has spoken in fatalistic terms of this tragedy being "God's will" or that God's hand was somehow in the act of violence. God's agency was in being present with the victims and later their families, rather than preventing the tragedy. Those interviewed do not speak of God's protection in terms of "magical thinking." God does not supernaturally rescue potential victims, but does work through relationships and community.

Despite the ease with which the interviewees would speak about God being the source of their security, this frame is tempered by a pragmatism

13. Robert J. Cottrol and Raymond T. Diamond, "The Second Amendment: Toward an Afro-Americanist Reconsideration," *Georgetown Law Journal* 80, no. 309 (1991): 353.

in preventing violence. There was speculation in the weeks following the tragedy in Charleston that African American churches would move toward having armed protection in worship.[14] According to journalistic accounts and my own research, African American churches have made changes toward securing worshipers, but these have largely been enhanced security systems rather than turning to guns. Indeed, the A.M.E. denomination issued a statement encouraging all of its congregations to review their security systems. Every African American congregation represented in this study had strengthened its security system after Charleston; only one reported that they had also incorporated armed guards in their security plan. Security enhancement in the last year usually included installing more security cameras, locking doors, posting "lookouts," having audio speakers at every entrance, and "men in suits" at doors and especially outside the "counting room" as "the money is usually counted by women." The one exception was an A.M.E. church that did have "armed security" because one or two retired police officers who attend the church often wore their guns to church. They were concealed, however, because, the pastor explained, "you just don't want to see guns in church." For this A.M.E. pastor, knowing there were a few guns as part of an enhanced surveillance system only added to the "feeling of security," and did not in any way undermine his commitment to God as the ultimate source of security. Further, all respondents were concerned there not be an impediment to worship. All were committed to "welcoming the stranger in our midst"—a commitment that Charleston had shown was so demonstrably risky.

Churches and the Urban Gun Culture

Gun ownership was not something often discussed in the congregation, but a few pastors reported they had preached about gun violence. A more troubling reality than the need to protect the congregation is the level of gun violence in the communities outside their walls. Black men are overwhelmingly the victims of gun homicides, and most of those murders are committed with illegally acquired weapons.[15] Acute awareness of the

14. See Tariro Meewa and Jessica Dinapoli, "African Americans Are Changing Their Views on Gun Control after the Charleston Massacre," Reuters, July 15, 2015; Tyler Pager, "After Charleston, Black Churches Straddle Fine Line between Security, Openness," *USA Today*, August 16, 2015; Tamara Audi, "Pastors Say Black Churches Need to Review Security," *Wall Street Journal*, June 18, 2015, among many articles on church security.
15. This is usually through a practice called "straw buying," in which someone who cannot pass the required background check (because of a history including felony conviction or involuntary commitment in a mental health institution) pays someone with a "clean record" to purchase guns.

carnage in black communities caused by gun violence could very well contribute to the strong support for strengthening gun regulation.[16]

Few of those interviewed, however, expressed any hope changes in gun control would address the issue of gun violence. They did not see guns as the problem; rather, most articulated a well-developed analysis of the "root causes" of gun violence: mainly, years of inadequate policies in education, housing, job creation, and health care have colluded with institutional racism to create conditions for urban gun violence and mass incarceration. Exacerbating these urban dynamics is the high-profile shootings of black men by police. This social analysis does not focus responsibility solely on individuals but systems. Police are not seen as a source of protection, but of threat. In turn, police have often kept their distance from poor neighborhoods, allowing a gun culture to flourish with its norms and enforcement.[17] Interviewees reflected a more sympathetic view of those caught up in the street life and the "prison industrial complex."[18]

Given the critical understanding of the causes and dynamics of gun cultures, and being affected by it, there is still a social distance between the congregations studied and the street culture within urban neighborhoods.[19] Some spoke of their sense of vulnerability, saying they were more fearful within their own neighborhoods, and less threatened by violence from whites. This is not surprising, in light of recent research on social mapping of perpetrators and victims of gun violence.[20] Interracial shootings are relatively rare; victims are overwhelmingly shot by those within their racial group. "You hurt people who are a lot like you," says David Kennedy, a professor and director of the National Network for Safe Communities at John Jay College of Criminal Justice in New York City. "That's how it works."[21]

16. Pew Research Center, "Gun Rights vs. Gun Control."

17. Jill Leovy, *Ghettoside: A True Story of Murder in America* (New York: Spiegel and Grau/ Random House, 2015).

18. See discussion of earlier studies in Yamane.

19. Jill Leovy, *Ghettoside: A True Story of Murder in America* (New York: Spiegel and Grau/ Random House, 2015).

20. See David Kirk, Andrew Papachristos, National Institute of Justice, *The Structural and Cultural Dynamics of Neighborhood Violence* (New York: Scholars Choice, 2015).

21. "Race and Homicide in America, by the Numbers," *U.S. News and World Report*, September 29, 2016, https://www.usnews.com/news/articles/2016-09-29/race-and-homicide-in -america-by-the-numbers.

Models of Response

Churches in Charleston and denominational groups such as the Episcopal Church, the Presbyterian Church (U.S.A.), and the United Methodist Church are among those that have focused efforts on changing gun laws. Nevertheless, most African American congregations I have interviewed recognize that changes in gun laws alone, however welcome, would not adequately address the urban gun culture. Therefore, some congregations are trying to address the problem of black-on-black violence, employing a variety of approaches to address the gun violence that has taken away so many young black lives.

For example, proceeding from the premise that we need to get guns off the streets, many congregations work with police and municipal governments to organize gun buybacks. Here people can get cash for turning in weapons, no questions asked. Often though, people bring in old (even antique) or broken guns, which are not the firearms perpetuating the violence. Also, the numbers of weapons bought back rarely make a dent in the large pool of guns in the community.[22] Guns are so ubiquitous and accessible in some neighborhoods, one public school teacher told me: "It's easier for my students to get a gun than a textbook."

A second faith-based strategy to raise the public profile of gun violence and mobilize advocates can be seen in efforts by an interfaith group called Heeding God's Call to End Gun Violence. This group sponsors "Memorials to the Lost," a traveling installation that displays marked T-shirts representing local victims of gun violence from the previous year, mounted on stands, and placed on the lawns of churches, parks, and schools. The memorial attracts media and pedestrians who are encouraged to "remember, pray and act."

Among other holistic approaches with documented success is the Ten Point Coalition in Boston. This is a faith-based organization credited with "the Boston Miracle"—a 79 percent reduction in violent crime over eight years in the most troubled part of that city. Pastor Jeffrey Brown described the disconnect between churches and street culture in his neighborhood as having been huge: "It's like we were in two different worlds."[23] He began to preach about gun violence and the need to build

22. Kate Masters, "Police Trade Cash for Thousands of Guns Each Year. But Experts Say It Does Little to Stem Violence," The Trace, July 17, 2015, https://www.thetrace.org/2015/07/gun-buyback-study-effectivness/.
23. Rev. Jeffrey Brown, "How We Cut Youth Violence in Boston by 79 Percent," TED Talk, May 2015, https://www.ted.com/speakers/rev_jeffrey_brown.

community, but after a teen died near his church, he realized he was leaving out a whole group of people in his efforts: the youth gangs. He and other clergy began to go out at night to develop relationships with these young people and were surprised to find they were not cold and ruthless, but were "overcomers." The Ten Point Coalition was able to build partnerships with the youth to address gun violence by building trust and a shared commitment to safety and, indeed, to life. Over time, they developed partnerships with other community sectors, including "some" police, social workers, and other local leaders. This evolved into Cease-fire, a holistic community antiviolence effort that draws on the resources of congregations as partners and agents and is now a strategy being replicated in some cities.[24]

San Francisco Bay Area pastor Michael McBride is also an advocate of a holistic and community-based approach to gun violence, heading an effort called Lifelines to Healing/LIVE FREE, which is affiliated with the People Improving Communities through Organizing (PICO) community organizing network. The program includes outreach workers or "violence interrupters," many of whom were formerly incarcerated. Focusing on building relationships with young men at risk (as both victims and perpetrators), these mediators have been effective in violence-prone communities.[25]

Concluding Thoughts

African American Christians have a lot at stake in the struggle against gun violence. Even as those in black churches are more likely to eschew guns and support stronger laws, they are conducting far too many funerals as young lives in their community are unnecessarily cut short. The cultural gulf between the pews and the streets can be wide, but the carnage in black communities is compelling many to transcend their fear, frustration, and social distance to transform their neighborhoods and cities. Their systemic analysis reveals the complexity of the gun violence problem. There will be no easy fixes. But community-based, holistic initiatives are showing promising results, especially as congregations step in as partners in those efforts.

24. D. M. Kennedy, *Don't Shoot: One Man, a Street Fellowship and the End of Violence in Inner-City America* (New York: Bloomsbury, 2011).
25. Michael McBride, "Gun Violence, Race, and the Church," February 7, 2017, https://www
.faithandleadership.com/michael-mcbride-gun-violence-race-and-church.

Chapter 24

Theological Listening and Learning in an HIV/AIDS World

Donald E. Messer

Deep in the heart of Zambia, I was challenged to preach a sermon and demonstrate a condom at the same time! Quickly Christian theology moved beyond theory to practice. Let me explain.

At the invitation of Dr. Ronald E. Peters in 2007, I accompanied a group to Zambia where we were exploring how theological educators were dealing with HIV and AIDS in the midst of a global pandemic. Zambia has a national HIV prevalence rate of 17 percent among adults ages 15 to 49. Young women ages 25 to 34 are at a much higher risk of being infected than young men of the same age. About one million Zambians are living with HIV and unknown numbers have died from AIDS. More than one million AIDS orphans have been left to struggle for survival. Reports indicate that "unprotected heterosexual sex drives the Zambian HIV epidemic, with 90 percent of new infections recorded as a result of not using a condom."[1]

A Young Woman's Testimony

The first day of our conference with Presbyterian and Reformed theological educators, male leaders of the seminaries reported how they were dealing with HIV. Repeatedly they condemned the use of condoms. As a United Methodist visitor, I was truly surprised, since nothing I knew in Protestant theology forbids the use of condoms to protect human life.

Members of our group, as well as other Zambians, were concerned. At breakfast the second day, someone said, "Don, you're an outsider. In

1. See http://www.avert.org/professionals/hiv-around-world/sub-saharan-africa/zambia.

your speech today, you have to say something about condom use." Wanting to be culturally sensitive, and yet scientifically evidence-based in my presentation on prevention, I chose to speak on the Gospel text of John 10:10 (NRSV).

With some hesitancy, I decided I would, at an appropriate point, display a condom, while I was talking about how Jesus had come to bring life abundant, and that HIV, AIDS, and poverty were modern-day thieves that came to "steal and kill and destroy."

I intended to slip it back in my pocket and continue my sermon. But, unexpectedly, a Zambian woman in the back of the room interrupted me by shouting, "Are you going to open it?" In a flash I had to decide what I would do. Thus, began my impromptu positioning of the condom on my thumb, even as I asserted it needed to be placed on the penis!

Immediately when I finished speaking, a young twenty-plus-year-old Zambian woman raced to my side and began her testimony. She reported she was HIV positive, thanks to being infected by her late husband. She expressed gratitude for the sermon and stressed to the church leaders and theological educators the imperative of using condoms to prevent HIV infection. Her witness left the audience spellbound. Her candor and courage tore away religious hypocrisy and forced honest discussion of theology and human sexuality. As a result, the conference continued with a new degree of honesty and realism, and not once again did anyone publicly declare condoms as being antithetical to Christian teaching or practice.

The Pedagogy of Practical Theologians

This incident illustrates the "pedagogy of the oppressed" articulated by the Brazilian educator Paulo Freire in his book by the same name.[2] An understanding of Christian truth and theology did not emerge in Zambia primarily from sophisticated academics or established church leaders but instead from the life and witness of a poor woman who was stigmatized, ostracized, marginalized, and victimized in her society. Yes, as a theological educator, I did speak, but it took the goading of an unknown African woman in the back of the room and then the dramatic first-hand testament of an HIV-positive woman to transform the dialogue and bridge the distance between theory and practice.

The methodology of urban ministry has always been to value the opinions of the overlooked and to draw upon the spiritual experiences of

---

2. See Paulo Freire, *Pedagogy of the Oppressed* (New York: The Continuum Publishing Company, 1970, rev. 1999).

those deprived of a voice in the rarefied sanctuaries of the religious establishment. Practical theology is not a matter of translating doctrine or Christian social teachings for the poor and oppressed. Neither is it simply the articulation through preaching and teaching of core theological convictions. Rather it involves an encounter with life where it is lived—in the streets, in the marketplace, in the bedroom, and so forth. It involves listening and learning, reading and reflecting, testing and trying to find meaning and insight amid everyday happenstances.

HIV and AIDS provide an excellent case context for realizing that talk of urban, suburban, and rural cannot be easily separated and segregated. Zambia illustrates how a disease like HIV flows geographically and cannot be isolated. In a global society, a new strain of HIV that appears one day in Thailand will soon find its way to Manhattan, Berlin, or an Alabama village. What happens in Lusaka does not stay in Lusaka, but spreads out across the countryside. Whether it is transported by a passenger on the next jet plane out of Asia or by a truck driver moving down the roads of Africa, HIV leaps boundaries and often finds a nesting place among the uneducated and impoverished.

Theological educators and religious leaders bear considerable responsibility for helping to fuel the HIV and AIDS pandemic globally. Their denial of the realities of human sexuality, and their propensity for either encouraging silence about sexual health or condemning persons for their sexual orientation and expressions, have made efforts to curtail the spread of HIV very problematic. Cindy Patton in *Globalizing AIDS* speaks of how "malign neglect has been the norm in a century of miracle cures. Millions of people had suffered or died of starvation and preventable diseases" at a time when intervention was possible.[3]

Instead of thanking God for condoms, church people have been too embarrassed to deal with sexuality, or too busy hypothesizing about the possibilities of promiscuity.[4] Instead of embracing family planning, reproductive health, and prophylactic methods for curtailing the spread of HIV, religious writers and speakers have dwelt in a spiritual fantasyland. As Melinda Gates once said, "In the fight against AIDS, condoms save lives. If you oppose the distribution of condoms, something is more important to you than saving lives."[5]

---

3. Cindy Patton, *Globalizing AIDS* (Minneapolis: University of Minnesota Press, 2002), xxii.

4. See Donald E. Messer, "Thank God for Condoms," in *Names, Not Just Numbers: Facing Global AIDS and World Hunger* (Golden, CO: Fulcrum Publishing Company, 2010), 93–112.

5. Melinda Gates cited in Donald E. Messer, *52 Ways to Create an AIDS-Free World* (Nashville: Fresh Air Books, 2009), 45.

At the heart of urban ministry is a commitment to save lives, not just from a spiritual perspective but in terms of reaching out to protect and preserve the mental and physical lives of people. Often understaffed and lacking sufficient resources, still churches in the heart of the city often epitomize the image of Jesus as the Great Physician, caring for those treated as "the least of these" by society.

Four Pedagogical Steps

The lessons to be learned from this incident in Zambia regarding pedagogy are at least four. First, there is the importance of immersion. Learning about life means stepping away from usual comfort zones and exploring unknown territories and venues in one's own neighborhood or in distant places. This is not a tourist theology, but a chance to listen and to learn from other cultures and people.

One summer when I was teaching a course on mission and evangelism, I learned my students numbered only four. I couldn't quite imagine my lecturing for hours every day and their being forced to sit endlessly at the seminary. So instead we turned my car into a classroom and we spent most of our time exploring the city, meeting people where they worked and ministered. Spending time in migrant second-language centers, talking with people lined up to get food, listening to the struggles of the homeless, and spending time in an AIDS clinic meant immersing ourselves into the Denver community. Textbooks were not abandoned, but our readings and discussions were supplemented with a reality that otherwise likely would have been absent.

Second, there is the value of involvement. Urban ministries inevitably emphasize practical internships that provide students an opportunity to be engaged in the community and church. During my seminary days at Boston University School of Theology in the 1960s, I had to choose between an assignment in a small Anglo suburban church or work in a struggling African American inner-city church. In retrospect, I realize how dramatically my life was changed because I chose the latter. I ended up working with a street gang of young boys, the "Grand Dukes," and became involved in the civil rights movement both in Boston and Selma. In Zambia, it was clear that those who only knew HIV and AIDS from a distance did not have the same perspective as the women who were involved personally with the challenges the disease posed to health and life in the church and community.

Third, there is the insight of experience. Doing theology requires various sources: Scripture, tradition, reason, and experience. Theological educators and seminaries often are heavy in Scripture and tradition but sometimes light on reason and experience. Early in the global AIDS pandemic, I was engaged in a workshop in India that was exploring the topic for the first time. One of the biblical scholars presented a paper tracing obscure ancient temple prostitution and asserted it had some relevance to the challenges facing India's health challenge.

I remember vividly my psychologist wife mumbling in despair about this "intellectual masturbation" that forfeited thoughtful practical theological assistance to an academic mishmash that may have sounded scholarly but offered nothing to promote the "abundant life" Jesus promised. Likewise in Zambia it was clear that the understanding of a young woman triumphed over the theological elders who were long into Scripture and tradition but short on experience and reason.

Fourth, there is the necessity of exposure. Understanding how God is at work in the world requires us to broaden our everyday exposure. All of us are limited by what we know and what we have experienced. The sociology of knowledge teaches us that we have all been shaped by our race, gender, culture, context, sexual orientation, nationality, and so on. Urban ministry particularly has been on the forefront of theological endeavors to move us at least a few steps beyond where we typically might be.

Elizabeth Pisani, in her book *The Wisdom of Whores: Bureaucrats, Brothels and the Business of AIDS*, challenged health scientists and policymakers to move beyond their statistical charts and be exposed to the world where people live and die. She writes that neither donors nor governments cared "about HIV unless we could show that it threatened the 'general population.'"[6] In other words, "the least of these"—the commercial sex workers, men who have sex with men, injecting drug users, transgendered persons, and the incarcerated—often have little value to either church or society. In Zambia today, like in much of Africa, data on "men who have sex with men (MSM) is almost nonexistent, with little knowledge of the HIV epidemic among this population." It is reported that "the illegal status, stigma and discrimination that MSM experience makes them a population that is difficult to reach with HIV prevention messages."[7] Thus, when I travel to Africa, I intentionally seek out members of the endangered LGBT community to offer support and also to expose my fellow travelers to the tragic and chronic human rights violations. What

---

6. Elizabeth Pisani, *The Wisdom of Whores: Bureaucrats, Brothels and the Business of AIDS* (New York: W. W. Norton & Company, 2008), 28.
7. See http://www.avert.org/professionals/hiv-around-world/sub-saharan-africa/zambia.

is always heart-breaking is that we can never tell people to turn to pastors for help because of the church's spiritual callousness.

The Journey from Head to Heart

Immersion, involvement, experience, and exposure deeply enrich the teaching/learning process. For many of us it is a long journey from our head to our heart—knowing what to do and actually doing it. These pedagogical steps help us broaden our horizons of human understanding and deepen our spiritual ties with God and neighbor. The unexpected visions and voices of the marginalized often speak with greater theological truth than those of us with years of credentials and yards of degrees. God often speaks through the cries from the streets and the voices of the incognito of our society.

Other times it is unexpected voices that rivet our attention, such as Elton John when he calls people to end stigma "rooted in moral or religious judgments," and to overcome our "intolerance and indifference" by preaching and practicing compassion. He claims an AIDS-free world is within our grasp: "We can cure this disease without a cure. We can end AIDS with love."[8]

Self-proclaimed as nonreligious, John yet speaks a theology rooted in biblical and Christian teachings. He points the way to health and hope by reminding us to practice what we preach and to embrace anew the non-stigmatizing ministry of Jesus, the great reformer, whose own pedagogy often reflected immersion, involvement, exposure, and experience. This conception of pedagogy bridges the gulf between theology and practice and allows us to participate in the transformation of the world.

In reframing urban ministry it is imperative to remember the words of Freire: "One cannot expect positive results from an educational or political action program which fails to respect the particular view of the world held by the people. Such a program constitutes cultural invasion, good intentions notwithstanding."[9]

8. Elton John, *Love Is the Cure: On Life, Loss, and the End of AIDS* (New York: Little, Brown & Company, 2012), 109, 213, 123, 207.

9. Freire, *Pedagogy of the Oppressed*, 95.

Chapter 25

Public Leadership and African Churches in the United Kingdom

Israel Oluwole Olofinjana

Black-majority churches in the United Kingdom (U.K.), of which African churches are part, have experienced phenomenal growth within a short period of seventy years. This growth began in earnest with the arrival of the *Empire Windrush*, the famous ship that brought Caribbean migrants in 1948. This growth trend has continued into the present, as evidenced by the expanding profile of one such church group, the Redeemed Christian Church of God, a multicultural, evangelical ministry that is the fastest growing denomination in the United Kingdom.

While the initial waves of black immigrants to the United Kingdom tended to come mainly from the Caribbean, African immigrants were arriving in increasing numbers by the 1960s, forming churches of their own upon their arrival in the United Kingdom. These African churches in the United Kingdom have come a long way since their inception in the 1960s, advancing from serving mainly as "sanctuaries" or "refuges" for marginalized African migrants to now more influential multicultural and multiethnic churches engaged with the community. In fact, less cautious toward their adopted U.K. context than perhaps initial waves of African migrants to the United Kingdom, contemporary African Christians within the U.K. context appear to be articulating a theology of reverse mission that now sees the United Kingdom as a mission field.

While all of these developments are commendable, African churches must also develop creative and innovative contextual ministry practices that will move us from simply providing social services to actively seeking the transformation of society. These churches have to address issues of structure in ways that will bring lasting socio-economic and political change within society. Social services such as food banks, winter night

209

shelters, and debt counseling are important, and African churches do these things very well. But bringing about systemic and structural change will mean doing more to address institutional racism, unemployment, poverty, underachievement in education, and inequalities in the health system, immigration policies, and the criminal justice system. These are issues that disproportionately affect three categories of people in Britain: migrants, deprived ethnic communities, and the white working class.

I consider four factors that can move African churches from provision of social services to affecting structural changes in society. These four factors are the development of transformational theologies, prophetic witness, training and development of professional laity, and intercultural ecumenical partnerships. The discussion of African churches in this chapter includes numerous types and varieties of African churches in the United Kingdom, such as African-initiated churches, African New Pentecostal churches, and African congregations within historic churches. In assessing the public leadership of these churches, I draw at points on the historical example of Daniels Ekarté (1890s–1964), a social activist and pioneering leader among African and Caribbean churches in Britain who migrated to the city of Liverpool in 1915 as a seaman.

Toward Structural Change in Society

An often voiced concern in the United Kingdom today is that churches within the nation, including black-majority churches, have become too middle class in their thinking to relate to the working class. It appears we are distant from people's existential realities as we worship in our comfortable megachurches or big Christian festivals and events. Churches in the United Kingdom must surely find ways to connect with the working classes.

African churches in particular must be concerned about people suffering from poverty, oppression, and injustice, given the disproportionate social hardships faced by African peoples locally and around the globe. African churches will need to espouse a new hermeneutic—a hermeneutic that will allow them to consider social action to be as scriptural a ministry as evangelism. The majority of African churches are actively involved in evangelism, but what is lacking among some is social action. Some of these churches view social action as good works that might not necessarily be God-inspired. This is a faulty hermeneutic considering the fact that Jesus sided with the poor. Jesus preached and taught the gospel, but he also fed the 5,000 with bread and fishes. The apostle James acknowledged that faith without action is useless (Jas. 2:14–26). Therefore, if African churches claim to be people of the book (the Bible), then they must take these teachings very seriously.

If they do embrace this hermeneutic their ministry will become more credible to the wider British society. But, whether that is the case or not, they will be fulfilling a necessary role as agents of transformation and liberation on behalf of those who are hurting and struggling within society. The financial power these churches amass through prosperity preaching can be directed to the cause of the poor and the oppressed. For example, there is an urgent need for churches to get behind efforts to abolish modern-day slavery and human trafficking impacting U.K. society and elsewhere, especially the victimization of large numbers of African women and children in the form of prostitution, child labor, organized crime, and drugs and arms dealing.

There are para-church organizations fighting these causes such as STOP THE TRAFFIK, Jubilee Action, A21 Campaign, and International Justice Mission (IJM). These para-church organizations often lack financial resources to battle the huge demands of the problems at hand. Some African churches have resources that could be used toward some of these projects. Making their resources available or using them to start similar projects would be a worthy cause to follow, but it seems that many prosperous African churches prefer spending money to promote their church festivals, conferences, and seminars rather than engaging in relief work.

Nevertheless, not all African churches neglect social and political action. Quite a few have recently risen to the task, such as Musama Disco Christo Church, whose social action projects include immigration services. Also, there are at least a dozen or so black-majority church leaders with noteworthy social action ministries and deep commitments to impacting the social context.[1] Much wider participation among black church leaders is needed, however, if we are going to move from influence

---

1. Those leaders would include Nims Obunge (founder of Peace Alliance), Celia Apeagyei-Collins (founder of Rehoboth Foundations), Les Isaac (founder of Street Pastors), Jonathan Oloyede (convener of National Day of Prayer, UK), Dionne Gravesande (head of churches at Christian Aid), Agu Irukwe (senior pastor of the Redeemed Christian Church of God's main congregation in London), Joe Aldred (Steering Group of National Church Leaders' Forum), Donnett Thomas (former chair of Churches Together in South London), Joel Edwards (advocacy director, Christian Solidarity Worldwide), David Muir (founder of Faith in Britain), Ade Omooba (director of Christian Concern for Our Nation), and Kate Coleman (director of Next Leadership). All have a made conscious effort to influence change in society.

to impact. In the words of Joel Edwards: "Impact goes beyond influence. I don't really care where you come from in the missionary enterprise, structural change is part and parcel of that mission, and that is a part of the challenge facing those of us from ethnic minorities. And I think this is about dialogue and partnership."[2]

How Can African Churches Affect Systemic and Structural Change in Society?

If African churches are to have an expanded social impact, firstly we must develop or adopt a theology that will have at the heart of its agenda the transformation of society. African churches today could look to an African church leader from a much earlier context of ministry within the United Kingdom for cues—Daniels Ekarté, who migrated from Calabar, Nigeria, to Liverpool in 1915. During Ekarté's early-twentieth-century ministry in Liverpool, black and Asian minorities in Liverpool suffered many effects of institutional racism, including poverty, unemployment, rejection of mixed-race children, and various forms of social deprivation. Ekarté as a socially conscious public and church leader responded to these urban challenges by founding in 1931 one of the first African churches in Britain, a socially active ministry called African Churches Mission (ACM).

Ekarté's reading of the urban ministry context of Liverpool in the 1930s led him to view God as the God of the poor and the oppressed and led him to engage in social action on behalf of the poor, including using ACM as an orphanage and a place for the marginalized and destitute. His understanding of God and his experience and knowledge of Africa's colonial history propelled him, like the Old Testament prophets, to speak out against inequalities such as institutional racism. It is worth mentioning that Ekarté was involved in the Pan Africanist and African Nationalist movements that led to the decolonization of African states from the late 1950s. He had good relationships with and supported African Nationalist leaders such as Nnamdi Azikiwe from Nigeria, Kwame Nkrumah from Ghana, Hastings Banda from Malawi, and Jomo Kenyatta from Kenya.[3]

As Ekarté's example suggests, developing a theology seeking to transform society will require African churches (including African Pentecostal

2. Israel Olofinjana, ed., *Turning the Tables on Mission: Stories of Christians from the Global South in the UK* (London: Instant Apostle, 2013), 220.

3. Marika Sherwood, *Pastor Daniels Ekarte and the Africa Churches Mission Liverpool, 1931–1964* (London: Savannah Press, 1994), 80. All these men later became presidents of their respective countries.

churches) to engage with broader activist discourses, especially via black British theology, African theology of liberation, and postcolonial theologies.[4] Theological development along these lines will require scholars and practitioners to overcome the dichotomies usually existing between them. National Church Leaders Forum (NCLF), a representative body of black churches in the United Kingdom, appears to be doing this at the moment by bringing together black British theologians and African leaders in order to educate and mobilize black-majority churches for political action.[5] Of particular note, NCLF has put together a black church political manifesto in 2015 whose objective was to encourage more active citizenship and advocacy on behalf of the common good by African and Caribbean churches and the wider black community.[6] The political manifesto, a first of its kind, addresses topics such as policing and criminal justice, mental health, voting and political mobilization, and international aid and development.

Certainly, being prophetic in advocating for the poor and against unjust structures will require boldness from pastors not only from the pulpit on Sundays but also in the public square during the week. But it is also important to understand, pastors cannot transform structures by themselves. We need professionals in our churches—politicians, doctors, lawyers, health workers, diplomats, bankers, professors, entrepreneurs—and we must also do what we can to help our members move into professional careers and leadership. Several African churches are doing this well, including the Redeemed Christian Church of God. One of its congregations, Trinity Chapel in London, includes the following tagline in its vision statement: "Developing Leaders: Influencing Society." Also, Jesus House in North London, the flagship church of Redeemed Christian Church of God in the United Kingdom, launched in 2013 a new

---

4. It must be clarified here that the Caribbean Pentecostal churches that started around the 1940s–1960s and some of the BMCs within historic churches are engaging with black and liberation theologies. Examples are Robert Beckford, whose background is Caribbean Pentecostal (Wesleyan Holiness Church), and Anthony Reddie, whose churchmanship is within the historic church (Methodist). It appears that it is the African Pentecostal churches that are distanced from these theologies.

5. NCLF is a national voice of the black church in Britain seeking to represent black-majority churches' interests and concerns through representation, advocacy, political education and action, and the media. It started in 2011 after the demise of the African and Caribbean Evangelical Alliance. The steering group is made up of church leaders, activists, and theologians from the African and Caribbean Christian communities.

6. National Church Leaders Forum, *Black Church Political Mobilisation: A Manifesto for Action* (produced by NCLF, 2014).

social enterprise, the Barnet Youth Business Incubator, to equip young people to start their own businesses. The project operates run in partnership with a youth charity called Elevation Networks and a governmental entity called Barnet Council. The project supports more than one hundred young people between the ages of sixteen and twenty-four who are interested in running their own business.[7]

In instances where African churches have influential professional leaders already existing in our churches, pastors and church leaders must encourage these leaders to engage with the sociopolitical issues affecting immigrants, deprived ethnic communities, and white working classes. African pastors cannot be content with simply having community leaders (including Members of Parliament or other political leaders) attending our Sunday services but then shy away from raising justice issues for these leaders to act upon. We must endeavor to speak truth to power even if it will mean losing some of these friendships and networks.

Last, African churches need to work in partnership with our white brothers and sisters to effect needed social change. It is interesting to note that Ekarté in his day cultivated ecumenical relationships with other churches such as the Church of England, the Catholic Church, and other church agencies.[8] Moreover, some of the people that worked at ACM were white.[9] Low-income whites also attended the services at ACM and benefited from its social activities. Ekarté's ecumenical commitments reveal that he recognized ACM was limited and that partners were needed to fulfill the church's mission.

Similarly, contemporary African churches will need to pursue more strategic leadership positions within U.K. church structures broadly speaking, including Bible colleges, mission organizations, and parachurch organizations. But these collaborations with white church structures cannot be done in a colonial manner, in which African Christians are still seen as inferiors. This will require that more of our African church leaders will need to undertake postgraduate studies, but any meaningful partnership with white churches will have to be based upon them seeing African church leaders as equals, including in educational attainment.

---

7. "Churches Raising New Generation of Entrepreneurs," *Christianity Today*, February 15, 2013, https://www.christiantoday.com/article/church.raising.new.generation.of.entrepreneurs /31645.htm.

8. Sherwood, *Pastor Daniels Ekarte*, 28–29.

9. Ibid., 38–39.

Concluding Thoughts

In conclusion, there is a clear need for African churches to become more engaged public leaders within British social affairs. To do so will require African churches to overcome unhelpful theological dichotomies between spiritual and social life, wariness toward theological training, and the wide chasm between black British theology and African church teachings and practice.

African churches in Britain must be challenged in the light of ACM's legacy and learn from their predecessor by engaging in systemic and structural issues in society. This will mean developing an authentic theology that can transform society, standing in the prophetic tradition and speaking against injustice, and developing professionals within the congregation. They will also need to recognize the need for partnership in God's kingdom. While African churches are still on a journey, there are signs such as the black church political manifesto that point in the right direction.

IV

Urban Ministry Adaptations

Chapter 26

Neighborhood and Congregational Renewal through Organization and Development

Phil Tom

I draw attention here to ongoing efforts by urban faith leaders to build broad-based and powerful coalitions for rebuilding the social, physical, and economic infrastructures of their communities. I have been a participant in these efforts, as learner, practitioner, leader, trainer, and now mentor for other faith leaders—committed to building urban communities and developing community partnerships between urban churches and community partners in the public and private sectors. I have had the opportunity to serve in small local organizations, churches, national organizations, and even the federal government. Each step of the way I have embraced and shared the lessons that allow us to empower communities through our faith.

During the 1950s and 1960s, as many whites and middle-class families fled major urban areas, these areas experienced significant loss of population and social capital, and economic disinvestment. It was said that the only institutions left in these communities were the liquor stores and the churches, and it became evident that if these communities were going to rebuild, then the key institution to lead the charge would be the churches. Many churches took up this charge and began reaching out beyond their four walls to mobilize their communities, addressing a variety of community issues such as abandoned and substandard housing, crime, inadequate city services, loss of jobs, and other persistent social problems. My first engagement with these mobilizations was in 1971 when I became involved with the First Presbyterian Church in the Woodlawn neighborhood on the Southside of Chicago—a neighborhood filled with abandoned and substandard housing, a significant loss of businesses and jobs, and experiencing numerous urban ills. Previously in 1960, First Church had worked with nearby churches, residents, and businesses to form The Woodlawn Organization (TWO) to address issues impacting the Woodlawn community. Like many Woodlawn residents, First Church members remained hopeful about their neighborhood, committed to rebuilding their neighborhood, block by block. For example, TWO successfully organized its community to battle the University of Chicago's plan to expand its campus into the Woodlawn neighborhood, which would have displaced low-income residents, the majority of whom were African American. TWO effectively used protests and boycotts to protect residents and advocate for their needs. Ultimately, a collaborative working relationship was established between TWO and the university that created new institutions in the Woodlawn area and gave residents a leadership role in decisions that impacted their community. During a time of major unrest in urban communities, TWO was the first of many urban broad-based community organizations across the country organized by the faith community.

As TWO and the churches in the Woodlawn neighborhood continued organizing their members and neighborhood residents to fight for justice, including pressuring the city of Chicago and other public and private institutions to improve the quality of neighborhood services, it expanded its mission to support community economic development. The coalition became a prime example of successful urban community building that incorporated both community organizing and development. TWO rehabbed and built houses, created jobs, and provided other essential services to the neighborhood in order to directly address some of the most pressing needs within the area.

As the community organizing movement grew, faith leaders learned from their organizing battles. It became clear for example that while you might win your fight with city hall to support the creation of more affordable housing units, you still had to fight to ensure the units were actually built, and by a trustworthy developer. We also learned that you could build new affordable housing units, but if the neighbors were not invested in the work of building up their neighborhood, then the economic gains for the community could become short-term.

In 1972, I continued my involvements with urban faith-based community building through participation in the Jesuit Agency for Organizing training program and through a position with the Community of United People (COUP), a neighborhood organization whose members consisted of African Americans, Hispanic Americans, and Latinos on the Near Westside of Chicago. There I met Tom Gaudette, who developed the

COUP training program in collaboration with the Archdiocese of Chicago to train priests and other faith leaders in organizing that effectively addresses issues impacting their urban communities. I also met Fr. John Bauman, director of COUP and later a cofounder of PICO National Network. These two men played a very significant role in shaping my ministry. I learned from them that it is essential to start with one-on-one conversations, to listen to people's dreams and concerns, to build relationships of trust, and to work on the issues raised by the people. These are the foundational steps for organizing and building community.

What I also learned in Chicago was the power urban congregations have to rebuild their communities through organizing and economic development work. I drew on these lessons and skills at the next two churches that I was called to serve: Dayton Avenue Presbyterian Church, a multiracial congregation in the inner-city Selby-Dale neighborhood in St. Paul, Minnesota; and then at Westminster Presbyterian Church, a smaller working-class congregation in Indianapolis, Indiana, whose neighborhood had experienced significant urban blight and flight. Both congregations worked with sister congregations and neighbors in addressing affordable housing limitations and economic disinvestment.

Unlike many urban congregations at this time preoccupied with self-survival, Westminster (a congregation with under one hundred members) was passionately committed to the vision and mission of building a strong and vibrant neighborhood for all of its residents. Westminster members believed its future vitality and health were intimately linked to the vitality and health of its neighborhood. Westminster helped create neighborhood organizations—the Near Eastside Community Organization (NESCO), then a few years later, Eastside Community Investments (ECI)—concerned with helping rebuild the neighborhood's housing and economic infrastructure. Over the years, ECI would build and rehab over one thousand affordable housing units, support the development of small businesses, and create new economic opportunities and jobs for many of its neighbors. Westminster members were heavily invested and involved with these two organizations.

During my thirteen years at Westminster Church, Westminster worked with its neighbors and community partners to develop a variety of community partnerships and ministries aimed at serving and strengthening its Near-Eastside community. Westminster helped create a new neighborhood association which successfully lobbied the Indianapolis City-County Council to designate its neighborhood as a site for federal block grant monies (funds that proved instrumental in helping the neighborhood rebuild its housing stock and public infrastructure). We worked with ECI to secure a $100,000 program-related investment from the Presbyterian Foundation (the first of its kind for the foundation) to help develop additional affordable housing. We forged a broad partnership with schools, churches, foundations, and businesses to create a health and mentoring program for teen mothers, an afterschool ministry for first- through sixth-graders, a legal assistance ministry, and a job training program for potential middle school dropouts. Working with eleven other congregations from the area and with a three-year grant from the Lilly Endowment, we formed the Near Eastside Church and Community Project (NECCMP), a project providing leadership training for congregations on neighborhood outreach and collaborative community building.

My experience at Westminster demonstrated that being a small church was not an obstacle to becoming an effective community builder. All of these ministries were vehicles for building relationships with our neighbors so that we could continue strengthening our community life together. Having vision, passion, a long-term commitment, and a willingness to get out beyond its four walls, to try to do something different, and to be willing to fail are essential qualities a church needs for urban community building. The combined effort of these congregations, working alongside community partners, transformed the life and mission of many of the congregations in this neighborhood.

Meanwhile, during the 1970s and 1980s, faith-based urban community organizing continued to gain momentum with the creation of national faith-based organizing groups such as PICO National Network in 1972, Direct Action and Research Training (DART) in 1977, and the Gamaliel Foundation in 1986. All of these organizations provided training for urban faith leaders on organizing and building up their communities. Along with the Industrial Areas Foundations, these four national faith-based organizing networks have continued to impact faith leaders in almost every major city in the United States and in cities abroad.

The success of the NECCMP led to the creation of the Church and Community Ministry Project in 1985, based at McCormick Theological Seminary in Chicago. This five-year project was funded by Lilly Endowment to work with forty congregations of diverse social, economic, racial, and denominational backgrounds in Illinois and Indiana to learn how to build social ministries that effectively meet the needs of their communities. Carl Dudley, professor of urban ministry at McCormick Seminary, served as director, and I served as codirector. Congregations learned to do direct outreach via one-on-ones with their neighbors, going from door to door or farmhouse to farmhouse.

One of the major insights gained from this undertaking was that money was not a primary factor in getting churches engaged in community building. While the project offered significant funding for the congregations that participated in the program, we were surprised at how many congregations turned down this offer. The congregations that wanted to rebuild their communities were led by pastors and leaders who were passionate about living out their faith by serving and strengthening their broader community. One success of this project was the Fountain Square Church and Community Ministry Project (FSCCMP) on the Southside of Indianapolis. Through direct conversations, neighborhood concerns over abandoned houses became apparent, and the project worked with the neighborhood on housing rehab. The first rehab was so successful that FSCCMP bought quite a few additional houses for rehab. This ministry continued to expand, and years later FSCCMP joined forces with another housing development organization in the neighborhood, rehabbing and building hundreds of affordable housing units and bringing significant economic resources and opportunities back into this once economically distressed neighborhood.

During the 1980s, numerous public and private entities such as the Ford Foundation, Enterprise Foundation, Lilly Endowment, the federal government's Housing and Urban Development department, state and municipal governments, the Local Initiative Support Corporation, and the Christian Community Development Association began to support and resource the work of faith-based community organizing efforts. My experience reflected this growing understanding of the importance of building relationships between public and private entities and between faith communities and neighborhoods.

I went on to serve as director of Community Development Corporations for the Indianapolis Neighborhood Partnership (INHP), a public-private partnership to rebuild the housing and economic infrastructure of many of Indianapolis's hardest-hit neighborhoods. Many faith leaders were passionate about helping to rebuild their communities but had not been provided through their pastoral or seminary experience with the necessary training. INHP provided the skills training to enable these leaders to turn their congregations into community builders. One of the many successes of this program occurred when neighbors and community partners created the Martindale-Brightwood Community Development Corporation (CDC), a neighborhood-level CDC that worked to rebuild its impoverished neighborhood by turning abandoned homes into safe and affordable units and by creating jobs and economic opportunities for its residents.

During the next thirteen years, I staffed the Urban Ministry Office in the national office of the Presbyterian Church (U.S.A.) where I was able to work with a wide variety of urban churches that in many cases were struggling just to survive. The Urban Ministry Office offered these congregations community organizing as a model for rebuilding their communities and for renewing and redeveloping their congregational life and mission. The office also provided funding, training, and technical assistance to assist these churches in becoming community builders. The training was provided in collaboration with IAF, PICO National Network, Gamaliel, DART, and other national advocacy organizations and drew many of the organizing techniques learned across several decades.

After many years of service from within churches and local community organizations, I was invited in 2010 to serve in President Obama's administration, working with the White House Office of Faith-Based and Neighborhood Partnerships as director of the Center for Faith-Based and Neighborhood Partnerships for the U.S. Department of Labor. With my colleagues at the White House and the other ten Federal Centers for Faith-Based and Neighborhood Partnerships, leaders of all faiths and national faith-based organizations were provided a wide variety of training and funding opportunities to assist them in addressing issues impacting their urban communities. At the Department of Labor, a common concern we heard from urban faith leaders was the lack of jobs and the deepening of long-term unemployment. Our office assisted these faith communities with partnering with local and state government entities, community colleges, local businesses, and the local workforce development board to develop strategies for effectively addressing job training and placement for their community residents. We also helped these faith communities organize or partner with the network of over 5,000 Job Clubs nationally that support and assist persons who are long-term unemployed.

Whether working at the neighborhood level or at the national level, my ministry has been devoted to assisting urban congregations in rebuilding their neighborhoods. Wherever there are passionate and committed faith leaders who by conviction of their faith feel it their calling to rebuild their communities, my calling has been and continues to be to support them as a partner and bridge builder that links them with the training, funding, resources, and potential partners that would assist them in fulfilling their community-building mission.

Chapter 27

Discernment, Attentiveness, and Church Planting in Urban Communities*

Christopher Brown

In the spring of 2014, a blogpost titled "Urban Church Planting Plantations" went viral among church planters and leaders of urban ministry.[1] Its author, Christena Cleveland, described how the economic redevelopment of Buffalo, New York, had attracted the interest of several wealthy suburban churches. Given the city's expected turnaround, these congregations started "planting" new ministries and churches back into an urban area they had once abandoned and neglected.

To those who have faithfully labored in urban environments through seasons of depression and desolation, this pattern of church planting smacks of colonialism, economic opportunism, and systemic racism. Lamenting the insensitivity of those who were founding and leading such new ministries, Cleveland wrote that across the United States she had repeatedly "seen predominantly white, wealthy suburban churches take an imperialistic glance at the urban center, decide that they are called to 'take back the city' and then proceed with all of the honor and finesse of a military invasion."[2] In Cleveland's observation, church planters who participate in these movements "charge into cities with blatant disregard

---

*This chapter contains content that was previously published in Christopher Brown and Johannes G. J. Swart, "Receptive to the Revelation: A Vision for the Future of the Church Planting Initiative at Pittsburgh Theological Seminary," *Pittsburgh Theological Seminary Journal* (Spring 2014): 15–24. Used with permission. The portions of that essay that pertain to the theory of church planting have here been adapted to be applied particularly within urban contexts.

1. Christena Cleveland, "Urban Church Planting Plantations," March 18, 2014, http://www.christenacleveland.com/blogarchive/2014/03/urban-church-plantations.

2. Ibid.

for the great ministry work that is already being done by under-resourced pastors and churches, blind to their own privilege and cultural incompetency, and accompanied by the arrogant empire-based idea that more money means more effective ministry."[3]

The trust that well-resourced suburban churches place in their wealth is revealed by their assumption that they can accomplish what under-resourced churches in the inner city cannot, despite vast cultural differences between their populations, most notably differing experiences of privilege and systemic injustice. When the church assumes that urban "families and communities are filled with needs that are best serviced" by outsiders, the church becomes "the essence of a consumer society."[4]

Conversely, the churches that trust in their wealth act as though increasing the number of giving units in their congregations will ensure future success in ministry. Such prosperous churches thus plant urban churches or satellite congregations in efforts to increase their market share. In a slip of the tongue that displays the way existing urban church leaders perceive the economic exploitation inherent in such movements, one Latina pastor described this pattern of imperialistic church planting as the formation of "urban church plantations."[5]

Cleveland's prophetic critique raises a number of significant questions about the theology and practice of church planting in an urban context. On what basis can Christian leaders presume to enter an existing community and claim any right to begin a new ministry? What postures ought such leaders take as they begin their work? How should a new ministry relate to existing ministries? Where is the Holy Spirit at work in the midst of such conflicts and questions?

The questions posed do not invalidate the entire concept or mission of church planting, but they do demand a fresh articulation of our theology of mission and an accounting of the potentials and perils of church planting in an urban environment. What is needed is a different vision of church planting, one which is rooted christologically in the humility of the incarnate Servant-Lord and grounded pneumatologically in the confidence that the Holy Spirit is already present and at work amid the communities to which God sends us. Accordingly, this vision of church planting calls us to surrender power and privilege and cooperate humbly

---

3. Ibid.

4. John McKnight and Peter Block, *The Abundant Community: Awakening the Power of Families and Neighborhoods* (San Francisco: Berrett-Koehler Publishers, 2012), 29.

5. Cleveland, "Urban Church Planting Plantations."

with God and God's people through practices of attentiveness and discernment. As John V. Taylor writes, "We must relinquish our missionary presuppositions and begin in the beginning with the Holy Spirit. This means humbly watching in any situation in which we find ourselves in order to learn what God is trying to do there, and then doing it with him."[6]

I explore these matters here as someone who has been involved with urban church planting and as a former director of the Church Planting Initiative at Pittsburgh Theological Seminary. The chapter draws on those experiences, and also points to examples of promising church planting practices in urban contexts.

New Ministry Contexts, New Relational Models

The church in the context of post-Christendom North America no longer occupies a privileged place in society. Rather, "Christianity in North America has moved (or been moved) away from its position of dominance as it has experienced the loss not only of numbers but of power and influence within society."[7] This means churches are being invited to adopt new forms of witness which can be practiced from postures of humility and powerlessness.[8] The cultural landscapes surrounding churches are also increasingly characterized by discontinuous change.[9] Factors such as rapid technological developments and movements of people groups combine in such a way that "uncertainty is the tenor of the times."[10] Such

6. John V. Taylor, *The Go-Between God: The Holy Spirit and Christian Mission* (London: SCM Press, 1972), 39.

7. Darrell L. Guder, ed., *Missional Church: A Vision for the Sending of the Church in North America* (Grand Rapids: Eerdmans, 1998), 1.

8. The term "missional church" was coined to describe the movement which is helping the church rediscover her missionary identity in a post-Christendom world. For tracing the development of the so-called missional conversation about the church's vocation in a post-Christendom North American context, see Craig van Gelder and Dwight Zscheile, *The Missional Church in Perspective: Mapping the Trends and Shaping the Conversation* (Grand Rapids: Baker, 2011). For more on the cultural dislocation of the church and changes facing the church, see also Patrick Keifert, *We Are Here Now: A New Missional Era* (Eagle, ID: Allelon, 2006).

9. In contrast to continuous change, which "develops out of what has gone before and therefore can be expected, anticipated, and managed," discontinuous change "is disruptive and unanticipated; it creates situations that challenge our assumptions." Alan Roxburgh and Fred Romanuk, *The Missional Leader: Equipping Your Church to Reach a Changing World* (San Francisco: Jossey-Bass, 2006), 7.

10. Alan Roxburgh, *The Sky is Falling!?!: Leaders Lost in Transition* (Eagle, ID: ACI Publishing, 2005), 40.

rapid discontinuous change seems to correlate to the destabilization of traditional church structures, forcing churches to become more nimble in order to respond to their varying contexts, whether urban, suburban, or rural.

As churches become increasingly aware of these changes, the Holy Spirit is also inspiring the development of new forms of Christian community with fresh expressions of worship and witness suited for these changing cultural contexts. As Darrell Guder has observed, "American indigenous churches" are proliferating across the country in myriad forms, including "so-called megachurches, as well as a staggering diversity of house churches, specialized fellowships, and genuinely new formations of Christian community."[11] These various forms of ministry have manifestations which affect urban contexts, often with varying degrees of positive and negative results.

Very specific leadership postures, habits, practices, and skills are required to initiate, cultivate, and sustain such new communities in ways that genuinely "seek the peace" of the neighborhoods in which they are situated.[12] These postures, habits, practices, and skills often stand in direct contrast to those employed by the more imperialistic models of church planting critiqued in Cleveland's article. Leaders who would humbly watch for what God is doing and seek to participate in the Spirit's formation of new communities must be formed and trained differently. With this in mind, Pittsburgh Theological Seminary developed an approach to initiating, cultivating, and sustaining new churches that could be described as *missional formation*.[13] Missional formation refers to the cultivation of the capacity to discern participation in the mission of God.[14]

---

11. Darrell L. Guder, "Leadership in New Congregations: New Church Development from the Perspective of Missional Theology," in *Extraordinary Leaders in Extraordinary Times: Unadorned Clay Pot Messengers*, ed. H. Stanley Wood (Grand Rapids: Eerdmans, 2006), 16.

12. On seeking the peace of the city, see Mark Gornick, *To Live in Peace: Biblical Faith and the Changing Inner City* (Grand Rapids: Eerdmans, 2002), 100–110; and Dan Steigerwald, *Growing Local Missionaries: Equipping Churches to Sow Shalom in Their Own Cultural Backyard* (Portland: Urban Loft Publishers, 2014), 37–79. For more on postures of leadership, see Tim Keel, *Intuitive Leadership: Embracing a Paradigm of Narrative, Metaphor, and Chaos* (Grand Rapids: Baker, 2007), 225–54.

13. The author served on staff as the Church Planting Initiative Coordinator at Pittsburgh Theological Seminary during the development of this approach. Faculty members who influenced this approach included Johannes G. J. (Jannie) Swart and Scott J. Hagley.

14. The term *missional* here refers to discerning participation in God's mission in the world. Formation refers to the cultivation of capacities such as postures, beliefs, attitudes, behavior, habits, practices, and skills.

In courses on church planting at Pittsburgh Theological Seminary, the components of this capacity were described with four "Fs": fellowship, focus, formation, faithfulness. Together, these four components include the primary postures, beliefs, attitudes, habits, practices, and skills to be cultivated for the sake of initiating and forming new Christian communities in the midst of the church's post-Christendom context.

This relational approach to formation puts *fellowship* at the core of what is at stake in forming Christian community.[15] Because the triune God is already at work in the world, the primary postures, habits, practices, and skills needed for leaders of new Christian communities are those which facilitate attentive listening to the Spirit so as to discern faithful participation in the mission of God. Thus we believe that the growth of new congregations that bear witness to Christ in their present contexts flows out of *fellowship* with the triune God and with the people *to* whom and *with* whom God sends us. As leaders pursue intimate fellowship with God and others, they cultivate the ability to sense and listen to the Holy Spirit's direction, sharpening their *focus* on the mission on which God sends them. Led by the Holy Spirit, these leaders participate in God's *formation* of a new Christian community among those to whom they are sent. These practices of fellowship, focus, and formation repeat continually throughout the ensuing life of the new community as its leaders dwell in *faithfulness* to God, to their calling, and to the people to whom God sends them.

In this approach it is clear that initiating, cultivating, and sustaining new Christian communities is first and foremost a matter of discernment in relationship with God and people rather than merely a functional matter of applying the right technology in planting a new church. According to John V. Taylor, "The main concern of any missionary training should be to help people become more receptive to the revelations of God."[16] Missional discernment refers to the church's capacity to receive God's gift of revelation in community with God and other people. This includes the ways in which churches or ministries operate in relation to one another. Church planting is by nature an ecclesial action. Therefore it cannot be carried out apart from the larger community of the Body of Christ. As Darrell Guder states, "It is clear from the New Testament

---

15. Fellowship here can be thought of in terms of the biblical concept of koinonia, implying the state of shared communion and joint participation which in the NT characterizes both the church as the body of Christ and the relationship of the church with the triune God.
16. Taylor, *The Go-Between God*, 70.

that God's Spirit forms a community for mission. God's call has always formed a people, a community, within which God was known, worshiped, made known, and served. . . . This community is, as ecclesia, called out and set apart for public witness, for demonstration before the world of the presence and power of Jesus the king."[17]

This "community for mission" is not just a given local congregation, but the entire church, for Jesus prayed that all his followers would be one so that the world would know he was sent by the Father (John 17:22–23). Leaders who are formed for missional discernment operate in community with the larger body of Christ in its myriad forms.

This approach to church planting emphasizes discernment and relationship and thus stands in contrast to approaches, methods, and models in which church planting is initiated by human beings and fulfilled through the sharpening of human skills. A church plant is not about a *commodity* we sell to other people; it refers to a *community* that God forms through us with other people. A church plant is not a vendor that *sells* religious goods to other people; it is a community shaped by *receiving* the gift of God's gathering of people. Church planting is not an *instrumental* matter of controlling and manipulating others into a new form of church; it is a *relational* matter of living faithfully in community with God and other people. Leaders who cultivate new Christian communities according to this approach must thus be formed relationally into people who attentively receive what God initiates and faithfully participate in the work God sustains.

New ministries which apply these principles in an urban context look remarkably different from services which import suburban models of church into urban neighborhoods undergoing gentrification. Instead, these new ministries humbly inhabit urban contexts and seek their peace in ways such as those Mark Gornick describes in his book *To Live in Peace: Biblical Faith and the Changing Inner City*.[18] Such new ministries begin with humility, seeking to remove the logs from their own eyes before addressing specks in others' eyes. As Gornick states, "Every church or ministry undertaking a development project needs to be acutely aware of the power of sin and the potential of the powers within its corporate identity."[19] Guarding against the sin of division in the Church, these new

---

17. Darrell L. Guder, *The Continuing Conversion of the Church* (Grand Rapids: Eerdmans, 2000), 68.
18. Gornick, *To Live in Peace*.
19. Ibid., 123.

ministries will also humbly operate in ways that listen to and seek unity with existing churches, ministries, and constituencies in a given context. From Gornick's perspective: "Reconciliation depends not on ignoring historic and present injustices, but on confronting them through the practices of repentance, forgiveness, and renunciation of status."[20] Members of such new churches then practice intentional "neighboring and friendship," developing authentic relationships which ensure that any plans for a new community "emerge out of genuine local ownership and responsibility."[21]

Faith Works, a ministry led by Presbyterian ruling elder Diane Anderson in Paterson, New Jersey, provides a positive example of the development of a new form of ministry in an urban context through practices of prayer, attentiveness, and communal discernment.[22] After learning about the Presbyterian Church (U.S.A.)'s 1001 New Worshiping Communities Initiative in 2014, Anderson found herself lying awake at night envisioning and praying about a new ministry which would connect her established urban church with those on the margins of society in their community.[23] Desiring to offer food and prayer for the prostitutes who worked the block behind the church building, Anderson first planned an event inviting the women into the church building for food. No one came. But Anderson treated the setback as an opportunity to seek guidance through prayer: "When we realized people were not going to come here for whatever it was we had, no matter how wonderful it was, then the Holy Spirit said, 'Get out of the box!'"[24]

Getting outside the box applied not just to the ministry, but to the very process of discernment Diane engaged in. While prayer-walking her neighborhood, Anderson noticed "people congregating at a Chinese restaurant, where the biggest seller was chicken wings."[25] Acting on her observations, Anderson decided to take chicken wings directly to the people to whom she was sent, meeting them on their own ground. What began as an evening of sharing chicken wings and taking prayer

20. Ibid., 86.
21. Ibid., 117, 120.
22. For a video depicting the ministry of Faith Works, see https://youtu.be/mV_pzcuV5KE.
23. For one report of Anderson's story, see Paul Seebeck, "Faith Works: New Worshiping Community Starts with 'Wings and Prayer,'" October 28, 2014, https://www.pcusa.org/news/2014/10/28/faith-works/.
24. 1001 New Worshiping Communities, "Faith Works: Wings and a Prayer," August 21, 2015, https://youtu.be/mV_pzcuV5KE.
25. Seebeck, "Faith Works."

requests—"Wings and a Prayer"—has turned into a ministry that now feeds up to a thousand people per month.[26]

Anderson's story is just one that displays the immense potential for faithful witness and community transformation that can be realized through practices of attentiveness to the Holy Spirit and communal discernment. In an interview with the Pittsburgh Theological Seminary Planting and Leading New Churches class in March 2016, Anderson emphasized the importance of listening to God in constant prayer. In addition to her own personal practices of piety, she and fellow people of faith meet regularly together to listen to God concerning their tasks and mission. After spending time in solitary worship and prayer, they come together to discern how to proceed in their ministry.

Similarly, the story of Faith Works displays the power of community in discernment. Faith Works operates using the space of and under the oversight of its parent congregation, the United Presbyterian Church of Paterson, New Jersey.[27] Other churches from the community partner with Faith Works across denominational lines, giving a sense of collaboration rather than competition in Christian outreach. Even more significant is the sense of collaboration Faith Works has with those whom it serves: the woman who was the "queen bee" on the block became Faith Works' greatest ambassador to the neighborhood, inviting others to receive food and prayer and vouching for the trustworthiness of the ministry.[28] This exemplifies the aforementioned "local ownership and responsibility" which should mark a locally discerned new ministry.[29]

As the story of Faith Works shows, when leaders of new worshiping communities in urban contexts discern a vision for a new ministry in collaboration with members of their neighborhood and other local church leaders, the new ministry can move forward in a way that genuinely seeks the peace of its context and earns the respect of its neighbors. Such an approach yields not plantations but new churches planted and watered by humble apostles and grown through the power and presence of the Holy Spirit made manifest in local communities.

---

26. As reported Diane Anderson in an interview with the Pittsburgh Theological Seminary "Planting and Leading New Churches" class on March 31, 2016.
27. In March 2016 Anderson was preaching regularly and leading the established congregation at the United Presbyterian Church of Paterson while they went through a pastoral transition.
28. Seebeck, "Faith Works."
29. Gornick, *To Live in Peace*, 120.

Chapter 28

Ministry, Diversity, and Community on an Urban University Campus

Jewelnel Davis

Almost forty years in university chaplaincy has allowed me to meet many young people who are struggling with issues of faith, spirituality, social justice, leadership, learning, and perhaps most of all, identity. Struggles with identity manifest both in the way students engage with the world based on their socio-demographic identity and in the way the world responds to them.

Student identities move along many trajectories—and those representations on a global research university campus in cosmopolitan New York City will be especially diverse. Students travel to Columbia University from many countries to study, and both the international students and American students are acutely aware of their personal and multifaceted identities. They come from varied religious backgrounds, as visible Muslims, Sikhs, or Jews. They come with various racial identities, ethnic identities, and sexual orientations.

They bring with them difficult questions about their lives. "I am addicted to heroin, and don't know what to do about it." "I met my boyfriend on a hook-up app and I don't know how to explain that to my parents." "I have been funding my education through a sugar mama or a sugar daddy." "I do not understand what my ex-girlfriend meant when she said I didn't respect her sexually and intellectually." "How do I tell my parents that I can't go home again and be the daughter that will tend to them in their old age?" "I never meant it to happen, but I am in love with someone who is of a different race or religion than my own; I do not know if I am able to manage my family's disappointment." These are the kinds of struggles students raise with university chaplains: struggles of heartache and their soul's pain.

233

Students who find their way to a university chaplain's office come seeking many things. They come seeking a sense of community, hoping to find other students like themselves and hoping to create fellowship spaces with likeminded individuals. Students want to see themselves mirrored in the student body and faculty, and expect administrators to take seriously the vulnerabilities that may attach to their specific identities. They wonder whether they will be safe, or how their education may be affected if they cannot find needed affinity group networks or support systems.

In response, I consistently wrestle with how an office of the university chaplain at a global research university can best serve a large cosmopolitan community of students, faculty, and administrators and meet this community on its terms. I must find ways to effectively communicate with these constituencies and authentically walk alongside them in their pursuits of the deeper meanings of their lives. I outline below additional details pertaining to the intensities of identity among cosmopolitan students and responses generated from a university chaplaincy.

Campus and Community Ministry Challenges

An office of the university chaplain at a global research university must see as its primary mission assisting students in their understanding of the connections between faith and learning. Availability for personal and pastoral counseling is important as students face crises, questions, and challenges in their academic and personal lives. Supporting spirituality in the broadest contours possible is essential for a university chaplain; this has to be authentic and it has to be reaffirmed regularly and publicly.

For our students, spirituality has mostly to do with dimensions related to personal meaning and purpose and rarely with matters related to dogma, rites, or rituals of a specific faith tradition. Students looking for the dimmest glimmer of spiritual guidance may very well talk with a university chaplain about the frayed edges of their hope, the depression that has overwhelmed their dreams, the frenzy of anxieties that have taken them to the brink of despair. A university chaplain is one more resource that students may trust to help them get the support they need from the university, from their families, from other resources in the neighborhoods surrounding the university.

The majority of young people on most university or college campuses in the United States are "unchurched," meaning they do not actively belong to any worship community. They attend no weekly religious services, no Bible studies, no community churches, or other houses of worship. Many approach Shabbat, the Sabbath, Saturday and Sunday, as time to relax, hang out with friends, sleep late, go to the mall, enjoy bottomless Bloody Marys while brunch hopping, catching up on the laundry, going for a run, or putting in a few hours of homework. Many students have had no religious upbringing except perhaps the annual trips to synagogue for the High Holy Days, the occasional visit to the church of a grandmother, the cultural experience of traditions like Diwali, Hanukah, or Christmas, the family gatherings for Passover Seder, the Eid feast, or Easter dinner. Students may occasionally watch a televangelist on YouTube, or even enroll in a humanities class that teaches the "Bible as literature."

Many students operate with unsystematic, hypercritical, stereotypical, or secondhand notions about religious faith or practice. Many believe faith communities have lost their integrity and their relevance. These students have been raised in environments where independent thinking is considered essential. The "do-it-yourself" attitude on the part of these young people, combined with a growing distrust toward institutions within the broader American culture, leaves many students wary of organized faith communities. These students opt instead for a more spiritual approach toward faith, or for more social or political avenues through which to express their faith instincts.

In response to these realities, I saw an urgent need to create a training space for new chaplains and established Religious Life Fellow positions within the university. These Fellows were recent seminary graduates who competed in a national search to fill these positions. These Religious Life Fellows, who are given substantial chaplaincy program responsibilities, are well positioned to relate to and interact with the student body based on proximities between their ages and life perspectives. The student body has been responsive to these Religious Life Fellows, as evidenced by increased student participation in programming activities and physical presence within the office—including for purposes of conversation with and counsel from Religious Life Fellows.

This is not to say there is not an active body of students participating in more traditional campus worship and ministry activities. Catholic campus ministries tend to thrive on university campuses. Sunday masses tend to be well attended, and priests are sought out for spiritual direction, personal counseling, and premarital advice. I have seen Mainline Protestant, clergy-led campus ministries struggle more than Catholics to attract and retain students. Regular participation in the activities of these ministries is likely to be less than twenty-five or thirty students a week—the exception being when these ministries include opportunities for community service such as tutoring children or serving in community lunch programs or local homeless shelters.

University students seeking affiliations with Protestant Christian communities tend to find themselves in student-led evangelical and nondenominational movements like the Intervarsity Christian Fellowship. Often students are attracted to culturally connected faith groups like Asian American Christian Fellowship and Asian Baptist Student Koinonia, or Faith in Action Sports, where faith is bundled into the reality of life. These various organizations across the university campus, including the more traditional denominational programs, are addressing the needs for greater demonstrations of intersectionality of faith, culture, and daily life.

Ensuring that students from across the diverse campus landscape view the university chaplaincy spaces and programs as welcoming and safe is a priority, especially given the more evident embodiments and expressions of cultural difference on cosmopolitan campuses such as Columbia. At Columbia, non-Christian and culture-specific student groups have become more vocal in the request to be acknowledged, represented, and protected within and by the university. In light of attacks on human life in Paris, Russia, San Bernardino, and across the globe, Muslim students have shared with us their increasing fears of being able to practice their faith safely within New York City's highly visible, closely watched urban setting.[1] Muslim women in particular, who choose to wear hijab, feel they are especially vulnerable to anti-Islamic sentiments.

To address this urgent need for support of Muslim students, we have provided spaces where students were free to voice their fears and concerns, be listened to and represented, and gather for prayer at appropriate prayer times throughout the day. Also, additional access to local Muslim Imams has been facilitated by adding a special adviser to the chaplain's office regarding Muslim life. Hindu and Native American students have also become more vocal about their needs, including requesting designated space for meditation, prayer, and quiet reflection. These spaces require allowances for smoke and candles, for example, which are essential for their ritual practice. Within the university setting, creating these spaces requires extensive planning and organization across many departments.

1. Eric Lichtblau, "Crimes against Muslim Americans and Mosques Rise Sharply," *New York Times*, December 17, 2015, https://www.nytimes.com/2015/12/18/us/politics/crimes-against -muslim-americans-and-mosques-rise-sharply.html.

Facilitating opportunities for students to act upon their faith is also essential.

Columbia University is known for being the most progressive of the Ivy League schools, possibly because the campus is located in upper Manhattan rather than in a small-town setting like many colleges and universities. The deep immersion in an urban setting has perhaps contributed to student awareness that their privileged university lifestyles are being undergirded by workers who barely make a livable wage. This dichotomy has motivated students to put their learning into action, with student activist groups on the Columbia campus vocalizing their concerns in 2016 about sustainable wages for those who work for the university system. Also in 2016, students joined in solidarity with restaurant workers of a nearby restaurant who were entangled in a lawsuit over stolen wages.[2] Not only wage insecurity, but food insecurity looms large in urban settings such as Columbia's upper-Manhattan setting—even for lower-income students attending the university. In response to student food insecurity, students have developed apps that allow food sharing among students.

As university chaplain, I also have to model this kind of responsiveness to the social needs of our students and community. When serving a student body consistently ready to interact with its surroundings with a humanitarian spirit, I must meet students halfway at least in order to stay useful and connected. Within the office of the university chaplain, providing a living wage has always been the keystone to creating an excellent team. Recently our office has answered the call from students by raising our base wage for student workers and increasing the wage for senior staff members. In addition, our office has made space to address emergency needs of students where financial limitations are paramount. Several years ago, we created an emergency discretionary fund for students. Gifts (no loans) up to $150 are distributed to students who have a need. If a dean of students contacts me and says a student is in need of emergency assistance, I provide debit cards ($50 per card) after meeting with the student in person. Being able to address these concerns promptly has connected our community and enhanced the meaning of chaplaincy in this complex urban campus.

2. George Joseph, "Indus Valley Restaurant Workers Protest," *Columbia Political Review*, November 10, 2012, http://www.cpreview.org/blog/2012/11/human-rights-start-at-home.

Concluding Thoughts

Students are multicultural, multiclass, they claim multiple identities, and they are aware of how these multiple identities overlap and inform each other. In the process, this can sometimes create dissonant and discomforting experiences within the university environment. A university chaplain may mediate diversities and disputes between subcommunities within increasingly intercultural, global interfaith settings, helping student groups and administrative offices to find the middle ground between closely held personal beliefs and passionately asserted political positions. A university chaplain must also assist students, faculty, and administrators who are seeking ways to understand their roles in matters of justice, civic responsibility, and campus leadership. Within these diverse settings, as students wrestle with ever more complexity while attempting to hold on to, discover, or cultivate religious and spiritual lives, universities must have the capacity and creativity to accompany students through the complexities they are facing. In these kinds of ways, universities (such as Columbia) are emblematic of the challenges confronting ministries in urban, cosmopolitan settings far beyond our gated campus communities.

Chapter 29

Prison Ministries, Voluntarism, and Relational Culture

Tami Hooker

The phone rings in the prison chapel. When I answer it, the person on the other end says, "I'm interested in volunteering there." It's a response that foretells a conversation filled with joy and possibility or one that is filled with awkwardness and disappointment. The answer to my next question is a good indication of which type of call this will be. So I ask with a bit of trepidation, "What are you interested in doing?"

In more than a decade as a prison chaplain, I have heard all types of answers. Some come from people who have a well-thought-out program meant to assist inmates in a spiritual or practical way or one that combines the two. Some come from people who want to bring their own religious or political agenda into a prison ministry setting. Some come from people who want to use the men under my care as a way to deal with an issue in their own past or present life.[1] Some make the amazing offer to help with whatever need we presently have. Finally, many insist they want to "bring Jesus into the prison."

Whatever the reason, throughout my years of chaplaincy, two things have been fairly constant. The first is that the person calling usually believes that they can most effectively minister by offering a praise and worship service that presents their church's or denomination's specific

---

1. While I have served as a volunteer and an intern in places where both men and women are incarcerated, my thirteen years in chaplaincy has taken place in state facilities that house only men. Throughout the chapter, the male nouns and pronouns are intentional and a reflection on my own experiences in those facilities.

understanding of Christianity.[2] The second is that the caller is unlikely to be from what would be considered a mainline denomination.

This lack of mainline denominational volunteers in prisons has been well documented.[3] Reasons that have been offered for this phenomenon range from a lack of seminary training related to prison ministry to the idea that avoidance of prison ministry by mainline denominations traces to the white middle-class theological sensitivities of mainline denominations.[4]

Let me begin by noting that I truly believe all of the people who call do so out of a heart that wants to help. I also believe many others would be interested in helping but believe they don't have the specific training or talents to help persons in prison. It has been my experience in speaking to Christian groups of numerous and varied churches that there is a great deal of compassion and concern for those behind prison walls, but people are unsure what is needed, how to become involved, and if they have the proper training and skills to be effective.

Becoming Part of the "Good Samaritans"

One of the most effective ways to be successful in a prison ministry requires no particular skills or knowledge. It is simply to show up regularly and consistently. One of the inmates' favorite volunteers, and one of the few I have worked with from a mainline denomination, was a man named Jim who regularly came on Sunday morning and sat with them in worship.

Jim was a white middle-class Presbyterian who didn't come from the kind of background most of the men in the facility did. He began coming to the prison as an official for the inmate's basketball games. But he wanted to come and get to know the men and embrace them as brothers in the faith, so he began attending worship. He didn't preach or sing or offer prayers. He didn't ask the men to come to understand or accept

2. Larry Nielsen, *Thinking about Jail and Prison Ministry: A Guide for the Lay Volunteer* (Ft. Pierce, FL: FBC Publications, 2005), 42.

3. James M. Shopshire Sr., Mark C. Hicks, and Richmond Stoglin, eds., *I Was in Prison: United Methodist Perspectives on Prison Ministry* (Nashville: The General Board of Higher Education and Ministry, The United Methodist Church, 2008), 11–25, 151–59. See also Richard Dennis Shaw, *Chaplain to the Imprisoned: Sharing Life with the Incarcerated* (Binghamton, NY: Haworth Press, 1995), 151–53; and R. N. Ristad, "A Stark Examination of Prison and Prison Ministries," *Dialog* 47, no. 3 (2008): 292–303.

4. Ristad, "A Stark Examination," 301.

the values of his community of faith. He came willing to learn about and understand theirs. He came in and talked with the men before service—asking about what was going on in their lives. He participated in the service from the pews sitting among the inmates. He assured the men that when people asked him where he went to church, he answered, the "Church of the Good Samaritan," which is what the church at my institution was named sometime in the distant past. Jim seemed happy and content to be welcomed as a member of their congregation, attending for years until he had to move away for his job. They loved him because he took time to come and be with them and they felt genuinely loved by him. It was enough.

When things go awry with people who want to volunteer or when people who are interested in serving don't think they would be able to do so, I think it is simply because people are unaware of how the church inside the prison functions, or they don't have a good idea of what prison life in general is like. Maybe they've seen too many TV shows or movies that depict life inside a prison and believe that's the reality that exists within our facilities. Irrespective of how their view of the life of the incarcerated may have been formed, many people seem surprised when they visit the facility where I minister.

One of the things that always seems to surprise people is that, except when they are required to return to their cells for count,[5] there are almost always inmates walking around. Their movements are controlled and monitored but nonetheless they move about the inside of the institution. A prison is like a small town or a city neighborhood. Men go to the dining hall three times a day to eat; they go to the commissary to pick up items they have purchased; they walk over to the infirmary for a dental appointment, or to the barber for a haircut, or to school for classes, or to the gym or yard for recreation. So on Sunday morning, they leave their housing units and walk over to the chapel for the weekly worship service.

When I entered prison ministry, first as a volunteer and later as a chaplain, I found a longstanding church already in place. When I became pastor of the "Church of the Good Samaritan," I found there were men there who had been members of the church for more than thirty years. They had seen volunteers and chaplains come and go. They would have

---

5. The counting of inmates numerous times each day is considered an essential activity in any jail or prison. It's absolutely imperative to ensure that every inmate we are responsible for is in fact still inside the prison. Inmates who are not where they are supposed to be at count time or who interfere with count in any way are usually disciplined.

certainly laughed had I told them I thought I was "bringing" Jesus to them as many of them had been walking a path of discipleship for decades. In this environment, men choose whether to sign up for religious programs. Most of the people who come to programs offered by volunteers already attend church regularly.

Fellowship as the Body of Christ

What's needed from outside are volunteer ministries that will help the men grow as disciples or people who will help men by giving them the skills to build a better life once they are released. What is needed are church volunteers willing to come and share fellowship with fellow Christians who happen to be behind prison walls. No one needed to bring Jesus into the facilities where I served. He had faithfully been there loving and caring for and supporting and comforting the men of the institutions since they were built. Walls and barbed wire do not keep God out. My work is to affirm how God has been and continues to be at work in their lives. If volunteers want to be accepted and heard, they need to learn to accept the prison church as it exists without requiring the prisoners to reflect the patterns of the churches the volunteers represent. They need to be willing to step out of their comfort zone, realize that they are being welcomed as guests to an existing church, and respond to that appropriately by putting in the time and effort to get to know the members of the congregation and to learn how that church functions.

A church inside a prison is, by necessity, much more ecumenical and diverse than most churches on the outside. Prisoners have one "church" available to them. If they do not agree with the doctrine or do not like the worship style or do not want to be in community with the others who attend there, they are not able to simply go down the street and find a church more to their liking. This necessitates honoring as many of the traditions represented in their community as possible. When people from Baptist and Lutheran and nondenominational and Methodist and Pentecostal traditions gather together for worship, each wants to feel that the service reflects their understanding of church. For me, that meant that even though I was ordained in the Presbyterian Church (U.S.A.), I needed to learn to give an altar call and to invite people up for prayer during service. And because I was willing to honor those traditions, I discovered that the men would be open and respectful when I introduced times of silence or guided meditation that appealed to different parts of our community. I learned that people would be willing to sing traditional hymns one Sunday without complaint if they thought service would include some gospel songs they were familiar with a week or two later. It is an amazing thing to see people from different races and classes and traditions gather to worship as one and to see the many parts of the body of Christ united in worship. It's an area where I think those in prison do a better job than persons in many churches outside the walls. This diversity also brings with it disagreements about things the church has often disagreed about. In order to function as a church, prison congregations need to agree to disagree in some areas and purposely remain focused on the things we can all agree upon. That means that volunteers are required to do the same. Prison ministry simply requires allowing and respecting other beliefs.[6]

The Prison Church of All Faiths

In fact, in a prison setting, respect and tolerance for other's beliefs need to extend further than across denominational lines to include those of other faiths. Prisoners are required to work with and to eat with and sometimes to live in a small cell with those who follow different faiths. If they were unable to do it with an attitude of respect for other's beliefs, it could lead to dangerous situations in a place that doesn't need additional security problems.

The only way to ask inmates to be respectful with any integrity is if we are willing to model it for them. If, at any time, staff or volunteers disrespect another's faith tradition, it implicitly gives inmates permission to do the same. For this reason, while we invite Christian volunteers to preach and teach Christian beliefs unapologetically, we ask them to refrain from commenting on any other religion's beliefs or practices. We maintain this same standard for any literature that is handed out to inmates or placed in our chapel library.

In the facility where I minister, I have intentionally structured the staff and activities so that interfaith work is encouraged and successful—not

6. Under the Religious Land Use and Institutionalized Person Act (RLUIPA), the Religious Freedom Restoration Act (RFRA), and the Civil Rights of Institutionalized Persons Act (CRIPA), inmates in both federal and state institutions retain certain rights to exercise religion. In a 2012 Pew Research Center's Study, "Religion in Prison—A 50-State Survey of Prison Chaplains," the majority of the state chaplains (84 percent) reported documenting religious affiliation of the inmates. While the relative size of the various religious groups were difficult to gauge, the chaplains response suggests that religious landscape behind prison walls is more diverse than the non-incarcerated adult population.

with everyone to be sure—but with many. It goes beyond ecumenical gatherings where Catholic and Protestant populations fellowship together, but also includes interfaith services on occasions such as Thanksgiving or staff worship services, or memorial services following deaths of staff or inmates. In these settings all faiths are invited, and all persons are made to feel welcomed. There is also a weekly group called Chapel Talk, which is a pastoral group counseling project where members of different faiths comment on topics based on what their faith teaches on the subject and what they believe. It is a place where men coming from their various faith backgrounds receive that information as gift rather than as something to be challenged or debated.

Unfortunately, many ministries don't want to take the time to learn anything about the prison culture. Instead, they wish to visit once or once a year for a worship service or a program. I can almost guarantee a good turnout for any outside individuals or groups who come in, if for no other reason than that prison life is routine and anyone or anything that offers something different is very welcome. But I don't believe having a variety of guests lead weekly services or having a onetime program provides many benefits in the long run. Without a chance to get to know the men and to converse with them as individuals (each and every one of whom is precious to God), volunteers sometimes revert to preaching "at" the men and telling them that they need to change.[7] That is something they are already painfully aware of.

Unlike many congregations, the men who I work with are unable to ignore the topic of sin altogether. Whether or not our services include a prayer of confession, their sins—at least the ones for which they have been incarcerated—are as we read in Psalm 51, "always before them." This is reinforced by their lack of freedom that is delineated not only by the thirty-foot-high wall around the institution but also by the clothes they are forced to wear, their lack of choices in their day-to-day lives, and their treatment by those who are part of their daily lives within the prison.

Judged and in Search of Grace

Even after spending as much time with these incarcerated men as I have, I am still unable to imagine what it would be like to have a major offense

---

7. Dennis W. Pierce, *Prison Ministry: Hope behind the Wall* (Binghamton, NY: The Haworth Press, 2006), 54.

I have committed listed in writing as a matter of public record, where anyone could view it and judge my worth as a person by that one fact of my past. The men I work with have already been judged by society. Many believe that they have also been judged by God and that God has dismissed them as unworthy.

They are by and large a people who struggle with some sort of brokenness. While that describes all of us, many of the men I have met in prison were raised in significant brokenness. Sometimes that included the brokenness of their family. Many were raised by people other than their parents. No matter how many times they were told that it wasn't their fault, I imagine many have believed there had to be something wrong with them if their parents did not want them. Many were raised in the brokenness of a society that categorized them as "lesser than" because of the color of their skin, their ethnicity, their neighborhood, their poverty, their lack of a decent education, or some combination of several of those factors. Many have struggled with drugs or alcohol problems. All were raised in a society that judges worth by power and wealth and where meaning and value have become harder to find. These are people in desperate need of hope. For them, knowing that God's love is greater than and independent of any past or present actions we have committed is an undeniable word of hope.

Our willingness to see and honor incarcerated persons as individuals and to take the time to listen to them does more than most sermons can in helping them to know God's love. A 2007 study of men and women who were county and state prisoners in Pennsylvania, conducted on behalf of the Pennsylvania Prison Chaplains Association, showed what many of the men and women prisoners surveyed in the study wanted most was time to speak to a chaplain one-on-one.[8] Surely such a request is a plea to be seen and heard and found worthy of someone's time and attention. It's a plea to be assured that someone in the church, and by extension God, still loves and believes in them.

With thousands of inmates and a limited number of chaplaincy hours in each institution, chaplains cannot hope to fill this requirement for all who want or need it. Meanwhile, the volunteers willing to help fill the staffing gaps should not feel as though they must have a background or history paralleling that of the prisoners to be effective in their work with these persons. For a community already accustomed to dealing with

---

8. Harry Dammer, "Chaplaincy Check Up" (presentation of research findings, annual Pennsylvania Prison Chaplains Association Conference, Columbia, PA, October 23–24, 2007).

diversity in their own population, all that prisoners require of persons ministering in these contexts is a heart acquainted with and willing to share God's love. The only other absolute necessity for participating in this ministry is a willingness to follow the security rules.

Perhaps the answer for current prison ministry programs lies in convincing both mainline and more evangelical Christians they do not need an awesome praise and worship band (although if they have one, they would be welcome to join—but not supplant—our inmate praise and worship group). Neither do they need knowledge of the latest therapeutic interventions or a degree in sociology to be effective in our prisons. Perhaps as chaplains we could do a better job of informing the church-at-large that what the men and women in our prisons and jails most want is simply to be seen as children of God, to have their stories heard, and to be shown that God and God's church care about them and about what happens to them next.

Perhaps then our prisons would be filled with volunteers from many parts of the church who bridge divides through an understanding that all stand in need of God's grace and we are indeed one in Christ. Perhaps our services could be filled with people like my friend Jim, who chose to show men in the prison he was honored to be welcomed into fellowship within their congregation. Perhaps if more churchpersons "outside the walls" were willing to leave their comfort zones and reach across the differences that divide us, every phone call to the chapel regarding volunteering would be full of joy and possibility.

Chapter 30

Martin Luther King Jr.'s Speeches and the Urban-Digital Context

Erika D. Gault

In the treatment of King's work, there is much on King as a theologian, as an activist, and as a revolutionary. This chapter explores King's influence as an artist, crafting a new context for our existential being in the world. In particular, it applies King's prophetic vision to the present urban-digital context. I first explore a few of King's speeches advancing the mid-twentieth-century civil rights movement and situated within a larger body of socially conscious performance art of the time. I argue that such speeches crafted new worlds of possibilities for audiences in mostly urban communities. This work continues in our own times. We must see the work of Millennials engaged in the arts and making use of online media tools as speaking to and about these same historical challenges in urban centers. Such online sites and their creative use offer urban dwellers important spaces to establish new identities and socially just communities. In coining these modern spaces the *urban-digital context*, this chapter articulates the unique way in which urban, more specifically marginalized African American, groups engage new media. Though the racial divide persists in both the acquisition and appropriation of all new technology,[1] I will explore how historically oppressed groups can and do make use of technology in crafting new worlds of possibilities, especially spiritually liberating spaces. But first, our attempt to understand the implications of Dr. King's speeches for our times must be guided by a deeper examination of the historical moment that called for his unique prophetic response.

---

1. Pew Research Center and Monica Anderson, Pew Research Center American Trend Panel, October 3–27, 2014; April 30, 2015. Raw data.

Nearly fifty years ago, Dr. King began the completion of what would ultimately be his last full-length work, titled *Where Do We Go from Here: Chaos or Community?* From February to March 1967, he spent much of his time in isolation in Ocho Rios, Jamaica. His opening chapter belies the chaos into which the United States had descended. Just two years before the historic signing of the Voting Rights Act of 1965, the country seemed to have turned down a much darker path. In a number of states, the Voting Rights Act proved ineffective in pressuring state and local governments bent on preserving white rule. Watts and other cities across the United States had erupted in riots. The weight of King's words "Where do we go from here?" further resonated later in 1967 in a speech to the Southern Christian Leadership Conference where he raised the same question. Presently, this inquiry persists in our urban spaces. The present moment is wrought with a certain chaos and complexity not unlike King's own times. Urban centers like Baton Rouge, Louisiana; Charlotte, North Carolina; and Tulsa, Oklahoma, all experienced police shootings of unarmed African Americans in 2016. And now comes heightened militarization against other communities of color in these same cities due to the immigration ban and the near silence from the Trump administration on criminal justice reform.

Artistry in Strategy

While others bemoaned the challenges and failures of the civil rights movement, King, like the eagle-eye prophet Isaiah, took the aerial view and articulated the stages of the movement. King demonstrated that the gains of the Voting Rights Act were only a first phase. According to Dr. King, "The absence of brutality and unregenerate evil is not the presence of justice. To stay murder is not the same thing as to ordain brotherhood."[2] This was the work of the second phase of the movement, where the realization of equality would occur with the dismantling of poverty. There was a particular artistry to interpreting the movement in this way. King's strategy here points to an understanding of the rhythm of justice that movements require. His vision of the movement was akin to a grand musical score or an exquisite piece of poetry; it requires its own ebb and flow. In other speeches Dr. King indicated that sometimes justice seemed silent in the universe. But then justice would strike up

---

2. Martin Luther King Jr., *Where Do We Go from Here: Chaos or Community?* (New York: Beacon Press, 1968), 4.

a chord again and even rise and fall before concluding with a spirited cadence. According to King, "The arc of the moral universe may be long, but it bends towards justice."[3] It was with that rhythm of justice that he sought to advance the movement.

In *The Prophetic Imagination*, Walter Brueggemann presents King as standing in the same prophetic tradition (on Vietnam) as the Old Testament prophets. Elsewhere Brueggemann argues that

> Prophets are people who, because of their roots in the theological tradition and because of some emancipatory experience in their own life, refuse to accept the definitions of reality that are imposed upon us by the socio-economic-political power structure. In ancient Israel, the prophets refused to accept the royal-priestly ideology of the Jerusalem establishment, and they kept saying that the radicality of the Torah was more definitive than what was going on in Jerusalem.[4]

This is precisely the site at which we find Dr. King, in the midst of an American Jerusalem refusing to accept the limited ontologies of racial hatred and white supremacy as well as the spirit of defeatism that seemed to have overtaken many within the movement. Instead, he seized the moment to speak prophetically, to criticize a political structure that promised a war on poverty, a campaign centered on addressing urban blight while pumping billions into a war on Vietnam. Simultaneously, he sought to energize his audience with the offering of an imaginative new space, a beloved community, a brotherhood, the kingdom of God. This prophetic lens is particularly important for the current urban-digital context. Language centered upon alternative communities or third spaces is dialectically opposed to the rhetoric of hate witnessed in the 2016 election cycle. This includes the Trump administration's embrace of groups like the alt-right or the fear of disembodiment at the hands of white supremacy which Ta-Nehisi Coates so eloquently discusses in *Between the World and Me*. There exist real creative potential in our times for thinking through the nation's darkest moments as potential sites for energizing communities toward alternative visions. This is an important act of resistance in addressing persistent urban issues. Like King, our

3. Martin Luther King Jr., sermon at Temple Israel of Hollywood, Hollywood, CA, February 26, 1965.

4. Bradford Winter. "A Conversation with Walter Brueggemann," *Image Journal* 55 (2007): https://imagejournal.org/article/conversation-walter-brueggemann/.

ability to respond to socially unjust strategies in the modern world will galvanize the creative potential of our counter communities which by their very presence and language imbue a prophetic capacity to criticize and energize toward change.

Artistry in Performance

A cursory read of King's philosophy regarding community might seem overly optimistic, if not naive. Yet it was an intentional movement toward physical, spiritual, and linguistic liberation. Like Langston Hughes, King was creating new worlds with his words. Outside of homiletics and Old Testament discussions of the prophet as performer, we rarely view King as the artist that he was. But he routinely made use of some forms both in his preaching and his approach to the movement. Nowhere was this more apparent than in the wonderful imagery derived from listening to his speeches and sermons. The array of metaphors sprinkled throughout his preaching demonstrates this. Consider the following example from one of King's speeches:"I have a dream that one day even the state of Mississippi, a state sweltering with the heat of injustice, sweltering with the heat of oppression, will be transformed into an oasis of freedom and justice."[5]

For King, these were not simply meant to be an assortment of metaphors. Metaphors are just one of an array of linguistic and performance strategies. Paul Ricoeur argues that it is through the metaphor that reality is redefined.[6] According to Henry Mitchell this redefinition "occurs as a result of the tension between the terms of a metaphorical statement. By moving beyond ordinary meanings, one is freed to form a new world."[7] King displayed the genius of his sermons and speeches in his intentional attempt to create a new world, an alternative vision for American society through language. We must consider every speech and sermon, then, as a performance of justice. In his vibrato, in the steady and methodical build-up to his final rapturous close, a developing rhythm toward justice, toward the fashioning of a new world took shape.

Several scholars have thought comparatively about other activists and scholars who were King's contemporaries. We must also consider the role of artists like James Baldwin, Mahalia Jackson, and others in either

---

5. Martin Luther King Jr., "I Have A Dream" (speech, Washington, DC, August 28, 1963), Government Archive, 4–5, https://www.archives.gov/files/press/exhibits/dream-speech.pdf.

6. Paul Ricoeur, *The Rule of Metaphor: The Creation of Meaning in Language* (London: Taylor & Francis, 2004), 5.

7. Henry Mitchell. *Celebration and Experience in Preaching* (Nashville: Abingdon Press, 1994).

fomenting or mirroring many of the ideas presented by King. Their work tells a similar story of performances of justice indicative of the moment. As an example, at the time King was writing *Where Do We Go from Here?*, Aretha Franklin was recording the single titled "Respect." Franklin, who had traveled with King at intervals since she was sixteen, recorded a track now synonymous with the civil rights and the women's movements. We must consider why that song became so essentially linked to these movements. On one hand its meaning is easy to grasp. Who doesn't like a little respect when they get home? But Franklin tapped into the same prophetic imagination we witness in King's artistic rendering. She demands something not always given to women, in a space known for its isolating and domesticating histories with women. The home becomes a new and liberated space where women are respected as equals. Like King, Franklin engages in creating this new world.

Couple this with the fact that "Respect" reminds us of the communal nature of performances. Its famous hook, imploring her love to "sock it to me," was originated by her sister Carolyn. The song itself was reimagined from the earlier version by Franklin's fellow riffter Otis Redding. Mark Anthony Neal has highlighted the communal nature, the fictive kinships, created in Redding's performance of this song and through his live performances.[8] Could it be that in their artistry these performers, like King, were creating counter spaces in which to critique the oppressive order of things and energize audiences toward justice? Every riff was set to the rhythm of justice, the making of a new world. Nina Simone tells us as much in "Feeling Good," released in 1965, when she pronounces, "This old world is a new world and a bold world for me."[9] Like Franklin's "Respect," later, "Feeling Good" had its origins in an earlier version of the song, performed as part of the British musical *The Roar of the Greasepaint* in which Cy Grant and later Gilbert Price, protégé of Langston Hughes, played the character of "the negro." "Feeling Good" comes after he has outwitted the slave master. His performance turns the slave hierarchy on its head and envisions a new world, a bold world. King joined this transnational concert occurring throughout the sixties that sought, through their performances of justice, to make the world anew.

8. Marc Anthony Neal. "'I Can't Turn You Loose': Otis Redding and the Kinship of Live Soul," *New Black Man (in Exile)*, December 15, 2017, http://www.newblackmaninexile.net/2016/12/i-cant-turn-you-loose-otis-redding-and.html.

9. Nina Simone, "Feeling Good," recorded June 1965, track 7 on *I Put a Spell on You*, Philips Records, 33-1/3 rpm.

In our own times, we continue to see the possibility for such new world making, such performative and transdisciplinary work aimed toward justice. The analysis of new futures in the scholarly and creative work now appears on sites such as Afrofuturism. The use of social media platforms for activism through hashtags like Black Lives Matter is another. Other examples include the album *Coloring Book* by graphic designer Brandon Breaux, and the making of communal and resistance spaces like Black Twitter, as aptly noted by Feminista Jones.[10]

Within the contemporary urban-digital context, the creative use of digital media platforms provides important sites for prophetic imagination. Criticizing and energizing today echoes the movement and linguistic strategies implored by Dr. King and others earlier in American history. This is the case for hip-hop star Chance the Rapper. While his lyrics demonstrate the urban influence of Chicago's Southside, his work also mirrors the role of new media in the creation of imaginative and liberatory spaces for Christian artists. Chance's third album made Grammy history, winning in three categories. This marks the first time streaming-only music was even allowed for Grammy consideration. Like the artistry in King's movement strategies, black Millennials like Chance the Rapper establish new strategies for articulating urban realities through the use of digital tools. These are not just accidental connections to the past, however, but an intentional nod to former leaders and their performances of justice. Chance notes as much in saying, "Being from the family I'm from—my great-grandmother marched with King—I have things that I have to do."[11] In the urban-digital context, new media figures largely in how one emulates King's activism and performances of justice. Chance's formation of #SaveChicago, to curb gun violence in Chicago, requires the use of such platforms in envisioning urban spaces differently. This strategizing and energizing can be viewed in his lyrics as well, centered as they are on Christian-centric visions of freedom.

The contemporary urban environment remains wrought with issues of over-policing, poverty, immigrant surveillance, and possible deportation,

10. In discussing the process for creating the first of Chance the Rapper's three album covers, Breaux describes first surveying the landscape of current rappers' album covers. His attempt was to fill what he saw as the missing "art and imagination" from other artists' covers. Through the use of digital painting Breaux achieved a distinct mein for the album, which has been highlighted for its futuristic look (see http://www.brandonbreaux.com/chance-page).

11. Tomi Obaro, "Chance the Rapper Is a Chicagoan of the Year," *Chicago Magazine*, November 17, 2015, http://www.chicagomag.com/Chicago-Magazine/December-2015/Chicagoans-of-the-Year-2015-Chance-the-Rapper/.

to name a few. Many of these urban realities speak to the persistence and relevance of King's prophetic vision and artistic use of language in our times. The artistic and scholarly work of many within the present generation continues that vision by seeking to create new worlds of possibility. This is cause for tremendous hope. For in their performances, we see the modulating rhythm of justice that King describes in saying the "arc of the moral universe may be long, but it bends towards justice."[12] The urban-digital context through performances of justice by artists like Chance the Rapper is bending us further toward justice.

12. A phrase adapted by and used by Martin Luther King Jr. in various speeches.

Chapter 31

Approaches to Ministry
in an African Prophetic Church in France

Aurélien Mokoko Gampiot

Kimbanguism is an African-initiated church that stemmed from the Baptist Church, of which its founder Simon Kimbangu was a member and a catechist. Today, it is considered as the largest African-initiated church, with an estimated membership of 17 million worldwide. It has been part of the World Council of Churches since 1969 and the Conference of African Churches since 1974. The existence of its French branch is a consequence of the strong global diaspora the Kimbanguist Church has had since the 1970s, specifically in Europe.

In France, Kimbanguist churches have had an especially strong urban ministry focus, and this chapter explores these aspects. The historical background of Kimbanguist migration from Central Africa to France is outlined first, followed by a focus on obstacles to the church's integration in France, and finally on expressions of Kimbanguist urban ministry in France.

Historical Background of Kimbanguist Presence in France

Kimbanguist religion may only be understood within the social, historical, and geographical context of its emergence. It was born in 1921 in the Belgian Congo, as a prophetic movement of struggle against the colonial order initiated by Baptist catechist Simon Kimbangu.[1] His campaign of miraculous healing and preaching against "the colonial situation of Blacks" impelled an unexpectedly durable revival movement.[2]

1. Efraim Andersson, *Messianic Popular Movements in the Lower Congo*, Studia ethnographica XIV (Uppsala, Sweden: Almqvist & Wiksells, 1958).
2. Georges Balandier, *Sociology of Black Africa: Social Dynamics in Central Africa*, trans. Douglas Garman (London: Andre Deutsch Ltd., [1955] 1970).

Indeed, after only six months of preaching and healing, Kimbangu and many of his followers were arrested on September 12, 1921. Their trial resulted in Kimbangu being sentenced to death and his followers to several years of imprisonment.

Nevertheless, Kimbangu was pardoned by the king of Belgium and his sentence converted to life imprisonment. He was promptly deported to Elisabethville (now Lubumbashi) at the other end of Belgian Congo, while 37,000 families of his supporters were likewise banished to other regions of the country. The main prophecy from his teachings that caused his imprisonment was: "The White man shall become black and the Black man shall become white." Kimbangu passed away in October 1951, after spending thirty years in jail, but the movement he initiated was kept alive and expanded under the leadership of his wife, Muilu Marie.[3] It obtained official recognition in 1959 by the Belgian government, thereby placing it on an equal footing with the Roman Catholic and Protestant mother churches.

The Kimbanguist Church nonetheless evidences a unique structure, especially its theology, which continues to be shaped by the quest for an answer to the oppression suffered by Congolese and other black peoples around the world. This particular theology of black liberation led the first Kimbanguist immigrants to France in the 1970s as a context in which to organize. Leaving behind the newly independent Republics of Congo and war-torn Angola to study in French universities, these students worshiped in Catholic or Protestant churches, but felt a nagging need to meet in a space that would be their own and provide continuity with the church services they knew back home. In 1975, Charles Kisolokele, Kimbangu's eldest son and the then deputy spiritual leader of the church, was in Switzerland for a medical check-up during the Christmas season. On his initiative, Kimbanguist followers gathered to celebrate the Christmas feast and decided during the occasion to create the International Kimbanguist Circle (CIK). The goals of CIK were twofold: first, to serve as a place of worship, biblical study, and exchange among the migrant Kimbanguist students living in Switzerland, Belgium, France, Portugal, and Spain; and second, to liaise between these members and the church's main headquarters, in what was then known as Zaire. Tracing their church's rootedness in all three Congos (before colonization by the Portuguese, the French, and the Belgians),[4] Kimbanguists today contend that the

---

3. Diangienda Kuntima, *L'Histoire du Kimbanguisme* (Kinshasa: Éditions Kimbanguistes, 1984).

4. The ancient kingdom of Kongo was divided by colonial powers, becoming the Belgian Congo (now Democratic Republic of Congo), the French Congo (Congo-Brazzaville), and Angola.

birth of their community in Europe also took place simultaneously in three countries—Switzerland, France, and Belgium. With the expansion of the community in France, the Kimbanguist Church eventually secured official recognition by the French Republic as a faith-based organization separate from the state. Nonetheless, this did not resolve the challenge of Kimbanguist acceptance and integration within France.

Challenges to Integration and Hurdles to the Ministry

In its home countries, the Kimbanguist Church has enjoyed official recognition and a certain degree of prestige and consideration from the broader society and from heads of state. This results in part from the iconic nature of Simon Kimbangu, who is now revered as a national hero in the Democratic Republic of Congo (DRC).[5] Also, in the DRC, Congo-Brazzaville, and Angola, the church band is regularly asked to provide music for occasions such as Independence Day or national worship services called for by the political authorities in times of national urgency. In its French diasporic context, however, the Kimbanguist community suffers from a lack of recognition although registered as a religious organization.

The Kimbanguist community in France comprises persons from three national origins (the two Congos and Angola), but church members must function as a coherent micro-society in order to adjust to a new environment where their religion is unknown and elicits indifference at best and suspicion at worst. For example, they must find ways to navigate social obstacles such as the absence of immigration documents and work permits, housing problems, or institutional race-based discrimination. But they must also make broader cultural and religious adjustments, having been socialized in the value system of their home countries, quite different from the individualistic, secular atmosphere of French society.

One expression of a vast cultural difference is in the absence of Kimbanguist temples in France, which are a common sight in their home countries. Instead, in France they have to rent warehouses at the outskirts of metropolitan areas to hold worship services or depend on the generosity of Catholic or Protestant clergy who sometimes offer to lend them churches for ceremonies. A second culture shock is in the gap between the two value systems. In their home countries, the church exerts a relatively tight form

---

5. Susan Asch, *L'Église du prophète Kimbangu, de ses origines à son rôle actuel au Zaïre* (Paris: Karthala, 1983).

of moral control, which is reinforced by the familiarity of their fellow Congolese or Angolans with the commandments and recommendations of the Kimbanguist faith. In France, conversely, the cardinal value is individual liberty and the dominant attitude is impatience with moral codes and constraints. After several years of residence in France, maladjustment morphs into an identity crisis for believers, torn between a French-style loss of personal identity and maintaining collectively embraced Kimbanguist moral standards (often leading to misunderstandings with the locals openly critical of religions with a strong communal dimension).

As a consequence, the Kimbanguist diaspora in France does not adjust easily to the customs of French society, shunning even participation in trade unions and political parties while placing a strong emphasis on group autonomy and collective self-help strategies. This commitment to mutual help is grounded in their racial consciousness, which is at the root of their religious worldview in the first place but is also heightened by their situation as racially othered migrants in a formerly imperial nation. The reference to Africa is therefore constant because it is central to Kimbanguist dogma and also essential to building and retaining their sense of identity and connectedness to Africa (accessed otherwise only via modern communications technologies or trips back to the continent).

Under such circumstances, integration in French society takes place mostly on an individual (rather than a collective) basis, by attending schools and universities, earning degrees, holding jobs, obtaining French citizenship, or marrying interracially. Members of the immigrant church community struggling to access these resources organize into informal networks, helping one another find employment opportunities or housing, as well as solutions for daycare or handling official paperwork. In the home countries, the Kimbanguist Church has its own schools from elementary level to the university, agricultural production units, and hospitals. In a diasporic situation, its members may have none of these communal resources. Among these African immigrant populations (concentrated mainly in urban contexts), ministry is put to the task in its efforts to respond to the challenges of church-building and social integration—while maintaining its messianic dimension.

Expressions of Messianism and Urban Ministry in a Diasporic Context

Kimbanguists view themselves as a missionary church, and as such they understand migration from the African continent as a response to a call to mission. Although most of the church members residing in France emigrated with other purposes than religious missionizing, faced with the difficulties of integrating French society they organized into communities that have tended to take precedence over individual aspirations. Communal ties are still rooted in the same traditional model as in the beginnings of the church in the 1920s, with a value system known as *Kintwadi*, a Kikongo term designating a sense of unity expressed by communal actions.

The religious life of the Kimbanguist diaspora in France is informed by worship services, religious ceremonies, memorial services celebrating historical landmarks in Kimbangu's life or his sons' lives, weddings, and funerals. All of these gatherings have kept enough structure and consistency to replicate their original formats from the home countries. Church members often travel across France or to other European countries to celebrate these events and, just as importantly, join their kin or friends for the organization of weddings and funeral wakes. If they are documented, some Kimbanguists even fly back home for feasts they consider particularly meaningful.

Mutual help in the Kimbanguist diaspora consists in providing the children from poorer families with the necessaries for school, encouraging the graduates from schools and universities, helping struggling students with free tutoring and mentoring, visiting the sick at home or at the hospital, and raising funds within the community for grieving families, which often need to fund the repatriation of their departed loved ones, or for members' weddings. Migrant Kimbanguist families generally comply with the traditions of their home societies with respect to engagements and weddings, and they are encouraged to do so by the church, insofar as this sacrament implicitly entails the payment of the dowry to the bride's family, which conditions all traditional weddings in Central African countries.

The close-knit nature of the diasporic community allows the members to remain focused on their motivations and the reasons for their presence in France. Their socialization is facilitated by the church's insistence, through hymns, speeches, and sermons, on reflecting and meditating on the racial oppression experienced by black men and women worldwide. Faced with the cultural rejection and institutional racism of French society, they find meaning, solace, and protection in the ideology and spiritual message of Kimbanguism. Indeed, this church offers a highly organized system of analysis and beliefs on racial domination and the material and metaphysical status of blacks. Kimbanguists see themselves as a sacred community of elects, like the biblical chosen people, entrusted with the mission of bringing about black people's redemption thanks to their testimonies on Simon Kimbangu's prophetic and messianic action. To prove the forthcoming advent of this redemption, Kimbanguist leaders prophesy the participation of black geniuses in totally novel, unheard-of inventions in the technological and scientific fields.

In France, the notion of race is simultaneously acknowledged and denied any political implication in the current constitution, which proclaims that the French Republic "guarantees the equality of all citizens before the law, regardless of their origin, race or religion." With regard to the various minority groups from Africa or other continents, the French Republic sticks to an assimilationist, universalist model, which absorbs all distinctive ethnic traits into a single system of social values that founds the French nation.[6] However, in reality, the denial of race as a social construct becomes utopian to the extent that it reinforces the various forms of systemic discrimination based on national origins. Under these circumstances, it is not surprising to observe a persisting use of racial rhetoric among Kimbanguist migrants, as they still experience the need for a black theology of liberation. The prevalence of racial analyses in their belief system causes them to be suspected by their native French friends and coworkers of following a racist ideology, even though these analyses help them cope with their minority situation.

In France as in the home countries, although the Kimbanguist community's unity is threatened by inner strife resulting from the church leadership competition and doctrinal tensions with mainline Christian groups, Kimbanguists' need for recognition and missionizing remains strong. They regularly organize marches on the streets of Paris, holding placards commemorating the deportation of the 37,000 families of supporters of Simon Kimbangu by colonial authorities, or preaching in public about their understandings of Christian dogma as redefined by their system of beliefs. In this way, the general ignorance of the European public about Kimbanguist faith is challenged on city streets by church members' quest for social visibility. When these street presentations are accompanied by musical performances from the church band, these are sure to draw the attention of passers-by and bloggers.

In this context, two ways of performing Kimbanguist identity may be distinguished. The first one is inscribed in an individual frame, which

---

6. Emmanuel Todd, *Le Destin des immigrés: Assimilation et ségrégation dans les démocraties occidentales* (Paris: Seuil, 1994).

combines the person's religious quest with his or her migratory experience. The other one is communal and embedded in a missionary dynamics, whereby the community is consciously centered on the roots and history of their religious traditions, cultivating a memory of the Kimbanguist epic, which also includes a meditation on the Transatlantic Slave Trade and the colonization of African countries. This is documented by the existence of active Kimbanguist publishing houses, which regularly print church members' research and sermons on aspects of Kimbanguist faith. The most significant example of these publications is the successful graphic novel series by Serge Diantantu, designed for second- and third-generation members of the community who were born and raised in France, often in neighborhoods with a strong Muslim presence. They narrate Simon Kimbangu's life and sufferings, and the history of Congo and the transatlantic slave trade, and sell by the thousands.

The diasporic community follows the church's three cardinal principles—Love, Commandments, and Work—and puts them in practice thanks to church fundraising (known as *nsinsani* in Kikongo). The essential source of funding for the church, it is organized by means of competitions between the choirs and men's, women's, or youth groups of which every man, woman, and teenager is a member. In the home countries and in the diaspora alike, an entire section of the Sunday worship services is dedicated to the collection of offerings, in a festive atmosphere where each group marches to the sound of the band, which plays the hymns of the church.[7] From its inception, the Kimbanguist Church has relied on self-financing in order to complete each of its great projects—namely, the building of temples, hospitals, schools, a university, studio apartments for foreign visitors in Nkamba, a lecture room, a television and radio station—most of them in the Democratic Republic of Congo. By this means, the church also purchases second-hand buses, musical instruments, computers and printers, and educational and medical material from charities or partner institutions in France.

Out of awareness of their common need for a durably safe space, several communities of the Kimbanguist diaspora in France have been planning to purchase a plot of land and secure authorizations for the building of a temple. The priority of Kimbanguist urban ministry thus appears to be a material and symbolical appropriation of the church's presence on French soil as a religious group, even if their future temple would not be

---

7. Marie Louise Martin, *Kimbangu: An African Prophet and His Church*, trans. D. M. Moore (Oxford, UK: Basil Blackwell, 1975).

endowed with the same sacred value as the various sites the church has been able to purchase in the home countries.

Concluding Thoughts

Kimbanguist ministry in French society is constrained by a variety of obstacles to integration, and is forced to implement strategies pertaining to adjustment rather than inclusion. Kimbanguist churches therefore work toward an integration of their members by offering them a form of relief from the systemic racism of a supposedly "colorblind" society. Within the safe spaces they provide, members can find healing and coping strategies.

This is also a migrant community which sees its mission as inscribed in a continuum with the priorities of the Kimbanguist Church in the home countries, and with its focus on maintaining a strong national and racial identity. As younger generations of diasporic Kimbanguists emerge who were born and raised in France, their understanding of Kimbanguism may be distinct from their parents' understanding. As a result, it is certainly possible that Kimbanguism will be reshaped in ways increasingly reflecting the urban French settings in which these younger generation Africans are being formed.

Chapter 32

Ministry to Ugandan Youth Affected by War and Conflict

James Okalo Ekwang

I outline here a decade of hands-on compassionate ministry work in Lira, Uganda, a city of approximately 100,000 persons in the northern part of the country. From 1988 to 2006, northern Uganda was embroiled in a violent rebellion led by Joseph Kony, the leader of a group referred to as the Lord's Resistance Army (LRA). Although the rebellion was put down by the government, and Kony and the LRA have retreated into hiding, northern Uganda is in an ongoing struggle to overcome the devastation caused by the conflict. The lives of many young people in northern Uganda were disrupted by the conflict, either as a result of their active participation as child soldiers, or as a result of educational and economic disruptions caused by the insecure nature of the social situation within the region. I have encountered many such young people in my capacities as founding pastor of Truth Evangelistic Fountain Ministries, Uganda and as country director of Children of the Nations–Uganda. Some of the services rendered by these ministries to young people in Lira are detailed here, after a brief discussion of the broader Ugandan social context.

Uganda Country Overview

Uganda, the "Pearl of Africa," boasts some of the best scenery in Africa, including magnificent lakes, rivers, and mountains, as well as semiarid lands. It is home to Lake Victoria, Africa's largest lake and the chief source of the Nile River.

The divide-and-rule British colonial policy created significant hardships during colonial rule and continues to be a source of Ugandan social

262

and political stumbling in post-independence Uganda. Uganda's people have endured much suffering in the wake of colonial rule. Between 800,000 and 2 million people died during President Idi Amin's post-independence dictatorship (1971–1979) and then the civil wars, tribal killings, and famines that followed his disastrous rule. The onset of the 1988 to 2006 Lord's Resistance Army terror clearly heaped on additional hardship and suffering. As the government forced the closure of Internally Displaced Persons (IDP) camps in 2007, most of the people of northern Uganda returned to their homes or communities. Countless communities, however, had been completely destroyed and families wiped out, leaving many with nowhere to go.

Today, Ugandans typically live in villages made up of small houses, often less than a couple hundred square feet. The houses in rural parts of the country are made of mud with thatched-grass roofs, though there is now an increasing number of houses with corrugated iron roofs. About 80 percent of all Ugandans work in agriculture. Nationally, they cultivate cotton, corn, tea, and coffee, though most farmers work at the subsistence level, struggling to grow enough to feed their families. They rarely have surplus food to sell for income that can provide other necessities like clothing and health care. The economy remains largely dual—with a small segment of the population extremely rich and a majority of the population extremely poor—but current government efforts could soon realize a middle-income economy.

Faced with these challenging social realities, our church moved compassionately in the community to serve the needs of orphans and widows. These groups were the hardest hit by the country's turmoil, having been left to fend for themselves either on the streets or in the remains of dismantled IDP camps. The following concerns needed immediate intervention:

- Health care was of great concern to families, with access to medical facilities persistently limited and costly. Access to even the most basic necessities or services is so limited that acute conditions such as malnutrition are rampant.
- Psychological and emotional stresses from unresolved trauma resulting from horrific war-time experiences continue to haunt adults and children alike.
- Children are in desperate need of improved educational opportunities to help them escape the cycle of poverty and open up a brighter future.

Program Involvements by
Children of the Nations–Uganda (COTN-UG)

After inviting partners to help the overwhelming rescue efforts, a combination of African and American trauma counseling teams visited IDP camps in and around key areas of northern Uganda. The teams provided grief and spiritual counseling, food distribution, and a daily presence in the community. After the war ended in 2006 and the governmental closures of the IDP camps in 2007, tens of thousands of refugees with nowhere to go were left to fend for themselves. COTN-UG registered as a National NGO and now cares for 723 children in northern Uganda, providing food, medical care, schools and education, sustainable development initiatives, clean water, Christian discipleship, a University/Vocational Program, and much more. Also, COTN-Uganda Ministry Center runs a primary school, the Marani Honors High School and dorms, children's homes, a farm with livestock, counseling services, a guest house, and staff offices. A few other programs are highlighted and outlined in greater detail here.

Saving Grace Street Kids Ministry

The plight of street kids in Lira was aggravated by the prolonged war, and we decided that they were a special category of children needing separate care and ministry. Our church created a partnership trust that began a highly subsidized program currently helping 456 children access quality, holistic education and shelter. Forty-five street kids are receiving free housing, health care, and education. The schooling we offer our kids is top-notch, as evidenced by Saving Grace Primary School's 2017 ranking by Uganda National Primary Leaving Examinations as the best performing primary school in Lira district.

Truth Vocational and Technical Institute

In 2013, the church realized there was a need to intervene in yet another area of community concern—students who had dropped out of school before completing required qualifications for employment. A common cause for dropping out of school was lack of money to pay school fees, but other causes included early pregnancies or various delinquencies. Consequently, we started a skills training center for these students, highly subsidizing their tuition or else partially or fully sponsoring short-term courses in areas such as block laying, carpentry, hairdressing, mechanics and driving, tailoring and garment cutting, and hotel management/ catering. These students are exposed as well to holistic ministry approaches, including a chapel program to help mentor them in areas of spiritual development. Many have embraced Christianity in ways leading to character transformation and to service in different capacities within the church and community.

My Sister's Keeper Outreach

This is a ministry to street sex workers, a target group not many tend to be enthusiastic about inviting into ministry programs. We found them, however, to be persons struggling with loneliness and who were led into their type of trade by circumstances mostly not of their own making. We began an outreach to these persons in 2014 through various forms of evangelism, and fifty girls left the street and embarked upon more productive and healthy lifestyles, and with some even serving in the church. For example, two have become very committed ushers in our church, play on our netball team, and participate in a revolving village savings fund program initiated by Samaritan's Purse which earns them income. This program (which also helps other needy people in our community) assists these girls in developing sustainable businesses and livelihoods instead of selling their bodies in order to survive.

Wheelchair Distribution to the Disabled

We believe that God's love is inexhaustible, and if we truly carry his love and passion, we should reach out to as many people as have need around us. Compelled by this, we identified a partner who supported us in giving out three hundred wheelchairs to the most disabled, including persons who lacked all mobility within their immediate context or beyond. After thorough assessments with the assistance of local government leaders, these persons were brought to the church in town, where we preached the gospel to them, counseled them, and provided them with new wheelchairs.

Crusades and Conferences

The backbone of all the aforementioned interventions has been a heart to win souls to God's kingdom. We hold gospel conferences and crusades that draw people from across East Africa and other countries. The High Voltage Miracle Conference has for the last fifteen years recorded more than 20,000 people in attendance each year for seven constant days. Up to 40,000 people attended our last crusade in February 2017! These crusades also give rise to various forms of service to the broader community. For example, a woman and her son from Idaho were both miraculously healed in one of our gospel crusades, and both decided to step out in service to some of our most needy communities. At least four times they have distributed locally packaged meals and hygiene packs and drilled water wells for the poorest and most neglected people of the communities, including the elderly, persons with leprosy, and other disabled people. This provided persons with a much-welcomed sense that they were loved and valued. One gentleman in his sixties said that he had never been treated as a special person until our church visited him. Everyone else looked at him as a burden.

It has, in fact, been the personal accounts and testimonies of persons served by COTN-UG and Saving Grace in Uganda that best describes our work:

- "Good Girl"[1] survived child abduction from her village when her grandma hid her in an empty water pot as rebels arrived at their home after having murdered hundreds of others already. Because the house was left open, rebels assumed all family members had run away. In 2010, COTN-UG brought Good Girl to town (Lira), and enrolled her in primary grade one. She is now in sixth grade and excited about the possibility of becoming a doctor in the future.
- "Acitel" escaped from rebels after being forced to drink the blood of her dying mother. When she was brought to the COTN-UG shelter in 2007, she would never smile at any one, despite the daily trauma counseling she received. After spending one year at COTN-UG, she broke through, becoming the most humorous child around.
- "Calvin" was traumatized after losing his parents in the war, and often behaved like a lunatic. His behavior made it difficult to take him seriously or to embrace him as a deserving orphan. His persistence in immersing himself in the COTN-UG program, however, overcame resistance to him as a program participant. Once given a full chance, Calvin surprised us by performing excellently in class, and he is now a composer, singer, and recorder of gospel music.

1. Pseudonyms are used to preserve privacy.

- Three of the girls participating in COTN-UG programs were rescued from situations of child labor, sexual exploitation, and eating from garbage bins in Lira town. All three girls later matriculated in a catering and hotel management course provided by one of the best institutions in Uganda, the Crested Crane Hotel Management Institute.
- "Peter," a street gang member, was known for such behaviors as breaking street fridges for sodas, grabbing guns from night guards, robbing unsuspecting town dwellers, and picking food from garbage. Nevertheless, at one of our feeding events he was won over to an active life in the church and also enrolled in and completed a carpentry course through our training institute. Peter has also won over fellow gang members, some of whom now serve in the church canteen and media department. "Jasper," who is Peter's street mate, has graduated from a primary teachers college and now teaches at Saving Grace Primary School, while "Oluge" has enrolled in a nursing course. Thirteen others who were once involved with street gangs have graduated from vocational institutes preparing them to start up private businesses.

In all these ways, we have attempted to live up to the ministry called for in an important Scripture passage, Isaiah 61:3. We hope we have been faithful to what this passage from the King James Version beckons us to do and that the testimony of our ministry encourages others to do likewise:

"To appoint unto them that mourn in Zion, to give unto them beauty for ashes, the oil of joy for mourning, the garment of praise for the spirit of heaviness; that they might be called trees of righteousness, the planting of the LORD, that he might be glorified."

List of Contributors

William Ackah is lecturer in the Department of Geography and programme director for Community Development and Development and Globalisation at Birkbeck University of London. He holds a PhD in government from the University of Manchester and was 2016–17 Fulbright research scholar at Pittsburgh Theological Seminary, where he researched the impact of gentrification on African American church congregations. He is a co-convener of the Transatlantic Roundtable on Religion and Race and is the co-editor of a Roundtable volume titled *Religion, Culture and Spirituality in Africa and the African Diaspora*.

Stephanie C. Boddie, PhD, is an assistant professor of social work at Baylor University with affiliations at the School of Education and the George W. Truett Seminary. She is also a senior fellow at the University of Pennsylvania's Robert A. Fox Leadership Program. Previously, she held research appointments at Carnegie Mellon University and University of Pittsburgh. She served as senior consultant for the Pittsburgh Theological Seminary's Metro-Urban Institute, a senior researcher at the Pew Research Center's Forum on Religion and Public Life, and on the faculty of Washington University. She is a widely published scholar in the field of social work.

Christopher Brown is pastor of First Presbyterian Church of Berthoud, Colorado. He previously served as a founding co-pastor of the Upper Room Presbyterian Church in Pittsburgh, Pennsylvania, and as the first Church Planting Initiative Coordinator at Pittsburgh Theological Seminary. He received his master of divinity degree from Pittsburgh Theological Seminary and his B.A. degree from University of Colorado–Boulder.

Randall K. Bush has served as the senior pastor of East Liberty Presbyterian Church since March 2006. Previously, he served as pastor of First Presbyterian Church, Racine, Wisconsin, and pastor of Lomagundi Presbyterian Church, Chinhoyi, Zimbabwe. He also has served as adjunct faculty at Pittsburgh Theological Seminary and at Carthage College in Kenosha, Wisconsin. He received a bachelor of music degree from the University of Kansas and theological degrees from Marquette University (PhD) and Princeton Theological Seminary (master of divinity). He has published extensively, including a book titled *The Possibility of Contemporary Prophetic Acts*. He is married with two young-adult children.

Peter Choi (PhD, University of Notre Dame) is director of academic programs at Newbigin House of Studies in San Francisco. A historian of eighteenth-century North America, his areas of specialization include transatlantic revival religion, early evangelicalism, and world Christianity. He is the author of *George Whitefield: Evangelist for God and Empire*.

Jewelnel Davis is the university chaplain, director of the Earl Hall Center, and associate provost at Columbia University. She came to Columbia in 1996 after receiving a bachelor of arts in religious studies from Brown University, being awarded a master of divinity from Yale University and a master of social work from the University of Connecticut, and completing a certificate program in higher education management and development at Harvard University. She is committed to the mission of Columbia's Earl Hall Center: *"Erected for the students that religion and learning may go hand in hand and character grow with knowledge."*

Katie Day, PhD, is the Schieren Professor of Church and Society at United Lutheran Seminary. She received her academic training at Gordon-Conwell Theological Seminary, Union Theological Seminary, and Temple University (PhD, sociology). She has published four books, the most recent being *Faith on the Avenue: Religion on a City Street*. She has co-edited two volumes: *Companion to Public Theology* and *Yours the Power: Faith-Based Community Organizing in the U.S.* She has conducted major sociological studies focusing on race and religion and has published results in a number of journals. She is ordained in the Presbyterian Church (U.S.A.).

Stephan de Beer, PhD, teaches practical theology and directs the Centre for Contextual Ministry at the University of Pretoria, South Africa. He directed the work of an ecumenical community organization in the inner city—the Tshwane Leadership Foundation—from 1993 to 2013. His passions are urban theology and urban community transformation, and his research interests include the church in the city, homelessness, housing, spatial justice, methodologies for doing child theology, and more recently, the gift of urban social movements. Stephan serves on the boards of a number of organizations committed to homelessness, social housing, urban change, and child theology.

Curtiss Paul DeYoung is the CEO of the Minnesota Council of Churches. Previously he was the executive director of Community Renewal Society (Chicago), professor of reconciliation studies at Bethel University (St. Paul), and a pastor in the Church of God. He is the author or editor of ten books on racism, culture and the Bible, and interfaith social justice activism. He has degrees from University of St. Thomas (EdD), Howard University School of Divinity (MDiv), and Anderson University (BA).

James Okalo Ekwang is the founder and senior pastor of Truth Evangelistic Fountain Cathedral, Lira, Uganda, with around thirty branches. He hosts international revival conferences and mass gospel crusades. He founded Children of the Nations–Uganda, serving as its country director from 2007 to date, raising orphaned and destitute children with holistic ministry. He is the board chairman of Saving Grace in Uganda, another holistic full board ministry to street children in Lira. He is also co-founder of Truth Vocational Technical Institute, Lira, helping secondary school dropouts access skills training. He received his master's degree from Fuller Theological Seminary. He is married to Agnes and is blessed with four biological and eight adopted children.

Aurélien Mokoko Gampiot holds a PhD in sociology from the University of Rennes 2 (France). He is currently a scholar at the CNRS-GSRL, Group Societes Religions Laicites (Sorbonne University, Paris). His research focuses on modern African religions, interethnic relations, and migrations in Africa and Europe. His fieldwork is based on African religions and African diaspora, particularly Kimbanguism and black Judaism in France. His most recent book is titled *Kimbanguism: An African Understanding of the Bible.*

Erika D. Gault received her PhD from the American Studies Department at the State University of New York at Buffalo. Her scholarly work focuses on the intersection of religious history, technology, and urban black life in postindustrial America. On the topics of hip-hop, religion, and digital ethnography, she has delivered and published a number of papers regionally, nationally, and internationally. She is an ordained elder at Elim Christian Fellowship and an assistant professor in Africana studies at the University of Arizona.

Kimberly Gonxhe serves as director of the Metro-Urban Institute at Pittsburgh Theological Seminary. She earned a bachelor of science from Ohio University and a master of divinity from Pittsburgh Theological Seminary, where she was the Valentour World Travel Scholar focusing on women's issues in a global context. She also serves as executive director of the Live Foundation, a global gender justice organization. Gonxhe has advocated for the marginalized in forty-three countries, spanning five continents. Her work has positively affected war-torn displaced people in Uganda and reformed sex workers in Indonesia, as well as married, mutilated, and uneducated young girls in Kenya.

Scott Hagley, PhD (Luther Seminary), teaches missiology at Pittsburgh Theological Seminary. Before coming to Pittsburgh, he served as the director of education for Forge Canada and the teaching pastor at Southside Community Church in Vancouver, British Columbia.

Interested in the way congregations adapt with their neighborhoods, he has published a number of articles on congregational mission and leadership and is currently working on a book-length study of an urban congregation. He lives in Pittsburgh with his wife and two daughters.

Tami Hooker works for the Pennsylvania Department of Corrections and has served as the chaplaincy director at two of the state's institutions. She received the department's Outstanding Performance Award in 2007, was nominated for the Thomas A. Fulcomer Award in 2013, and is a past president of the Pennsylvania Prison Chaplains Association. Tami has a BA from Duquesne University, an MSW from the University of Pittsburgh, and an MDiv from Pittsburgh Theological Seminary, where she was recently honored as a distinguished alumna for excellence in specialized ministry. She also serves as a quarter-time pastor at the Presbyterian Church of Mt. Washington and is enrolled in the DMin program at Louisville Presbyterian Theological Seminary.

Herb Kolbe is the part-time director of leadership initiatives at the Pittsburgh Leadership Foundation and a full-time campus minister with the Coalition for Christian Outreach (CCO) at Duquesne University. Herb served with Young Life for sixteen years in Pittsburgh, Bermuda, and New England before joining the staff of the CCO in 1990. He held a variety of leadership positions in the CCO before returning to direct involvement in urban and student ministries in 2007. He completed an undergraduate degree at Penn State University and a master's degree at Fuller Theological Seminary. He has been married for forty-one years and has two adult daughters.

Felicia Howell LaBoy, PhD, is the lead pastor of St. John's United Methodist Church, a multiracial, multiethnic congregation in Oak Park, Illinois. With over eighteen years of urban pastoral ministry and over thirty years of business experience, she is the former associate dean of Black Church Studies and Advanced Learning at Louisville Seminary and former assistant professor of evangelization at United Theological Seminary. With expertise in the fields of faith-based community and leadership development, evangelism, and race relations, she weaves her academic, pastoral, and business education and experience to lead diverse groups in achieving better churches, communities, and organizations.

Michael A. Mata has led and equipped others in community and church-based urban transformation for more than thirty years. He is director of the Transformational Urban Leadership Program at Azusa Pacific Seminary. Mata also serves as community transformation specialist for Compassion Creates Change Inc., and was the director of Tools for Transformation for World Vision's U.S. programs. Prior to his work with World Vision, Mata held the Mildred M. Hutchinson Chair in Urban Ministries at Claremont School of Theology. He has nearly twenty years of experience in urban pastoral leadership and holds degrees in biblical literature, religion, and urban planning.

Michael McBride is a native of San Francisco and has been active in ministry for over twenty years. He serves as the lead pastor of The Way Christian Center in West Berkeley, a ministry that he planted. In March 2012, he became the national director for Urban Strategies/LIVE FREE Campaign with the PICO National Network, a campaign led by hundreds of faith congregations throughout the United States committed to addressing gun violence and mass incarceration of young people of color. He is a graduate of Duke University's Divinity School, with an emphasis in ethics and public policy.

Donald E. Messer, President Emeritus and Henry White Warren Professor Emeritus of Practical Theology at the Iliff School of Theology, serves as executive director of the Center for Health and Hope, Centennial, Colorado. Author of sixteen books, Messer holds a PhD from Boston University in social ethics. After twenty-nine years as a university and seminary president, he founded the center, which promotes education, prevention, care, and treatment of persons infected and affected by HIV and AIDS around the world.

Kang-Yup Na is an associate professor of religion at Westminster College, Pennsylvania, where he teaches courses on the Bible, biblical interpretation, and Reformed theology. His area of specialty is the New Testament (Paul's letters in particular) and hermeneutics. The son of first-generation Christians in South Korea, he is a teaching elder in the Presbyterian Church (U.S.A.) who has lived, studied, taught, and served churches in various places in New Jersey, Korea, Atlanta, Germany, and New York City. He earned an AB at Princeton University, an MDiv at Princeton Theological Seminary, and a PhD in New Testament from Emory University.

Setri Nyomi, PhD, a Ghanaian theologian, was General Secretary of the World Communion of Reformed Churches (WCRC) (formerly World Alliance of Reformed Churches—WARC) from March 2000 to August 2014. The WCRC is the worldwide church family of Presbyterians, Reformed, Congregationalists, Waldensians, and some united churches bringing together more than 80 million Christians in 106 countries. He and his wife, Akpene Nyomi, are now back in Ghana where he is the district pastor of Evangelical Presbyterian Church, Adenta, Accra, and a senior lecturer at Trinity Theological Seminary, Legon.

Israel Oluwole Olofinjana is the founding director of Centre for Missionaries from the Majority World and is an ordained and accredited Baptist minister. He is the pastor of Woolwich Central Baptist Church, a multiethnic, multicultural, inner-city church in Southeast London, having previously pastored two other churches in London. He holds a BA in religious studies from the University of Ibadan, Nigeria, and a master of theology from Carolina University of Theology. He has edited or authored several books and published several academic articles or chapters on the subjects of reverse mission, African Christianity, mission and theology, and black-majority churches.

Ronald E. Peters, EdD, is an internationally known preacher, educator, and adviser on social witness policy and urban theological education. His writings, including his popular textbook *Urban Ministry: An Introduction* (2007), reflect his commitment to enhancing the quality of life for "the least of these" through interfaith collaboration for justice advocacy. He served as president of Interdenominational Theological Center, Atlanta, Georgia; Henry L. Hillman Professor of Urban Ministry and founding director of the Metro-Urban Institute at Pittsburgh Theological Seminary; pastor of New Covenant Presbyterian Church, Miami, Florida; and founding pastor of Martin Luther King, Jr. Community Presbyterian Church, Springfield, Massachusetts.

Anthony Rivera is an ordained minister of the Word and Sacrament with the PC(USA) and native New Yorker. He earned his master of divinity and master of theology degrees with a concentration in biblical studies from Princeton Theological Seminary. He is currently working on completing the Urban Change Focus Doctor of Ministry degree at Pittsburgh Theological Seminary. His essay is devoted to theological education in the urban context and is dedicated to his wife and daughters.

Laurel E. Scott, PhD, is an activist minister leading the Newman Memorial United Methodist Church in Brooklyn, New York. While working on her doctorate at Boston University School of Theology in the early 2000s, she was active in justice ministries in the Boston area and has pastored congregations in Massachusetts and Connecticut. She returned to her home in New York in 2013 and is engaged in pastoring, preaching, teaching, writing, and a $2 million church restoration project.

Lisa Slayton is chief executive officer at Pittsburgh Leadership Foundation, where she oversees all strategic initiatives and partnerships. She has designed and launched the Leaders Collaborative and delivered organizational development consulting, training, and coaching services to a wide variety of organizations, including NetHealth, CTR Systems, Akina, GrowthPlay, Prominent, Careform, Light of Life, Truefit, and WabTec, as well as a number of local congregations. She also serves as a board director for SIMA International. She received her undergraduate degree from Mount Holyoke College and a master's degree in social and civic entrepreneurship from Bakke Graduate University. She has been married to Roger for thirty-six years and has one adult son, Zachary.

R. Drew Smith is professor of urban ministry at Pittsburgh Theological Seminary, and is co-convener of the Transatlantic Roundtable on Religion and Race. He has published widely on religion and public life, having edited or co-edited eight books and four journal collections and having written more than fifty articles, chapters, and reports. He has recently completed writing a forthcoming book on contemporary black clergy activism.

He earned his bachelor's degree from Indiana University and a master of divinity as well as a master of arts and PhD in political science from Yale University. He is a Baptist minister and has ministered in various parish contexts and prison ministry contexts.

Jean Stockdale grew up in Ohio, then lived in various parts of the United States and worked in various industries. She settled in Highland Park, New Jersey, to raise her daughter. Mistakenly believing the collection of tasks she had done in previous jobs gave her sufficient background to confront societal issues, she found that it's not background but courage that's needed. Her faith community, the Reformed Church of Highland Park, focuses and sustains her activism, far exceeding any results she might have achieved without it.

Phil Tom has served urban congregations in Chicago, St. Paul, Indianapolis, and New York City. He has also served as the national staff for the Presbyterian Church (U.S.A.)'s Urban Ministry Office; co-director of the Church and Community Ministry Project at McCormick Theological Seminary; and in the administration of President Barack Obama as director of the Center for Faith-Based and Neighborhood Partnership for the U.S. Department of Labor. He received his master of divinity degree from McCormick Theological Seminary.

Angelique Walker-Smith, DMin, is national senior associate for Pan-African and Orthodox Church Engagement at Bread for the World based in Washington, D.C. She has extensive experience as a faith thought leader, journalist, speaker, preacher, and author. She has received awards from President Bill Clinton and Senator Richard Lugar and from two of her alma maters, Yale Divinity School and Kent State University. She is a recipient of the Indiana Sagamore of the Wabash, which is one of Indiana's highest civilian awards. She served as executive director of the Church Federation of Greater Indianapolis and as a volunteer assistant chaplain at the Indiana Women's Prison.

John C. Welch, a Pittsburgh native, received a BS in chemical engineering and economics from Carnegie Mellon University, a master's of divinity from Pittsburgh Theological Seminary, and a PhD from Duquesne University in health care ethics. With twenty-seven years of ministry experience, including as a pastor, he is vice president for community engagement and student services, and dean of students at Pittsburgh Theological Seminary. He is an adjunct professor of business and health care ethics and is chief chaplain for the Pittsburgh Bureau of Police. He is married with four children and three grandchildren.

Index

urban community formation and, 90,
93, 97–103, 145
urban conceptual worldviews and, 17,
19, 27, 35, 39, 44–45
urban ministry adaptations and, 231, 250
urban social policy and, 153, 190, 210,
215
See also death-dealing forces/realities;
specific topics and events
integration
challenges to (Kimbanguist, in France),
254, 256–57, 261
See also desegregation
integrative ministries, 123, 128
interfaith work, 114, 155, 201, 238, 243–
44. *See also* ecumenism
Internal Dimensions of Church
Connectedness to Community
(Bush), 109–14
Internally Displaced Persons (IDP), 263
International Justice Mission (IJM), 211
International Kimbanguist Circle (CIK),
255
International Missionary Council, 40
Internet, 25, 114, 252
intersectionality, 1, 6, 28, 31, 34, 37, 62, 236
Intervarsity Christian Fellowship, 236
involvement, 206
Iraq, 55n3
Iraqi war, 114
Isaiah, 70, 99n5, 149, 248, 267
Islam, 24, 64, 106, 236. *See also* Muslims
Ivy, Archie, 171–72
I Was in Prison and You Came to Visit Me
(Walker-Smith), 120

Jackson, Jesse, Jr., 172–73
Jackson, Jesse, Sr., 91
Jackson, Mahalia, 250
Jacobsen, Dennis, 153
Jamaica, Queens, NY, 49
James, Apostle, 210–11
Japan, 55–56, 135
Jennings, Willie James, 28–29, 31–32
Jerusalem, 178, 249
Jerusalem church, 35–36, 41
Jesuit Agency for Organizing training
program, 220
Jesus Christ, 57, 70

the cross, 161
as Great Physician, 206
identity of, 102
as Immanuel, 57
as King, 230
mission and purpose, earthly, 102
power of, 230
as servant, 99n5, 226
as Word of God, incarnate, 57–58, 162
See also Christianity; Christology;
Trinity
Jews. *See* Judaism
Jim Crow/Jim Crow laws, 98, 117, 179
Job, story of, 56–58
jobs. *See* work (employment)
Johannesburg, South Africa, 3, 67, 138n2,
158
John, Elton, 208
John, Gospel of, 57–58, 163–64, 204, 230
Johnson, Lyndon B., 180
Jones, Feminista, 252
Jones, Gregory, 184
Jubilee Action, 211
Judaism, 22, 57–58, 63–64, 114, 185, 233
Judeo-Christian forms of religion, 24
"no longer Jew or Greek," 60
judgment, 244–46
The Jungle (Sinclair), 6
justice, 60, 70, 149
the Accra Confession, 158–66
all nations called to, 149
communities, just, 165, 247
God of, 164
spatial, 145
theological tools for, 161–62
See also criminal justice; *dikaiosynē*;
economic justice; injustice; racial
justice; social justice
Justice for Our Neighbor (JFON), 130

Kairos Prison Ministries, 115n1
Keifert, Patrick, 42n21
Kelsey, David, 42n21
Kennedy, David, 200
Kenya, 23, 123, 212
Kenyatta, Jomo, 212
Kimbangu, Muilu Marie, 255
Kimbangu, Simon, 254–61
Kimbanguist religion, 254–61